VOLTAIRE
PHILOSOPHICAL
DICTIONARY

VOLTAIRE

PHILOSOPHICAL DICTIONARY

*Translated, with an Introduction
and Glossary by*
PETER GAY

Preface by André Maurois

A – I

BASIC BOOKS, INC.

PUBLISHERS · NEW YORK

THIS BOOK IS FOR
Sarah, Sophie, and Elizabeth

PREFACE

UNQUESTIONABLY, Voltaire and Victor Hugo have been France's two most widely popular writers. Voltaire's last trip to Paris, the enthusiasm of the crowds, the famous performance of *Irène* at the Comédie Française where the audience watched the author and not the play, the acclaim of the Académie, the meeting with Benjamin Franklin, the ferment aroused by his illness and death, all this conjures up a picture almost unparalleled in literary history—except for the funeral ceremonies of Victor Hugo, the coffin beneath the Arc de Triomphe, the candelabra veiled in crepe, and the long murmur of a whole people rising like the tide toward the sleeping poet.

It is rare that literary glory shines with such luster. Usually it is conferred by an elite, by disciples, that is, by a restricted group. But in these two cases the writer had been, in his lifetime, the symbol and the inspirer of a struggle. Hugo had defended political freedom against the Empire; Voltaire had defended freedom of thought and toleration. Each had acquired a singular prestige by a long, voluntary exile. Voltaire at Ferney, smiling and emaciated, stooped in his armchair; Hugo on his feet on his little island facing the ocean—these are two unforgettable images, two statues which France welcomes into its Pantheon even today.

Not unanimously. Voltaire and Hugo were the heroes of the Third Republic and the French Left; both have been ill-treated by the Right. Voltaire above all was violently attacked every time a clerical party came to power. He had battled against the Church; his memory paid for this rashness. Even writers who were neither believers nor clericals reproached him for a philosophy that was too simple, too deliberately contemptuous of every metaphysical anguish. In *Madame Bovary*, Flaubert made the pharmacist Homais into a Voltairian, as narrow and intolerant in his way as the abbé Bournisien. Empress Eugenie said: "Voltaire? I don't like that man who makes me understand things that I shall never understand." This feminine remark is not without acuteness. It recalls the formula of the critic Faguet: "A chaos of clear ideas." Doubtless each of Voltaire's ideas, taken individually, appears luminous, wittily expressed, adroitly proved. "But," say his adversaries, "on the next page he will set forth the opposite idea, no less shrewdly. Voltaire is a marvelous polemicist; he is not a philosopher. He is clear; he is not profound. He has no doctrine; he has prejudices."

No book is a better answer to these reservations, these reproaches, than the *Philosophical Dictionary*. *Candide* is a more finished work of art, but with the preconceptions and the mystery of every work of art. A dictionary offers a convenient device for touching on a thousand different subjects. The alphabet takes care of the composition, which would be disconnected if the philosophy of the author did not spread a single color over everything. And Voltaire, whatever one may say, has a reasonably stable philosophy. People ask: "What does he believe? Sometimes he assaults the Church; sometimes he argues that it is necessary. Sometimes he seems to be a deist; then he goes so far as to build a church: '*Deo erexit Voltaire*'; sometimes he announces that the canaille needs a God, which implies that he does not need one. Sometimes he is a pessimist and ridicules Leibnitz's and Pangloss's 'All is for the best in the best of possible worlds'; sometimes he is an optimist and affirms, like Rousseau, that man is born good and that it was only the bad example set by kings and priests that has perverted him. Sometimes he is for equality; sometimes he adds: 'On our miserable globe it is impossible for men living in society not to be divided into two classes, one the rich who command, the other the poor who serve.' "

Indeed, a chaos of clear ideas—how can we find our way through it?

First of all the reader must take account of a very important factor: prudence. Voltaire was much afraid of persecution, and we must concede to him that he had good reasons to be afraid. People have asked: "What did he have to fear, and against whom did he battle? Were not his contemporaries, whom he seems to try to persuade, all persuaded already? Freedom of thought? It had been won. Who thought more freely about religious matters than certain men at Court? Political equality? We shall see a little later, during the night of 4 August 1789, that the young nobility itself will take the initiative." The objection has no weight. The injustices against which Voltaire campaigned existed, and they were monstrous.

The name of père Le Tellier, confessor to Louis XIV, had become execrable in Voltaire's time, but the great men he had crushed had none the less ended their days in exile and want. In a relatively recent past, the wise Charron had been threatened with loss of life; the learned and generous Ramus had been murdered; Gassendi had been compelled to retire to Digne, far from the slanders of Paris. Closer to Voltaire, the philosopher Bayle—he too the author of a dictionary—had been persecuted and reduced to poverty. And why? He had been reproached for not praising, in his article on *David*, the atrocious actions and injustices of that king! In 1713, Fontenelle had been on the point of losing his position and his liberty for having edited a *Treatise on Oracles* that had alarmed the fanatics. In France and Prussia, Voltaire

himself had been able to measure the dangers of absolute
power. In his youth he had been beaten by the lackeys
of a great lord whom he had offended, and he, not the
guilty men, had been imprisoned in the Bastille. He had
never forgotten the pain and the shame of this beating.
It was not in the thirteenth century, but in the eighteenth, that the chevalier de La Barre, a young man with
much sense and great hopes, convicted of irreligious
behavior, was condemned by the judges of Abbéville to
have his tongue torn out, his hand cut off, and his body
burned in a slow fire. It was not in the thirteenth century, but in the eighteenth, that French Protestants had
no civic status, and could neither be legally married
nor buried. This is what merited the indignation of a
philosopher and justified the prudence of an old man.

A philosopher. . . . Does the *Philosophical Dictionary* truly define a philosopher? I think that the answer
must be affirmative, whatever Faguet may say, and that
this philosophy was a scientific one. Voltaire was not a
scholar, but he had studied more than one science and
thought very much like a scholar of his time. He believed in the facts of experience, and in reflection about
facts; he did not believe in metaphysical reveries. "O
man! God has given you understanding so you may
conduct yourself well, and not to penetrate the essence
of the things he has created." Hence an ethics and not a
metaphysics. But the existence of God? Is not this already a metaphysical idea? No, because God, for Voltaire, is a fact of experience. The world appears to us
like a well-made and well-regulated clock; hence there
must be a watchmaker. "Who does a piece of work but a
workman? Who makes laws but a legislator? Hence
there is a workman, an eternal legislator."

This God cannot modify his own laws. If he did so, he
would recognize that he had been mistaken; he would

not be God. Hence he does not act by particular acts of will. There are not, there never have been, any miracles. Or, rather, everything is a miracle. "The marvelous order of nature . . . the activity of light, the life of animals—these are perpetual miracles." But the violation of these immutable laws would be a contradiction in terms. A law cannot be immutable and violable. Still, all nations have reported incredible prodigies. Voltaire challenges these accounts. "It would be desirable that a miracle, for the sake of being fully verified, should be performed in the presence of the Academy of Sciences in Paris, or the Royal Society in London, and the Faculty of Medicine, assisted by a detachment of the regiment of Guards." Everything that goes beyond the worship of a supreme Being is superstition, and "the most superstitious times have always been the times of the most horrible crimes."

Thus, "physical laws are immutable. . . . Everything is regulated, correlated, circumscribed. Man can only have a certain number of teeth, hairs, and ideas; there comes a time when he must lose his teeth, his hair, and his ideas. . . . Imbeciles say: My doctor pulled my aunt through a mortal illness. . . . Your doctor saved your aunt; but he certainly didn't negate the order of nature to do so: he followed it. It is clear that your aunt couldn't prevent herself from having a certain illness at a certain time, . . . that she must call a certain doctor, that he had to prescribe the drugs to her that cured her." Still, this immutability of destinies in no way prevents a man from being moral, for morality is within him; it is part of his destiny. What is essential in morality is common to all men. People everywhere respect their father and mother, have pity for oppressed innocence, regard freedom of thought as a natural right. Here the philosophy of the *Dictionary* becomes quite weak, for if to respect morality is to accomplish one's destiny, surely evil and immoral men too accomplish the destiny that is within them. How would they be what they are not? How would they want what is contrary to their nature? On this point Voltaire offers little explanation. On freedom and the will he is infinitely less penetrating than Descartes was before him and Sartre is today.

But his practical morality is simple and sound. It is the morality of Confucius, whom he admires; it is that of Christianity when it says: "Love thy neighbor as thyself." His quarrel is not with Christian ethics; it is with the metaphysics of Christianity and, even more, with its historical truth. On the absurdities and improbabilities of the Old Testament he is inexhaustible. Educated by the Jesuits, intense reader of the Bible and its commentators, he knows, or thinks he knows, everything about these subjects. To argue with theologians excites him. He is wrong to attack them on the plane of the literal truth of the sacred books; he has no trouble finding in them improbabilities, contradictions, and a barbarous morality which shocks him. Moses, Solomon, David, are his favorite targets: he judges them in the name of a morality which could not have been theirs and which derives, partly, from the Stoics and, partly, from the Gospels. His excuse is that his adversaries are fundamentalists who defended the historicity of the sacred texts down to the most minute detail. That gave the scoffer a fine opportunity. He misused it.

Voltaire's principal error was not to have recognized the positive contribution of Christianity to our civilization. His picture of universal history is precisely the reverse of Bossuet's majestic tapestry. For Voltaire, humanity has traversed a pagan period which was one of simplicity of manners and a relative tolerance; then, starting with Christianity, a time of cruelty and intolerance; it will see a golden age in the future. How would this paradise on earth be established? By the diffusion of enlightenment, by science, by liberty. We can see why the Third Republic in France should have honored Voltaire as one of its sages. The philosophy of the regime was that of Ferney: anticlerical laicism, belief in progress, liberalism, respect for acquired positions, and search for happiness. We can see, too, that the present generation, having once again taken up a taste for various forms of mysticism, much less certain than its predecessor of the power of reason, less accustomed to the charms of life, more familiar—alas!—with cruelty and intolerance, no longer finds complete nourishment in Voltaire.

But it would be wrong to neglect what it can find in him—a lively and witty manner of deflating certain absurdities. The morality of Voltaire is not sublime; it is modest and humane. More than anything it is conscious of the pettiness of our anthill. Ants were not made to explain the Universe; it is enough for them to live as honest ants. "It is very sad to have so many ideas and not to know precisely the nature of ideas. I admit it; but it is much sadder and much more foolish to think you know what you don't know." That amounts to saying, like Montaigne: "What do I know?" Montaigne said it with less violence, perhaps because he had fewer enemies. Voltaire does not content himself with saying, "What do I know?" He sends forth a "What do you know?" addressed to metaphysicians. He "grandly clears aways earthly illusions." On this empty terrain we can build. What? A human world, one a little less evil, a little more tolerant. *We must cultivate our garden*—that is to say, Kings fight one another and Churches tear one another to pieces: let us limit our activity and let us try to perform our task as well as we can. Scientific and bourgeois conclusions. They announce modern man and the wisdom of the engineer, incomplete but effective wisdom.

The influence of the *Philosophical Dictionary* was profound, its success immediate and lasting. Still, the ideas it expressed were clichés in its epoch. Gassendi, Fontenelle, Bayle, had said all that. But they had neither Voltaire's prestige, nor his "prodigious genius to make abstract ideas vivid." A dictionary cannot have the poetry—just a little mad—which lends *Candide* so much grace. Nevertheless its form is adroit and varied. The dialogue, in which Voltaire excels, occurs in it frequently. Irony serves him at once as arrow and shield; it furnishes him with the means of expressing dangerous ideas, pretending that he does not believe them himself, which appeases scruples in his accomplice-readers. Let us add that a dictionary allows him, above all, to take up the same, very simple themes over again, and to drive the nail into the spot with repeated hammer blows; and that it also authorizes, as Julien Benda has so well said, "an absence of order which is far from being a fault," for it permits him to arouse attention ceaselessly. Let us say, finally, that Voltaire's battle is not finished, that the dead he has killed are doing far too well, that we are seeing in our time a revival of fanaticism and intolerance, that the golden age seems farther away than ever, in short that it remains necessary, more than ever, to reread Voltaire, from time to time, in order to weed the ground—before the sowing.

ANDRÉ MAUROIS
of the Académie Française

CONTENTS

EDITOR'S
INTRODUCTION

THE MAN IN HIS BOOK

THE BIOGRAPHY OF A
BESTSELLER

A CENTER OF CONCERN AND
A VARIETY OF METHODS

EDITOR'S
INTRODUCTION

THE MAN IN HIS BOOK

Voltaire's *Philosophical Dictionary* is not a dictionary: it is too episodic, too passionate, too personal
for that. Rather, it is a polemical tract, in turn sober and
witty, sensible and outrageous, sincere and disingenuous.
It is sometimes angry about the wrong things, sometimes superficial in its explanations, and sometimes almost as cruel as the cruelty it lacerates. But behind the
savage humor and partisan analysis there stands a passion
for humanity and decency, a hatred of fanaticism and
stupidity, which Voltaire would not have been embarrassed to acknowledge—and which we should not be too
detached to recognize—as moral. With its errors and its
erudition, its dazzling variety of tactics and brilliant
unity of style, the *Philosophical Dictionary* is Voltaire's most characteristic work. Practically everything
he knew found its way into it.

When Voltaire wrote its first articles in the fall of
1752, he was a glittering display piece at the court of
Frederick the Great and the most famous literary man
in Europe. His every work was hopefully awaited by
the literary world, appreciatively read by a wide public,
and shamelessly pirated by unscrupulous booksellers. He
turned out successes with monotonous regularity in
practically every genre of the literary and journalistic
repertory, arousing the wonder of his friends and the
envy of his competitors. He was, and he liked to think
that he was, a sickly man, yet his energies and his stores
of inventive imagination were inexhaustible: he was

fifty-eight when he launched on the *Philosophical Dictionary*, and while he drew on all his previous experience to compile it, in structure and intention it was a novel venture. Voltaire was perhaps the only man in Europe who could have written it, and he probably could not have written it much earlier. He would not have known enough.

Voltaire learned many of the right things early, including the habit of disguise. He had been born François-Marie Arouet in Paris on November 21, 1694, in the latter, less glorious half of the long reign of Louis XIV. His parents, solid and prosperous middle-class people with social pretensions and useful connections, sent their precocious son to Louis le Grand, a Jesuit *collège* favored by the wealthy and influential aristocrats of Paris. Their motive was tactical rather than pedagogical: they wanted François-Marie to become a fashionable lawyer, perhaps rising into the nobility of the robe, and Louis le Grand had the right clientele, the right social tone, and (what with the disfavor into which the Jansenists had fallen) the right political position.

But young Arouet disappointed both his parents and his teachers. True, he made friends, and from the highest social strata, but he wanted them to read his manuscripts, not his briefs. True, he was an outstanding student, but he was to use his enormous talents to turn against Christianity the learning he had acquired from Christians. He was supposed to become a lawyer and became a poet; he was supposed to become a compliant Christian and became a pugnacious pagan.

In the eighteenth century, an admirer of the classics need not have been, and often was not, a pagan. While the Jesuits catered to their spoiled charges and suavely tempered the severity of Christian teachings in a time when rigorous piety was out of style, they taught the Latin and Greek classics with Christian admonitions, and used elegant pagan doctrines and splendid pagan virtues as pedagogical gateways to higher Christian truths. The more scandalous Latin writers, like Ovid, were expurgated, and ancient philosophy was solicitously surrounded with the warning that it was sound only when it anticipated or imperfectly expressed the sublimities of Christian teachings. These tactics were not insincere subterfuges: the Jesuits were true, although modern, Christians, and the classicism they taught so well was rhetorical, literary, social. Classical education was class education: it provided delightful objects of aesthetic enjoyment, interesting subjects for concentrated study, and, above all, a common language for the educated. A well-placed tag from Horace, like a well-turned French epigram, marked the man destined for polite society anywhere in eighteenth-century Europe. "Classical quotation," said Samuel Johnson, "is the *parole* of literary men all over the world."

But Voltaire's appreciation of antiquity went far beyond a hero-worship of Cicero, the quoting of Latin lines half-remembered from school-days, a playful or even serious pedantry. His rejection of all Christianity—of the God-man, of miracles, and even of specifically Christian morality—was the confluence of many streams, including modish impiety, the theory of experimental science, the study of history sacred and profane. But his paganism was also a recapture of antique styles of thinking. Voltaire complacently, and correctly, exalted modern over ancient science and had little patience with ancient systems of thought, but his critical temper and his concern with ethics were the temper and the concern of ancient philosophy.

Voltaire spent six happy years, from 1704 to 1710, at

the Jesuit *collège*, and it is here that we must seek the
first roots of the book he began to write in 1752 and
published in 1764. In the *Philosophical Dictionary*, paganism appears in many forms. It is decorative, as in the
article SONGES, which opens with a quotation from Petronius. It is a polemical device, as in the article JULIEN
LE PHILOSOPHE, which contrasts the sober, decent humanity of the pagan emperor with the malicious fanaticism of his Christian slanderers; or as in several other
articles which contrast the educated Romans, who de-
spised and tolerated all religions, with barbarous Christians, who persecuted everyone including one another.
But beyond that, paganism informs Voltaire's style of
thought, and guides his pen in every article: it speaks
through his criticism of authority, his skepticism of the
miraculous, his admiration for men who suffered nobly
without hope of heaven or fear of hell, his program for
a humane, tolerant society, and his plea for a religion
without priests, without ritual, and without nonsense.
When Voltaire calls his article on SUPERSTITION a "chapter taken from Cicero, Seneca, and Plutarch," he is listing his spiritual ancestors.

It would be naive to portray Voltaire's education as a
matter of rigid stages. Voltaire's mind was far too lively,
too alert to new currents of thought, too eager to experiment with ideas or literary forms, to pick up its fur-
nishings in discrete packages: he dabbled in literature
before he published his first play, he admired English
philosophers before he went to England, and he smug-
gled political notions into his poems a quarter century
before he wrote his first political pamphlet. Yet when
we look back from 1752, trying to understand the man
who was about to begin the *Philosophical Dictionary*,
we see each period of his life dominated by a guiding

interest. Paganism was the first step in his education; literature was the second.

Upon his graduation from Louis le Grand, Voltaire launched himself into the great world. These were the last years of Louis XIV, and there was an expectant mood in the air. In 1715, when the old king's death liberated French society from somber repression, young Arouet was frequenting fashionable circles which fed on feline malice, scurrilous epigrams against Jesus, deist poems so daring that they could not even be written down and were recited in *salons* by individuals endowed with a retentive memory. The debauchees leading this society, who instructed Voltaire while he amused them, were growing elderly and repetitious, and there was room for a fresh talent, a youthful poet. Not surprisingly, the elder Arouet failed first to tie his son to a career in the law, and then to diplomacy: the competition of literature, deism, and long visits to *châteaux* was too strong. In 1718, at twenty-four, the young worldling firmly and finally repudiated paternal guidance: he changed his name to de Voltaire, and he finished his first tragedy, *Oedipe*.

These two events were peculiarly linked: in 1717, he had been imprisoned in the Bastille for some rather strong verses against the Regent. He had denied writing them, and for once his denials may have been true; but true or false, he was incarcerated for eleven months, treated well, and given leisure to finish his ambitious tragedy. When he emerged from prison he had a new name and a great hit. His career as a playwright was launched. Poetically enough it ended where it had begun, in Paris, in 1778, the year of his death, with the performance of *Irène* in his aged presence.

When we reflect on Voltaire's literary reputation, we

are tempted to make Voltairian observations about the ephemeral nature of fame and the unpredictable course of taste. His plays and poems, which we find intolerably tedious in our time, were hailed as masterful in his own. His favorite tragedies have shrunk to footnotes in histories of French literature; the *Henriade*, his long epic poem on his favorite French king, Henri IV, to which he turned not long after *Oedipe*, was compared by some readers in the 1720's to Vergil and is now practically forgotten. Today, Voltaire is much admired, or at least much invoked, as a haggard, quixotic knight of tolerance, but except for *Candide*, he is little read.

Yet the evidence of his literary gifts speaks to us from every page of the *Philosophical Dictionary*. To be sure, the subject of literature is slighted. There is an article on CRITIQUE, which tells us much about Voltaire's taste and even more about his distaste for critics who affect to despise what they cannot hope to equal. There is a rather less revealing article on literary men, LETTRES, GENS DE LETTRES, OU LETTRÉS, which shows Voltaire in one of his frequent moods of self-pity and says nothing of Voltaire's pioneering efforts to improve the social standing, the personal dignity, and the financial lot of professional writers, including himself. But the fact remains that much of what Bayle had tried to do a half-century before with four ponderous, tortuously written, and elaborately circumspect folios, much of what Diderot and his troop of collaborators were trying to do with an enormous encyclopedia—much of this Voltaire was trying to do with one slight book, small enough to fit into the pocket: the first four editions of the *Philosophical Dictionary* advertised it to be "*portatif*." To combine a maximum of explosive power with a minimum of space, to educate without boring, and to persuade without annoying, required genius in the ability to economize, to select, to conceal, and to entertain. With Voltaire, such genius was the marriage of natural endowment and life-long attention to the details of his literary craft: he was artful enough to conceal his art, but he lavished all his literary skill on the *Philosophical Dictionary*.

In the winter of 1725-1726, Voltaire, now a literary celebrity in his early thirties, had a famous quarrel. He had some words with the chevalier de Rohan, fatuous offspring of an old noble house, and in February 1726 he was lured from a dinner party and beaten up by Rohan's men before Rohan's contemptuous eyes. To Voltaire's dismay, his aristocratic friends turned their back on him, and in April the government sent Voltaire once again to the Bastille, largely, it would seem, for his own protection.

The incident was a valuable if rather drastic lesson: it was a reminder that the realities of a stratified society remained realities, even for him. The successor to Corneille and Racine, the heir of Vergil, the intimate of the great, the beneficiary of royal pensions, was nothing but plain Arouet once he dared to challenge the system.

This was the first benefit of his beating; his visit to England was the other. Voltaire was released from the Bastille in May 1726 and immediately embarked for England, where he stayed for over two years. The visit was of decisive importance for him: its echoes were to reverberate all through his life.

There used to be vigorous controversy among Voltaire scholars over this visit. Some, chiefly English, once argued that it made a man of him, and a thinker; others, chiefly French, that it did no more than supply him with material, and confirm religious and philosophical views he had picked up from French deists and skeptics. To-

day, scholars have arrived at a cosmopolitan consensus
appropriate to such a cosmopolitan as Voltaire: Voltaire's English visit did not produce a conversion; his
writings of the early 1720's show signs of his concern
with toleration, his doubts about Christianity, his rather
rudimentary interest in natural science and empirical
philosophy. But his English years, nevertheless, had a
profound influence. They were a period of urbane activity and thoughtful leisure for him, of reading and observing. England appeared to Voltaire's dazzled vision
the realization of some utopian hope: peculiarly sensitive, after his recent humiliation, to social realities, he
was delighted to see commoners honored by the state
and bourgeois rising to positions of eminence; increas-
ingly aware of literature as a craft above base propa-
ganda or servile entertainment, he was delighted to see
English writers, no matter what their social origins, rich
and respected. England, he wrote to his friend Thieriot
late in 1726 in his newly acquired English, was a "nation
fond of their liberty, learned, witty, despising life and
death, a nation of philosophers."

The glow of England never faded, and all his life
Voltaire good-humoredly pleaded guilty to the charge
of "Anglomania": English philosophers, English deists,
English scientists, gave firm and informed direction to
his youthful discontent, polite skepticism, and amateurish
passion for politics. Some of his acquisitions bore ready
fruit: when he returned from England late in 1728, he
had a rich accumulation of notes and ideas for a book on
English civilization. Others, especially deism, went underground and were fused with his later reading to produce his highly personal critique of Christianity, of
which the *Philosophical Dictionary* was the most celebrated specimen.

The *Philosophical Dictionary*, indeed, is suffused with

the warmth of Voltaire's Anglomania: like his paganism, it appears both in numerous details and in the intellectual style of the book. The imaginary dialogues which make up a good portion of the *Dictionary* often have Englishmen for their heroes: in LIBERTÉ DE PENSER, free expression is vigorously upheld by an English officer named Boldmind; in CATÉCHISME DU JAPONAIS, the Japanese who defends toleration is obviously an Englishman; *L'A, B, C*, the long dialogue which Voltaire wrote in 1768 and liked well enough to include in the 1769 editions of the *Philosophical Dictionary*, has a "monsieur A" as its most active protagonist, and he too is an Englishman. In fact, Voltaire could think of no higher praise for *L'A, B, C* and its boldness than to call it, in a letter to Madame du Deffand, an "English roast beef."

There are many other reminiscences: memories of a meeting with Berkeley, quotations from Shaftesbury, kindly references to Quaker pacifism. But more pervasive than all these are Voltaire's intellectual debts to Locke, champion of philosophical modesty, empirical inquiry, and associationist psychology; to Newton, enemy of vain hypotheses and creator of the true system of nature; to Hume, philosophical unmasker of miracles, penetrating psychologist, and natural historian of religion; and to critical deists like Woolston. Not only *L'A, B, C* but the *Philosophical Dictionary* as a whole is an English roast beef, served up with the subtlest of French sauces.

Voltaire's distillation of his English years, the *Lettres philosophiques*, came out in Paris in 1734, and was burned by the hangman as subversive and irreligious. Naturally, it was an immense success, but Voltaire, who had completed the book some time before, was off on other tacks. In 1731 he had published his first major history, the *Histoire de Charles XII;* in 1732, after other plays of indifferent merit, he scored a dramatic and critical triumph with *Zaïre,* which has aptly been called "a tender tragedy." It was dedicated, with pointed bluntness, to Voltaire's English friend Everard Fawkener, *"marchand anglais."* Here was François-Marie Arouet's first revenge on the chevalier de Rohan. There were to be more.

But in the early 1730's, revenge was far from Voltaire's mind. He was occupied, rather, with love and with its improbable companion, scholarship. In 1733, he had become Madame du Châtelet's lover, and in the summer of 1734, escaping possible trouble over his book on England—his "philosophical, political, critical, poetical, heretical, and diabolical letters"—he moved to her *château* at Cirey in Champagne, reassuringly close to the frontiers of Lorraine. There he stayed, but for occasional trips to Holland, Prussia, and the French court, for fifteen years, until the death of his mistress.

Madame du Châtelet is such an extraordinary person, with her ungainly frame, the masculine aggressiveness of her scientific conversation, her thirst for men (which Voltaire could never hope to satisfy), her irresponsible lust for gambling, that it is all too tempting to treat her fifteen-year liaison with Voltaire as a comical interlude. It was, in fact, anything but that. The lovers worked hard, kept rigorous hours, and collaborated in studying mathematics, making scientific experiments, and doing research in theology. Madame du Châtelet was a bluestocking, but she was not a dilettante. She translated difficult English works with more than average competence, learned languages faster than Voltaire, knew her classical philosophy, studied Newton and Leibnitz with evident comprehension, and took a professional interest in the major philosophical and theological questions then agitating educated men all over Europe. She read hard and wrote much; some of the finest mathematicians of the century, like Maupertuis, improved her algebra and warmed her bed.

This woman was the source of great vexation, but also of great delight, for Voltaire. In her presence, with her help, or for her sake, he consolidated what he had learned before and struck out in new directions. The list of his writings, or of writings nearing publication, shows the widening range of his interests and an increasing capacity for connecting the facets of his education to a central view of life. In 1738, he entered the debate between the Cartesians and Newtonians with his *Eléments de la philosophie de Newton*. In England, Newtonianism had triumphed readily; but on the Continent, Descartes' physics and methods of reasoning still had overwhelming support. Voltaire was not a scientist and had only indifferent abilities as an experimenter, but with his unfailing grasp for the essential, he understood that natural science was the most significant single development in the Europe of his time and that Newton's theory of gravitation, as well as his much-discussed "refusal to make hypotheses," would become the basis of the modern world-view and the heart of the Enlightenment. During his English visit, when he had witnessed Newton's funeral at Westminster Abbey and adopted the insular opinion that Newton was the greatest man who ever lived, he had still thought it possible to reconcile Newton with Descartes. Now, in the *Eléments*, neither the first nor the most rigorous, but probably the most influential popularization of Newtonian physics and Newtonian empiricism in the eighteenth century, Voltaire, for all the survival of Cartesian and Leibnitzian conceptions in his thinking, made himself the prophet of Newtonianism.

The *Philosophical Dictionary* is a thoroughly Newtonian book: its world is a world of unchanging and
unchangeable natural laws, created by a God who dis-
dains miracles as paltry admissions of his own ineffi-
ciency or impotence, a world of basic constituents like
mind or matter whose nature is unknown to us but
whose obedience to eternal natural law we can understand and admire. Voltaire transcended Newton's formu-
lations in one respect: he no longer needed to explain
the observed irregularities of the solar system or of
comets with Newton's notion of occasional divine intervention into the workings of the world. Mathematicians
like Maupertuis, Clairaut, and d'Alembert (all acquaint-
ances of Voltaire) were confirming and extending the
truth of Newtonian theories with dramatic measurements,
equations, and experiments, and fitting these irregularities into a universal system even vaster than Newton
had dreamed of. Newton had been a Christian, but his
scientific theories led men to a world-view irreconcilable
with Christianity. Voltaire went beyond Newton, and
the Newtonian scientists of Voltaire's century went beyond Voltaire into a thoroughgoing naturalism. While
Voltaire, the true deist, never surrendered his belief in
the Divine Watchmaker, the scientists preached Newton's physics without Newton's god.

For Voltaire, Newtonianism was more than a scientific
system: it was an intellectual method implying a social
policy. It taught us, he wrote a young man in 1741, to
"examine, weigh, calculate, and measure, but never
conjecture." Newton had never made a system; "he saw,
and he made people see; but he didn't put his fancies in
place of truth." Such Newtonian modesty led men to
focus on what they could know, and to be tolerant. If
we do not, and cannot, know the essence of things (as
Voltaire insists in ÂME, BÊTES, MATIÈRE, and elsewhere),

we will not persecute others, who are as ignorant as we are. Thus scientific method and religious toleration, Newtonian physics and the attack on fanaticism, are aspects of a single enterprise.

The scientific revolution, then, had its rewards, but even for a deist like Voltaire it raised troublesome questions in metaphysics and ethics. He grappled with both in his years with Madame du Châtelet, first in the *Traité de Métaphysique* of 1734, then in the *Discours en vers sur l'Homme* of 1738, and less systematically but far more fatefully in his private correspondence with Frederick of Prussia, initiated by the crown prince with an adulatory letter in 1736. Voltaire, never a systematic thinker, gradually worked his way to a deterministic view of life (vividly reflected in the dialogue DE LA LIBERTÉ) and a common-sense view of ethics, a kind of shorthand secular decalogue of human decency without dogmas or quibbles (repeated, in various forms and with varying emphases, throughout the whole of the *Philosophical Dictionary*).

All this sounds rather portentous, but Voltaire's education never lacked its playful side. In the Cirey period, he wrote some of his most famous plays and most of his delightful philosophical tales. Even his paganism found playful expression in the scandalous—or what the devout thought scandalous—defense of pleasure and luxury, the poem *Le Mondain*. This poem, like almost everything else, eventually contributed to the *Philosophical Dictionary:* the article LUXE curtly, and sensibly defends the cultivated ease of Athens against the military rigor of Sparta, and coyly quotes two lines from *Le Mondain* as lines the author of the article has "read somewhere."

Even more significant for the *Philosophical Dictionary* than this array of publications of the Cirey period

are the writings published after it closed and the studies
which never found their way into print at all. In the
first group are Voltaire's two historical masterpieces,
the *Siècle de Louis XIV*, and the *Essai sur les moeurs*,
which Voltaire undertook to prove to his mistress that
history had utility as well as charm. In the second
group are inquiries into the logic, coherence, dates,
sources, and moral value of the Bible.

Voltaire's interest in history began early, and his epic,
the *Henriade*, was a first, immature product of that
interest. The *Histoire de Charles XII*, still a racy and
informative book, was, for all its power, little more
than the biography of a romantic adventurer. With his
accounts of the reign of Louis XIV and the growth of
Western civilization he found his method and made his
major contributions to the discipline of history. Voltaire
was the first to make civilization the subject of historical inquiry; one of the first to be rigorously secular in his analysis of causes; and a thoroughgoing, although not always happy, critic of his sources. Voltaire's
histories are histories of the "mind" of an age; they
portray an interconnected network of institutions in
which political forms, social ambitions, artistic production, and foreign policy all act upon one another and
are all, collectively and separately, more important than
details of battles, court intrigue, or the history of the
Chosen People.

The defects of these writings are well known—Voltaire's critics have seen to that: he lacked sympathy with
ages alien to his ideal of cultivation or hostile to his theological convictions, and his persistent campaign to improve his readers often interfered with his efforts at
objectivity. Yet even a hasty reading of the *Philosophical Dictionary* shows that its author has mastered the
craft and the materials of history. His critical use of

Herodotus in CIRCONCISION, his skepticism of improbable tales, his relish for the revealing incident, his easy allusion to historical characters and events from many ages and many civilizations, his dislike of mere chronicle and insistence on what is important—all these show the historian at work.

In the *Philosophical Dictionary*, to be sure, Voltaire exercises his historical skills chiefly on the Biblical Jews and the early Christians, and historical analysis shades into theological criticism. When Voltaire came to Cirey, he already had a general position on religion: he was in favor of toleration and simple, reasonable beliefs, and he opposed fanaticism, persecution, and superstition. In a notorious early poem, *Epitre à Uranie*, probably written in 1722 but not circulated until much later, Voltaire had attacked the idea of a cruel God and, visualizing himself as a modern Lucretius, declared war on the "Sacred lies that fill the world." The *Henriade* had singled out Henri IV's tolerance as his finest virtue, while the book on England, the *Lettres philosophiques*, had praised the Quakers and offered as an explanation for English power and prosperity the happy coexistence of many religions: one religion, he wrote, threatens to lead to despotism, two cause religious war, but the English "have thirty, and they live happy and in peace."

All these notions were the staples of advanced freethinkers for whom religious war was an anachronism, religious enthusiasm a lower-class aberration, and religious dogma a myth. But now, at Cirey, Voltaire refined his instruments of criticism and sharpened his weapons of attack: the commonplace freethinker became an accomplished Critical Deist.

Deism, which attracted many nominal Christians in the early eighteenth century, had two faces: on its Constructive side, it drew on the speculations of Chris-

tian humanists, latitudinarian clergymen, and modern
Stoics. True religion, it argued, is as old as creation; it
consists of a few simple maxims about the fatherhood
of God, the regularity of nature, and the brotherhood of
man; it preaches peace and kindness, and despises ritual,
sects, and intolerance; it depends for proof on the natural revelation of human reason and draws strength from
the unanimity of philosophers: Chinese literati, Persian
sages, Roman Stoics, and Jesus, the ethical teacher, were
all regarded as deists.

This Constructive Deism is the foundation of Voltaire's positive religious convictions, and its characteristic tenets open article after article of the *Philosophical
Dictionary*. "Almost everything that goes beyond the
worship of a supreme Being and the submission of one's
heart to its eternal commands, is superstition"—thus
begins SUPERSTITION. "What is toleration? It is the endowment of humanity. We are all steeped in weaknesses
and errors; let's forgive each other our follies; that is the
first law of nature"—thus begins TOLÉRANCE. "Every
sect, of whatever kind, is the rallying point for doubt
and error"—thus begins SECTE.

But Constructive Deism gets its cutting edge from
Critical Deism, that peculiar mixture of science and
hostility which undertakes to examine Christian documents to prove their absurdity, Christian history to
prove its cruelty, and Christian ritual to prove its dependence on pagan rites. This is what Voltaire and
Madame du Châtelet did at Cirey, with the greatest
gusto and with the largest possible battery of scholarly
support. They borrowed freely from Bayle's *Dictionary*, used arguments from subversive manuscripts that
passed slyly from hand to hand, imported Critical Deist
works like Thomas Woolston's *Six Discourses on the
Miracles of our Savior*, read orthodox apologetics like

La Bletterie's *Vie de l'Empereur Julien* in order to refute them, and relied heavily on dom Calmet's pious commentary, the enormous *Commentaire littéral sur tous les livres de l'Ancien et du Nouveau Testament*, which they shamelessly pillaged and ungratefully ridiculed.

The result of the lovers' exhaustive, verse-by-verse study of the Bible was a sizable manuscript by Madame du Châtelet, the *Examen de la Genèse*, which, despite the modesty of its title, is an examination of the whole Bible, from the Book of Genesis to the Book of Revelation. Voltaire's precise share in the enterprise will never be known, but it seems to have been considerable, and there is good evidence that at Cirey he wrote, or at least drafted, some of his most vehement anti-Christian writings published only much later, in the 1760's, when he could operate with relative security from his strategically located *château* at Ferney.

To be sure, the *Philosophical Dictionary* is not merely an alphabetical compilation of Critical Deist attacks on the Bible; its assault is far more comprehensive and far more varied. But again and again, the *Examen de la Genèse* reads like a first draft of a passage, or an argument in the *Philosophical Dictionary*.

Thus (to offer but a few gleanings from a far larger harvest): in order to throw doubt on the veracity of the translators, who begin Genesis with an affirmation of monotheism—"In the beginning God created the heavens and the earth"—Madame du Châtelet quotes dom Calmet to the effect that the original Hebrew text speaks of "gods." This sally from the *Examen* found its way into the article GENÈSE in the *Philosophical Dictionary*, where Voltaire suggests with characteristic lightness of touch that anyone with the slightest education knows that Genesis has "gods" and not "God" in its opening sentence. Again, Madame du Châtelet ridicules the two incompatible stories of the creation of man and woman and the creation of the sun three days after light and darkness had been separated. In GENÈSE, Voltaire raises the same objections, using Madame du Châtelet's observation that the stories demonstrate little more than abominable ignorance of natural science.

The Bible is not only incorrectly translated and swarming with contradiction; it is also filled with immoral stories, vicious conduct held up as exemplary, foolish and puerile myths. The *Examen* makes much of Abraham passing his wife off as his sister, and the *Philosophical Dictionary* devotes a large part of its article ABRAHAM to this patriarchal lie. The *Examen* professes horror at David—bandit chief, murderer, and adulterer—and the *Philosophical Dictionary* has a short but powerful article on DAVID which repeats all these charges. Again, Madame du Châtelet condemns the Book of Proverbs as boring, repetitious, infelicitous, and inelegant in its many images, and Voltaire adopts these criticisms in his article on SALOMON.

The New Testament offered an equally fertile field for skepticism: the *Examen* wonders over the two contradictory genealogies of Jesus, the many apocryphal gospels, the darkness covering the earth for three hours at the Crucifixion, the reprehensible behavior of Paul in returning to the temple, and dozens of other riddles. All of them find their place in the *Philosophical Dictionary*, especially in CHRISTIANISME, significantly the longest of the articles. Dozens of other examples are available, but I think I have said enough to make the conclusion inevitable: it was once thought that the guardian angel (or, if you will, the evil spirit) of the *Philosophical Dictionary* was Frederick the Great, but it should now be clear that behind that work stands someone else—the robust, intelligent shade of Madame du Châtelet.

I say "shade," for in September 1749 this extraordinary woman died, as scandalously as she had lived, after giving birth to a girl fathered neither by her husband the marquis du Châtelet, nor by her official lover, Voltaire, but by another lover, the poet Saint Lambert, to whom she had been driven by the demands of her passionate heart and her awkward body. Bereft, Voltaire moved to Paris, and there, late in 1749 and early in 1750, he added another dimension to his experience—politics.

His activity was neither a new interest nor a sudden caprice; he had followed diplomatic and domestic politics in Europe for over thirty years. What he had written on politics—in the *Henriade*, his book on England, and his correspondence with statesmen—showed him a hard-headed relativist, as ready to see the blessings of constitutional government as the virtues of centralized authority; Voltaire was not a doctrinaire admirer of "Enlightened Despotism." But in the political infighting in France, Voltaire was on the side of the king, and had been a royalist all his adult life. His reasons for this position were based not on abstract principle but on the harsh realities of French history. As a French royalist, Voltaire opposed the privileged bodies in the state—nobility and clergy—and objected to powerful particularist and provincial tendencies which kept the country from unifying its weights and measures, rationalizing its taxes, and improving its legal procedure. The system of venality, under which military, administrative, and judicial posts were bought, sold, traded, and treated as private property, created centers of power within and against the state. These centers, as Voltaire grimly noted, consumed without producing, escaped taxation, obstructed governmental efficiency, and in general resisted the most essential reforms. Voltaire's admiration for the French crown was more limited than some of his pronouncements might indicate, but he committed himself to it, for only the king and his ministers, supported by an alert public opinion, could pursue the policies the country so desperately needed.

When Voltaire came to Paris after Madame du Châtelet's death, Louis XV was embroiled with the clergy in a major struggle for power; here was a fine opportunity to express political opinions to a large public. But it seemed that Voltaire would have to be a royalist without, and perhaps even despite, his king, for his position at court was rather ambiguous. In the mid-1740's, Voltaire had turned courtier: he had been appointed Royal Historiographer in 1745, and in the following year, after a shameless campaign, he had finally been elected to the Académie Française. But he was too irreverent and too indiscreet to remain popular at court, and when he appeared in Paris in the fall of 1749, he had few close friends there. It did not matter: the fight between king and clergy was too interesting to be resisted.

The issue was taxation. The clergy, as the First Estate of France, and as a major owner of real estate, had a vast income but no obligations to pay taxes. Every five years, at the quinquennial Assembly of the Clergy, it offered a "voluntary gift" to the crown, but in 1749 Machault d'Arnouville, the aggressive finance minister, had persuaded his king that this gift was not enough. Accordingly, Louis XV issued an edict imposing a five per cent income tax on all Frenchmen, including the privileged orders. In 1750, when the clergy met to consider this imposition and offered resistance, a war of pamphlets began, and Voltaire was joyfully in the midst of it. In some light-hearted sallies, Voltaire ridiculed clergymen as fat, debauched, useless, lazy; but in May or early June 1750, he wrote a full-scale political tract,

La voix du sage et du peuple, which moved from lampoon to a serious attack: the clergy deserved no exemptions and it should have no power in the state, either in politics or over individuals. Clerics were no better than tutors: they should be allowed to teach, but told what to teach and how to teach it.

La voix du sage was Voltaire's first systematic statement on the political position of the clergy and on the wide gap between Voltaire's ideal and French actuality. The articles in the *Philosophical Dictionary* which bear on these and other political questions are little more than elaborations of this first tract. Reading *La voix du sage* side by side with such articles as LOIS CIVILES ET ECCLÉSIASTIQUES, or PRÊTRE, is to see the Paris of 1750 in the book of 1764.

In 1764, such ideas were becoming widespread, thanks partly to Voltaire's intervention in 1750. But in 1750, his radicalism seemed extreme and excessive even to the king in whose behalf it had been expressed; to the timorous and vacillating Louis XV, this kind of royalism concealed—or rather revealed—the most dangerous kind of anticlericalism. Unwelcome at court, Voltaire resolved to leave France. His education was complete, or nearly complete, and his ties with his old world were severed, or nearly severed. Frederick II, who had long wanted to "possess" Voltaire, now had his chance: Voltaire was willing to come to Prussia, perhaps to stay.

It seems right somehow, or even inevitable, that the *Philosophical Dictionary* should be conceived in Prussia, in the uncertain twilight of semi-exile. All of Voltaire's experience, as I have said, is in the book, but it would seem that the thin air of an alien environment was the atmosphere best calculated to create, or at least confirm, the recklessness needed for his final, public break with the established order.

THE BIOGRAPHY OF A BESTSELLER

The precise origins of the *Philosophical Dictionary* are lost in obscurity. This is appropriate for a book so expert in concealment, so rich in evasions and false cues. Colini, who was Voltaire's secretary during this period, reports that Frederick the Great suggested such a dictionary to his dinner companions on September 28, 1752, when Voltaire had lived at the Prussian court for over two years. Colini is an unreliable reporter, but there is nothing inherently improbable in his account: Frederick was as anticlerical as his celebrated guest, and far more impious; he was not without a certain literary ingenuity, and he had a pitiless sense of humor capable of conceiving such a vast practical joke.

It is just as likely that the father of Voltaire's *Philosophical Dictionary* was Voltaire himself. He was equipped to compile it and inventive enough to think it up. Indeed, its first articles have a striking literary and psychological affinity to his notorious anti-Christian pamphlet, the *Sermon des cinquante*, not published until 1762 but written either in Prussia or shortly before. The *Sermon* is Voltaire's declaration of war against Christianity: the Bible is contradictory and childish; Christian mysteries like Transubstantiation are absurd; the Jews are ignorant, savage, and mendacious, and their God is cruel, petty, and altogether hateful. The man who could write such inflammatory things was certainly in the mood to write the *Philosophical Dictionary*.

Clearly, the idea was in the air at Potsdam. On September 5, 1752, Voltaire wrote to the king, then in Silesia reviewing his troops, that his companions were living together peacefully, awaiting his return. "We have," he added, "fine projects for the advancement of human reason." Then, on September 29, the day after

the dinner reported by Colini, Voltaire asked his intimate friend, the countess Bentinck, to send him "the
Bible dictionary of dom Calmet, with all the volumes of
his commentaries," and promised to take good care of
the books: "This vast collection of sacred nonsense is
full of remarkable things." Calmet had been invaluable
to Madame du Châtelet in her *Examen de la Genèse*; it
was only natural for Voltaire to appeal to the same
authority as he began to write his *Philosophical Dictionary*.

This is not very solid; still, it is all we have and are
ever likely to have. But whatever the share of Frederick
the Great in thinking up the *Philosophical Dictionary*,
it is certain that he was its first reader and most enthusi-
astic critic. Through October and November 1752,
Voltaire submitted his first articles to the king; "Beel-
zebub's theologian," as Voltaire called himself, was de-
liriously happy to hear that Frederick considered his
articles "very good," or "very fine," or "well done."
Fired with the excitement of a daring enterprise, the
approval of his companions, the memories of Cirey, and
the information drawn from Calmet, all went smoothly
for a while: ABRAHAM, ÂME, ATHÉE, and BATÊME followed one another in rapid order.

Then for several years nothing went well, and the
Philosophical Dictionary was put aside. The reasons for
this intermission are not hard to find: Voltaire quarreled
with Frederick in the winter of 1752, and for over three
years led a wandering existence. Rejected by Potsdam,
rejected by Paris, he traveled restlessly, visited friends,
lamented his lot, carried on a passionate affair with his
niece, and searched for a home. During his wanderings,
he entered this charming story into his notebooks: "Today, 23 June 1754, dom Calmet, abbé of Senones, asked
me what was new; I told him that Madame de Pompa-

dour's daughter had died. 'Who is Madame de Pompadour?' he replied." To readers of the *Philosophical Dictionary* the name of dom Calmet is familiar enough; he appears in it as a benighted, superstitious relic of a darker age. But this is just another trick of Voltaire's ungrateful trade: Calmet was kindly, learned, and by no means unwilling to allow his impious visitor to stay in his abbey for a month and use his library.

But while an abbey was a good place to visit, Voltaire did not want to live there. In the winter of 1755, he finally discovered his natural habitat, the neighborhood of Geneva. For the next few years he busied himself with acquiring several properties there, and by the end of the 1750's he was settled in Ferney, a *château* on French soil near the Genevan border. He was happy again. He was very rich and very purposeful; his house was far from Paris, but with its stream of distinguished visitors and its unceasing flow of correspondence, it became a kind of literary government in exile. Where Voltaire was, *there* was Paris.

During these years of readjustment, Voltaire's radicalism deepened and grew more pointed. The dreadful Lisbon earthquake of November 1, 1755, and the Seven Years' War, which began in 1756, permanently alienated him from whatever remnants of cosmic optimism he had left. He puzzled over these events in his poem on the Lisbon earthquake and in *Candide*, and he remembered them in the *Philosophical Dictionary*. In *Candide*, he coined the much-quoted phrase that we must cultivate our garden; at Ferney, in the twenty years that remained to him, he made clear that for him the phrase did not mean Epicurean indifference but humanitarian meddling. He did not neglect literature—he would never do that—but he grew more passionate about social reform. His new slogan, *écrasez l'infâme*, expressed his new intensity, and as he planned his major assault on *l'infâme*, he turned once again to the *Philosophical Dictionary*.

He had never wholly forgotten it; even in the dark, aimless years of the early 1750's he had put thoughts into his notebooks which were either intended for the *Dictionary* or later found their way into it. As we read these casual entries, we encounter Asian gods, like Xaca or Fo, who haunt the pages of the *Dictionary*; we read the observation that "there are virtues and vices as there is health and illness," which is elaborated in CATÉCHISME CHINOIS; we find tantalizing lists of paradoxes and contradictions that are the germs of some of the theological articles. As the supreme professional, Voltaire wasted nothing but rewrote everything. A felicitous phrase in the notebooks would not be thrown away; it would appear, still more felicitous, in the *Philosophical Dictionary*. Thus:

NOTEBOOKS	AMOUR-PROPRE
L'amour-propre est comme cette partie qu'il faut cacher et dont il faut se servir, qui est agréable, nécessaire et dangereuse.	*Cet amour-propre est l'instrument de notre conservation; il ressemble à l'instrument de la perpetuité de l'espèce: il nous est nécessaire, il nous est cher, il nous fait plaisir, et il faut le cacher.*

The fifties, then, were a time for making phrases and storing up ideas, the early sixties a time for using them. To judge from his infrequent and circumspect allusions in his correspondence, Voltaire resumed concentrated work on the *Philosophical Dictionary* late in 1762, through 1763, and early in 1764.

Everything was propitious. Voltaire was old, inde-

pendent, and relatively safe. Should trouble arise with
the French authorities, he could move to Les Délices in
Geneva; should Genevan pastors object to his theatrical
performances or political interference, he had Ferney in
France. Now if ever was a time to speak out. Others
were speaking out, although, as Voltaire noted with some
complacency, less well than he. Diderot's *Encyclopédie*
was nearing completion: it was a vast undertaking with
which Voltaire collaborated, which he defended, but
from which he expected little. The *Encyclopédie* was too
bulky, too clumsy, too adroit, too expensive, to produce
the propagandistic effect he wanted to produce. Diderot
hoped to "change men's ways of thinking" and so did
Voltaire, but Voltaire was convinced that *l'infâme* was
strong, solidly entrenched, truly built on a rock. It could
be blasted loose only with simplicity, clarity, brevity, and
rage: as he wrote his articles for Diderot, he inevitably
thought once again of his own, one-man *Encyclopédie*.
This is what he meant when he wrote in 1765: "Twenty
folio volumes will never make a revolution: it's the small,
portable books at thirty *sous* that are dangerous. If the
Gospel had cost 1,200 sesterces, the Christian religion
would never have been established."

In 1762, Voltaire received a fresh piece of evidence
concerning *l'infâme* in action: the Calas case. Voltaire's
imagination, always touched by the concrete and the
dramatic, was aroused by the affair. Marc-Antoine Calas,
the eldest son of an obscure Huguenot cloth merchant
in the city of Toulouse, had been found hanged in his
father's shop in October 1761. Jean Calas was convicted
of the murder of his son, tortured, and executed in
March 1762. It was widely believed that he had committed this outrage to prevent Marc-Antoine from con-
verting to Catholicism. When Voltaire first heard the
story late that month, it struck him as a fine specimen

of Christian fanaticism, no matter whether Jean Calas was guilty or innocent. Guilty, Jean Calas demonstrated the length to which a superstitious Protestant would go to prevent his son from turning Catholic; innocent, Jean Calas demonstrated the stupidity of Catholic magistrates who believed that Huguenots committed ritual murders. Gradually, Voltaire moved from his rather callous, pragmatic view of the case to a general, humane, principled critique of the French judicial system. He became convinced that Calas had been wrongfully imprisoned, wrongfully convicted, wrongfully tortured, wrongfully broken on the wheel, and began a campaign to rehabilitate the old man's memory and, broadening his aim, to reform the French legal code.

Voltaire never stopped learning. What the Calas case taught him was that it was not enough to expose the crimes of religion—politics and law must be reformed as well. But, conversely, to concentrate exclusively on legal reform was to treat the symptom and leave the infection untouched. Thus from 1762 on, as Voltaire wrote petitions on the Calas affair and polemics on French law, he did not forget his broader cause. The *Philosophical Dictionary* rapidly took shape. He importuned his friends for books: in December 1762, evidently working on articles like CHRISTIANISME, he asked his Paris correspondent Damilaville to send him *"presto, presto"* a recently published *Dictionnaire des conciles.* "Theology," he wrote acidly, "amuses me; that's where we find the madness of the human spirit in all its plenitude." Again, in May 1763, he asked Damilaville to return the article IDOLÂTRIE; he wanted to insert it in the forthcoming *Dictionary.*

It took another year. Finally, in June 1764, a small octavo volume of 344 pages appeared in Geneva, bearing a false London imprint. It contained 73 articles and was entitled *Dictionnaire philosophique portatif*. Its success was immediate, enormous, and predictable: Voltaire had expended all his talents on it. In September, Grimm reported in the exclusive newsletter by which he informed and entertained royal and aristocratic subscribers all over Europe that "there exists a *Dictionnaire philosophique portatif*, a volume of over three hundred pages, published through the indefatigable zeal of the patriarch of Les Délices. But this is true only for the true faithful; as for the malicious, it is proved that this great apostle had no hand in it. Anyway, the entire edition of this precious gospel is down to perhaps twenty or twenty-five copies. Lucky the man who can get one!"

Voltaire gloried in his success and frantically denied his authorship, with as much vigor as he had put into the writing. In letter after letter he begged people to believe that he had not written the book, that he had not even read all of it, that evil-minded enemies were trying to get him into trouble. "I implore you to shout that I've had no hand whatever in the *Portatif*," he wrote to d'Alembert on September 7, and he repeated this injunction almost daily for months.

But it could not be denied—and Voltaire would have been displeased if it could have been denied—that the *Dictionary* showed the master's touch on page after page. Hence Voltaire shifted to a new line: the *Philosophical Dictionary* was nothing but a collection of harmless pieces designed for respectable publications, a collection "by several hands" to which English divines and English deists had made major contributions. This alibi was not a complete lie; rather, it was a partial truth reiterated to produce the effect of a complete lie. At least one of the articles, MESSIE, was in fact by Voltaire's friend, the Swiss pastor Polier de Bottens; at least one article, IDOLÂTRIE, was actually printed in Diderot's *Encyclopédie;* a handful of articles, like CONVUL-SIONS and MIRACLES, were patterned closely after the Critical Deist writings of Middleton. But everyone, including Voltaire, was perfectly aware that such judicious borrowings, far from softening, only increased the revolutionary impact of the *Dictionary*.

Voltaire's transparent mendacity has often been severely criticized. It has been taken as a symptom of a kind of malicious inability to tell the truth, or as part of a good-natured charade in which an author denied the book everyone knew to be his and the government burned the subversive work in a harmless ritual designed to impress the ignorant public with the government's earnestness without frightening the author. But such criticism gravely underestimates the power of censorship in continental Europe. Authors *were* frightened: witness Diderot's unwillingness to publish any of his more daring productions after his imprisonment in 1749; authors *were* harassed: witness the fate of Rousseau, who signed everything he published and was hounded from refuge to refuge. Voltaire could never be sure that lax censors or pro-*philosophe* officials would remain in office, or that a policy of leniency might not be suddenly, drastically, reversed.

The *Philosophical Dictionary* made a great stir. The first edition was rapidly sold out, and fortunate owners passed their copies to their friends. Outraged ecclesiastics set to work compiling anti-Philosophical Dictionaries, a tribute to Voltaire's power. He was called a "ferocious beast," an enemy to Christian men, a threat to the Christian community. In September 1764, the Genevan government ordered all copies of the book seized and burned; in December, the same ceremony took place at The Hague; on March 19, 1765, the *parlement* of Paris followed suit; and on July 8, 1765,

the book was proscribed by the Holy Office at Rome.
Voltaire's response to the first of these condemnations
was the wry remark that the Genevan government was
welcome to burn a book in which he took no interest,
as long as it did not burn him. He promptly began work
on a second, enlarged edition.

For two years it seemed improbable that Voltaire
would share the fate of his book. But then, in June 1766,
the chevalier de La Barre, a foolish and undisciplined
youth, was burned at the stake for some adolescent im-
pieties. He had refused to take off his hat to religious
processions, sung obscene songs about the Virgin, was
accused of mutilating a large wooden crucifix, and certainly read scatological anticlerical pamphlets. His pathetic little library was thrown into the flames with his
body, and among the books was his copy of the *Philosophical Dictionary*. Here was tragic vindication of the
prudence of Voltaire's subterfuges.

His notoriety and his fame moved Voltaire to inter-
mittent fits of panic and, at the same time, to aggressive
euphoria. For five years, from 1764 to 1769, he reprinted, revised, and enlarged the book. There was a
new edition in December 1764, yet another in 1765 in
two duodecimo volumes, a fourth in 1767. Then, in
1769, the book appeared in its largest form: two solid
volumes with 120 articles, including the long dialogue
L'A, B, C, and with the new title, *La raison par alphabet*. It was reprinted several times in the last nine years
of his life, under its final title, *Dictionnaire philosophique*. It is this edition, the most comprehensive collection of Voltaire's articles that can properly be called
the *Philosophical Dictionary*, that is printed here.

As the *Philosophical Dictionary* expanded, so did
Voltaire's sympathies. He was in his seventies, and fully

entitled to intellectual retirement. But he refused to live off his capital. Living in and near Geneva, in close touch with Genevan patricians, publishers, and physicians, he could not help meddling in Genevan politics. In the two decades that Voltaire was concerned with them, Genevan politics were enlivened, and embittered, by an intricate party struggle verging on civil war. A patrician party, anxious to retain the government of the small republic in the hands of an exclusive elite, faced a bourgeois party determined to broaden participation in political decisions to their own group, without however granting the lower orders, the so-called "*Natifs*," any share in the state.

In this complicated fight, Voltaire's natural allies were the patricians. They were his friends, and besides he had spent most of his life saying that the masses were incapable of casting off superstition, were unworthy of self-government. But the more he learned of Genevan history, law, and politics, the more convinced he became of the merits of the bourgeois case, and he shifted his support, which was not without weight in this republic, in accord with his new convictions. But then, in 1766, well after the third edition of the *Philosophical Dictionary* had appeared, the *Natifs* entered the scene, and to the dismay of both patricians and bourgeois, Voltaire made himself their champion. He did not become a convert to democracy but, as always in the past, he listened to his experience. These sturdy workmen, gardeners, carpenters, and watchmakers spent their leisure time reading—even reading Voltaire—and Voltaire was moved to modify his facile, snobbish assumption that the poor must be governed by lies and the fear of hell.

This shift toward radicalism, toward appreciation of

the possibilities of universal enlightenment, is subtly reflected in the succeeding editions of the *Philosophical
Dictionary*. In the first edition, the articles ÉTATS and
ÉGALITÉ demand government by the rule of law but
appear resigned to drastic inequality as inevitable and
even useful. It is only in FRAUDE (characteristically a
dialogue, for the issue was unresolved in Voltaire's
mind) that one of the speakers suggests the need for
honesty with all citizens, even the lowliest. But some of
the later articles take a more radical line. TORTURE recalls the Calas and La Barre cases in its assault on
French legal practice; and *L'A, B, C* is even prepared
to toy with the possibility that democracy is the best
form of government. The Voltaire of 1769 was no
longer the Voltaire of 1764.

   This is the biography of the *Philosophical Dictionary*
—or almost all of it. In the last eight years of his life,
from 1770 to 1778, Voltaire's inventiveness declined,
but not his vigor. He was active against *l'infâme* to the
last, and now published some of the Critical Deist
works he had begun thirty years before. And the con-
tinuing success of the *Dictionary* gave him a formula
which he adopted, to the confusion of his later editors,
in another work. Starting in 1770, he brought out
another dictionary, a nine-volume alphabetical compendium entitled *Questions sur l'Encyclopédie*. It contained
and expanded some of the articles from the *Dictionary*,
and scores of new ones, fighting the same battles over
again. When he returned to Paris in February 1778,
very old and very feeble, he was *l'homme aux Calas* to
the thousands who acclaimed him: a social reformer, a
humanitarian, a radical anticlerical. Only the cultivated
remembered, or cared, that he had written tragedies or
comedies or dramatic criticism. That this shift in the

image of Voltaire should have occurred was the result
of his labors of the last twenty years. The man of *Zaïre*
had become the man of the *Philosophical Dictionary*.

A CENTER OF CONCERN AND
A VARIETY OF METHODS

I said at the beginning that the *Philosophical Dictionary* is not a dictionary. The remark has its risks: it
invites the witticism that the book is not philosophical
either. But to make it would be to miss the significance
of philosophy for the *philosophes*. For the men of the
Enlightenment, philosophy was not one discipline among
many but *the* discipline—the mobilization of sound
thinking for the sake of right living. With repetitive
and almost obsessive vehemence, the *philosophes* denigrated metaphysics and joked about system-makers. In
fact, they were so preoccupied with practicality that
they sometimes skirted close to philistine anti-intellectu-
alism, a trap they avoided only by their comprehensive
definition of what was practical and by their pleasure
in the play of mind for its own sake. Yet, for all their
playfulness, they viewed the task of philosophy with
grim seriousness; and first in the order of priority was
the destruction of error. Locke, whom Voltaire made
the hero of the continental Enlightenment, had thought
it "ambition enough to be employed as an under-
labourer in clearing the ground a little, and removing
some of the rubbish that lies in the way to knowledge,"
and Voltaire's *Philosophical Dictionary* was perhaps the
most savage rubbish-clearer of the age.

Still, for the *philosophes* the names "Age of Philosophy" and "Age of Criticism" (which they applied to
their century with sublime self-confidence) were not

alternatives but synonyms. They accompanied the most unsparing criticism with the most persistent concern for moral and political construction; they accepted Cicero's dictum in *De officiis* that "no man not concerned with ethics can call himself a philosopher"; and for them (as for him) ethics was virtue in action.

This conjunction has often been overlooked; the *philosophes* have often been accused of being "merely negative" or "merely destructive." To be sure, some of their belligerent language makes this interpretation plausible, but in fact the energy that animated them was a drive for knowledge and control, a restless Faustian dissatisfaction with appearance. Their favorite instrument was analysis; their essential atmosphere, freedom; their goal, reality. The most popular metaphors of their writings were not merely metaphors of battle but metaphors of penetration: they spoke of the light that pierces corners of darkness, the blow that levels barriers of censorship, the fresh wind that lifts the veil of religious authority, the surgical knife that cuts away the accumulation of tradition, the eye that sees through the mask of political mystery-mongers. If philosophy was destructive, that was because destruction had become the precondition of construction.

I am far from suggesting that hostility or destructiveness were absent from the *philosophes'* mode of thought; indeed, I strongly suspect that most of them, Voltaire among them, rather relished both. But negativity was not an end in itself. Disingenuous as the *philosophes* may have been in expressing regret at the necessity for war, their assumption that war was inevitable was correct enough. As self-appointed knight errants of truth, the *philosophes* found the makers of myth and the forces of privilege planted like grim-faced guardians before a precious hoard. And the identity of the enemy was, as it were, emblazoned on their shields: it was Christianity.

Voltaire for one always came back to that: it was to the interests of ecclesiastics everywhere to keep men in the condition of ignorant and submissive children; it was to their interest to immolate human victims, stamp out rational dissent, enforce a deadening uniformity, and reject sound science; it was to their interest to quibble about meaningless philosophical constructions and waste the time of educated men on ridiculous theological controversies. In a word, the church was the implacable enemy of progress, decency, humanity, and rationality. For the first time in history, a happy society, based on power over nature, was within the grasp of men, but Christians were exerting all their energies to obstruct its realization. The vicious interests of Christianity, Voltaire argued further, were matched by its power, cleverness, and lack of scruple. Christian notions were inculcated early and reinforced by dire threats; hence they were hard to uproot. They were handed on from generation to generation; they paralyzed the powerful and seduced the intelligent. These are the despairing themes of several articles in the *Philosophical Dictionary*, and they dictated its tactics.

The battle of the *philosophes* with Christianity is a commonplace in intellectual history, but we must understand its intensity before we can really understand the *Philosophical Dictionary*. For, despite the crystalline clarity of its writing and the immediate appeal of its wit, the book is in many respects opaque to the twentieth-century reader. Why should a popular polemic devote at least half of its space to abstruse technical questions of theology, church history, or man's knowledge of the soul? Why should Voltaire, who was not a compulsive crank but a rational man of letters, concentrate his energies and expend his venom on matters that would arouse only a small group of students today?

The answer is that the eighteenth century was very different from our own. Theology was still important and still familiar; theological controversies had far more than academic interest—they went to the heart of daily concerns, to the very meaning of existence. It is no longer fashionable to speak of the warfare between science and theology, and in truth the seventeenth and eighteenth centuries produced a finely shaded spectrum of beliefs and tolerated close alliances between scientists and theologians, God and nature, the pulpit and the laboratory. Nevertheless the notion of two parties, of believers against unbelievers, retains much validity. A man could be a scientist and a Christian at the same time, as Newton, the greatest of them all, demonstrated. But a man could not at the same time regard Christianity as uniquely true and subject it to the kind of rationalist critique he directed against other religions; he could not at the same time think of the Jews as God's Chosen People and investigate their history as objectively as the history of ordinary nations; he could not at the same time revere the Bible as *the* Book and read it in the same way that he read all other books.

Voltaire's logical, historical, and textual exegeses were thus more than an intellectual game. The task of persuasion, to which the *Philosophical Dictionary* addressed itself, was (as the *philosophes* would have liked to say) practical, but it was also (as Voltaire often said) far from simple. Christianity was not only a mighty but also a many-sided enemy. It had a sacred predecessor, the Jews; it had an authoritative text, the Bible; it had an ethics of humility and self-abnegation; it had a history filled with affecting martyrs and impressive miracles; it had a philosophy of science and a theory of politics. In the *Philosophical Dictionary* Voltaire attacked them all, rather like a modern Hercules face to face with a modern Hydra.

The stakes in this attack on Christian theology were higher than the fate of theology itself: to discredit Christianity was to take a decisive step in the direction of a secular, modern civilization. The 1760's, the decade of the *Philosophical Dictionary*, was a time of great beginnings. It marked the quickening of mechanical inventions, improvements in agricultural productivity, and the establishment of an industrial discipline that we are once again calling (after some shifts in fashion) the Industrial Revolution. It saw the beginnings of what R. R. Palmer has recently called the "Age of the Democratic Revolution," a widespread rebellion against time-honored constituted authority, a rising demand for self-government, and rudimentary essays in popular political activity. It was the decade in which Rousseau published his most revolutionary books, the *Contrat social* and *Emile*, Diderot completed his *Encyclopédie*, and Holbach deluged Europe with his atheist tracts. Voltaire had angry contempt for the first, cool respect for the second, and (as the article ATHÉE shows) vehement disagreements with the third of these men; but Rousseau, Diderot, Holbach, and Voltaire, an improbable team of reluctant allies, were yoked together in a single enterprise: the movement for modernity.

The *Philosophical Dictionary*, therefore, could fire its shots from a sheltered position; it was a single cannon in a sizable battery. Many of the resonances evoked by its arguments could be evoked because Voltaire belonged to an impressive tradition of revolutionary dissent. And yet, for all its borrowings, for all the reinforcements it received from his contemporaries, for all its family resemblance to other works, it was a deeply personal book. Much of its power was generated by Voltaire's style, for that style was unique.

The eighteenth century was pervasively engaged with style. It was Voltaire's contemporary, Buffon, who coined the celebrated maxim that *le style est l'homme même*. What Buffon meant by suggesting that style was the man himself was that it depended on more than artifices, graces learned in school, conventional devices, or participation in a literary tradition. It was an alliance of talent and craftsmanship, general cultivation and specific information. That is why when we speak of Voltaire's style we must begin by speaking of his knowledge. This is the burden of Diderot's perceptive remark to Catherine the Great: "What is it that particularly distinguishes Voltaire from all our young writers? Instruction. Voltaire knows a great deal, and our young poets are ignorant. The work of Voltaire is full of matter, their works are empty." Clearly, what applied to poetry applied even more strongly to polemics.

In a century of voracious readers, Voltaire was remarkable for his inquisitiveness and intelligence, for the excellence of his library, the rationality of his working habits, and the energy of his research. It hardly needs pointing out that his scholarship was rarely disinterested, and the *Philosophical Dictionary* shows that it was far from impeccable, too. There are wrong dates for the Bar Kochba rebellion or for Justin Martyr; there are mistranslations. Professional archeologists or classicists greatly surpassed him in their own specialties, and sometimes, when these scholars were as belligerently Christian as Voltaire was belligerently pagan, they publicly convicted him of some embarrassing errors. Yet, considering his status as an amateur and the spectrum of his writings, his knowledge is nothing short of admirable.

It shows to good advantage in the *Philosophical Dictionary*. Here he commands an enormous vocabulary and moves with ease from theologians' jargon or lawyers' cant to classical allusions, Italian literature, English expressions, and popular doggerel: the opening line of the first article, ABBÉ, is a quotation from a contemporary song. Voltaire can slyly mine and casually refer to "the learned Fabricius," whose scholarly Latin editions of the Gospels, canonical and apocryphal, were in his library; he gives his own version of Jewish history or Jewish views of Christianity by citing Basnage's voluminous *Histoire des Juifs*, a French translation of Josephus, or a compilation of Jewish writings, *Tela ignea Satanae*, by the seventeenth-century scholar Wagenseil. Sometimes his information is out of date, but usually he consults the most recent writers: in the article RELIGION, he courteously and anonymously dissents from Hume's *Natural History of Religion*, which he owned in a French translation of 1759.

But, as Voltaire knew better than anyone else, a merely learned treatise, no matter how anticlerical its implications, could never touch *l'infâme*; the dry dust of learning needed the alchemy of style to be converted into a living threat to Christianity.

Voltaire's style is a celebrated but surprising instrument: beyond its obvious virtues, to which I have freely referred, it is full of concealments. It appears straightforward but is richly allusive; it appears coolly rational but is an admirable vehicle for the expression of passion; it appears disarmingly simple but contains the most powerful agents of persuasion. In his subtle analysis of Voltaire's style, Erich Auerbach points to Voltaire's "method of posing the problem so that the desired solution is contained in the very way in which the problem is posed," and to his "searchlight technique, which over-illuminates the ridiculous, the absurd, or the repulsive" in his opponent. These techniques, writes Auerbach, are not new, but Voltaire gives them special power by "his tempo."

In the *Philosophical Dictionary*, Voltaire employs his tempo with masterful versatility, although, impressively enough, his variety never leads him into incoherence of tone. In all his stylistic tricks and clever turns of phrase we recognize a single mind: Voltaire could never convince anyone that he had merely edited the contributions of several hands. He had a wide repertory of roles at his command, but his performances were dominated by a single, pervasive technique: irony.

Irony is more searching than sarcasm, more serious than playfulness, and more honest than a lie. It consists of saying one thing and meaning another, like a lie; but unlike a lie, which seeks only to deceive, irony seeks to clarify. The ironic effect is achieved when both actor and spectator recognize the role as role, and the deception as the path to reality. Irony says what must be said and cannot be said; it illuminates by reflected light. It is, as Goethe says, the pinch of salt that makes food palatable, but it does more: irony reveals by concealing.

Voltaire's irony lies in his adopting poses which he, and his readers, understand to be inappropriate to him, or in exploiting poses which are appropriate but dramatized for the sake of effect. These devices permit Voltaire to expose what he could never expose directly; they permit him to approach forbidden territory under cover of darkness. In a world of censorship, of ecclesiastics hunting heretics, and of influential readers to be appeased, irony was an agent of twofold liberation: it freed the writer to speak the truth, and it freed the reader to see it. Voltairian irony was itself an ironic counterpoint to Jesus' assertion that the truth shall make us free.

For Voltaire's contemporaries, his irony was delicious, because it was adroitly executed and reassuringly familiar. Today we are in danger of overlooking the brilliance because the familiarity has faded. It may therefore be useful if I offer some program notes to his ironic self-dramatization, a short guide to his roles.

The Bewildered Believer. Voltaire often tries to discredit Christian doctrines by pitting conflicting assertions of theologians against one another. In ARIUS he appears confused and outraged by controversies over the nature of the Trinity. This pose is doubly ironic: a sincere believer, seeking theological clarity, might well be bewildered by quarrels over "hypostasis" and "generative power," but there is not an ounce of sincere search in Voltaire. Merely by listing them, he depicts all positions on the Trinity as equally absurd and all controversies about it as equally futile. His aim is to destroy, not to understand. Again, Voltaire, probably with conscious irony, is parodying an ancient Christian tactic; many centuries before, the Fathers of the Church had attracted pagans to Christianity by unmasking the unending disagreements of pagan philosophers on the most important questions.

The Clever Prosecutor. Turning Christian arguments against Christianity is first cousin to turning statements from believers against belief. As the clever prosecutor, Voltaire puts unfriendly witnesses on the stand and compels them to condemn themselves by their own words. In JEPHTÉ he cites Judges to convict the Biblical Jews of practicing human sacrifices; in CONCILES he quotes from the emperor Constantine's letter to Hosius to convict the Church Fathers of pettiness and pride. This pose, apparently so straightforward, also has its ironic overtones. Voltaire relies on his unfriendly witnesses only when they confess their own crimes or castigate the crimes of their fellow-believers, but he refuses to accept their testimony when they speak well of themselves or their brethren. As the first Christian emperor, Constantine is a hypocrite and an assassin, but Constantine berating other Christians is heard with respect and transformed, for a brief moment, into a *philosophe*.

The Grand Inquisitor. The role of prosecutor is not free from difficulties. Its rationale, advanced in JEPHTÉ, is that we can judge nations only by their own archives. But since neither Jews nor Christians had ever claimed to be perfect, proof of imperfection is no argument against the religion these sinners practice. To be sure, Voltaire does not rest his case against religion entirely, or even chiefly, on the sins of its devotees; he expends much ingenuity unmasking the illogic of religion itself. But he never forgets the consequences of religious beliefs and institutions; a century before Dostoyevsky's Grand Inquisitor, he takes the position that the effects of Christianity have been the tragic opposite of its program. This too is an ironic role: Voltaire has little use for Christian morality even at its purest, but he is willing to use the Sermon on the Mount to demonstrate how far Christians have fallen from the announced aims of Christ. Voltaire strikes this pose, at once belligerent and despairing, in the very first article: the true ABBÉ, as the name implies, is a father, not a lazy wastrel; and what has happened to the vows of poverty and obedience? Again, as he writes in MIRACLES, a religion based on the true miracles of Our Savior has been degraded by the fantastic and laughable claims of recent priests. Voltaire, as the reader well knows, believes neither the "true" ancient miracles nor the false modern ones, but this insincerity (which depends for its effectiveness on its transparency) does not weaken his point: even if Christianity, at the beginning, was humane and impressive, it has turned, and had to turn, into its opposite.

The Beleaguered Catholic. Few pleasures are as pure as quoting enemies against themselves, but Voltaire was perfectly ready to vary his tactics and quote allies against enemies. He had to be cautious, for his allies were often dangerous company: pagans, freethinkers, rakes, or Unitarians. If they were to be quoted, they must be censured, no matter how feebly; they must, as it were, be praised with faint damns. Here, Voltaire is the beleaguered Catholic, troubled by what appear to be persuasive arguments by heretics, schismatics, or infidels. Thus in ANTITRINITAIRES Voltaire deftly expounds the Unitarians' denunciations of the Trinity for more than two pages, and then, with bland piety and deliberate ineffectiveness, dismisses these arguments as inexcusable, since Church Councils have decided that they are wrong.

The Subversive Anthropologist. Voltaire was a real cosmopolitan, fond of England, impressed with China, attached to pagan antiquity. But when he praises all these in the *Philosophical Dictionary*, he is doing more than giving way to affection; he is using the method of invidious comparison and exploiting his own feelings: at once involved and detached, he manipulates them as though they were not his own. For "England is free and happy because it has free speech," read: "France, which has censorship, is miserably backward." For "the Chinese literati have an admirable religion free from superstitions and the rage to persecute," read: "Catholics have a despicable faith, steeped in superstition and stained with persecution." When, in MORALE, Voltaire scornfully denies the imputation that ancient pagans had no morality, he is not only defending his beloved Cicero and Marcus Aurelius, he is asserting their superiority over Christians, who father such ridiculous slanders but have embarrassingly little morality of their own. In TOLÉRANCE he even uses the Jews as models: the Jews in the Roman Empire, he writes, stubbornly clung to their deity, but they did not resent the gods of others. We happen to know from his correspondence that for once his praise of the Jews was sincere, but in the *Philosophical Dictionary* his point is that the Jews, bad as they are, are far better than the Christians: "The Jews didn't want the statue of Jupiter in Jerusalem; but the Christians didn't want it in the Capitol." Reader (as Voltaire would say), draw your own conclusions.

The Intelligent Ignoramus. The great ironist of antiquity was Socrates, and his most effective pose the pose of ignorance. Voltaire, who admired Socrates without wishing to emulate him, used ignorance with similar intentions and similar results. In Voltaire's hands, ignorance was at once a working principle and a weapon. As I have said, Voltaire was a good Lockian and a good Newtonian: he was convinced that there is much we do not and cannot know, that we must concentrate our energies and bring the knowable to bear on the formulation of rational policies. But his insistent reiteration of ignorance is also an ironic pose: if as educated and intelligent a thinker as Voltaire is puzzled by so much, other men must be equally in the dark. Hence all dogmatic theology, all tales of miracles, are thrown into doubt: theology depends on the unknowable, miracles depend on the undemonstrable. A Philosophical Dictionary is in and of itself an ironic place for the pose of ignorance, and some of Voltaire's happiest inventions in the book match this larger irony. Thus in EZÉCHIEL Voltaire lends his cloak of ignoramus to a learned rabbi, who expatiates at some length on obscure passages in

Ezekiel and Hosea, and then confronts Voltaire: " 'But do you know what all this means?' 'No,' I told him. 'Neither do I,' said the rabbi."

The Outraged Humanitarian. Voltaire's humanitarian activities are a matter of public record, but the purity of his motives has often been put into question. Such suspicions may be petty and are certainly wrong, but they are not useless: they point to Voltaire's self-dramatization. The *Philosophical Dictionary* is filled with outraged humanity; much of its energy comes from diatribes in which Voltaire expends his fury on Inquisitors who burn heretics, Calvin who "assassinated" Servetus, rulers who gaily destroy flourishing countries in irresponsible war, judges who condemn accused men to torture, scholars who denigrate the Emperor Julian, ecclesiastics who impose Lent on the poor. In FAUSSETÉ DES VERTUS HUMAINES he falls on a priest who has written a book denying human virtue, thus libeling all non-Christians by implication. Does this mean, asks Voltaire, that Epictetus was a rascal just because he was a pagan? "I'll say no more about it, lest I grow furious."

Was this fury real? To judge from his notebooks and the testimony of his most intimate friends, there can be no doubt that it was; its reality is not jeopardized and its value is not diminished by our discovery that it is used by a controlled artist. Rage and pity are all the more impressive when they are eloquent; they are particularly powerful in a writer notorious for his light touch and petty malice, for in him they are a dramatic change of pace. They come as an unforgettable shock. No doubt Voltaire enjoyed his rage, but his ironic detachment from his emotion did not kill that emotion —it converted incoherent exclamations into firmly pointed polemics. Voltaire the outraged humanitarian is playing a role, but he is playing himself.

Not one of these devices was new; they were familiar instruments of controversy in an age in which Gibbon could write his celebrated footnotes, or David Hume could remark in his essay on miracles that "The Christian religion not only was at first attended with miracles, but even at this day cannot be believed by any reasonable person without one." Much of their power—I cannot insist on this enough—rested on their familiarity: they established immediate communication with educated readers and facilitated communication with the new reading public. Unlike our own century, the eighteenth did not make a fetish of originality; it enjoyed writing "imitations" and liked to soften the strange idea by the familiar form, the radical proposal by the traditional manner. That is why Pope could define "true wit" as

> Nature to advantage dressed,
> What oft was thought but ne'er so well expressed.

That is why Voltaire, rather than inventing techniques, combined and varied known techniques.

But—I must say once again—these techniques had never been so skillfully employed. Consider his insistent, almost painful repetition of a single word to establish an inescapable mood (in HISTOIRE DES ROIS JUIFS ET PARALIPOMÈNES he uses the word "assassinate" fifteen times in one sentence to convict the Biblical Jews of bloodthirsty cruelty); his witty transposition of one issue into another (in CATÉCHISME DU JAPONAIS he ridicules the quarrels of Christian sects over theology by depicting schools of cooking disputing over recipes); his deft injection of piquant speculation to keep interest high (the article AMOUR NOMMÉ SOCRATIQUE is an amusing examination of homosexuality, DES LOIX exalts equity over legal fetishism with a very funny story about double incest, and JOSEPH playfully considers various types of eunuchs); his use, rare and more enjoyable for being rare, of scatological material (as in EZÉCHIEL and his famous "lunch"); his straight-faced sentences which begin in one key and modulate into another (the first sentence of CONCILES begins "All councils are doubtless infallible," but ends "for they are composed of men")— these are Voltaire's inimitable, unmistakable signature.

All this preoccupation with tactics raises a final and uncomfortable question: are not all of Voltaire's roles eclipsed by another role, that of the Dirty Fighter? Irony is all very well, but can distortion be covered by so polite a word? Can the fight for truth be won with so much lying?

The *Philosophical Dictionary* is sprinkled with distortions. Thus in the fifth conversation of *L'A, B, C,* Voltaire sarcastically discusses the "art of surprising, killing, and robbing," and offers as an early instance of this despicable art the story of Dinah. According to Voltaire, the son of the king of the Shechemites was "madly in love" with Dinah and wanted to marry her. Dinah's brothers then proposed that the Schechemites be circumcised, so that all would become a single nation. The Shechemites agreed, submitted to the ceremony, and then, when they were asleep, Simeon and Levi fell upon them and killed them all while "ten other patriarchs" robbed them. Voltaire offers no reason for this mass slaughter beyond saying that the two "lovers" had "slept together," and the reader must conclude— and is expected to conclude—that the Jews were a thieving, murdering horde. Genesis, xxxiv, confirms the general outlines of this story, including the killing and robbing, but gives the reason for this terrible act, not once, but over and over again: Dinah had been raped.

The prince saw Dinah and "seized her and lay with her and humbled her"; and Jacob told his sons when they came home from the field that their sister had been "defiled," and "the men were indignant and very angry, because he had wrought folly in Israel by lying with Jacob's daughter, for such a thing ought not to be done." Even after the slaying and robbing, Genesis emphasizes that all this was done "because their sister had been defiled." Thus Voltaire converts the primitive revenge of a vile outrage into an act of wanton and cowardly cruelty.

He plays the same game with the Christians. In PIERRE, Voltaire—hiding behind two scholars—condemns St. Peter for causing the death of Ananias and his wife Sapphira. As he tells it, Ananias had sold some property and given money to St. Peter, but "held back a few écus for himself and his wife to pay for their necessities, without telling him." For this Peter made him die "of apoplexy," and a little while later did the same to Sapphira. This, Voltaire concludes curtly, "is harsh." But read in the Biblical context, the incident acquires a rather different meaning. Acts, v, supports Voltaire's version of the incident but Acts, iv, shows that he has, once again, omitted the central point: "Now the company of those who believed were of one heart and soul, and no one said that any of the things which he possessed was his own, but they had everything in common. . . . There was not a needy person among them, for as many as were possessors of lands or houses sold them, and brought the proceeds of what was sold and laid it at the apostles' feet; and distribution was made to each as any had need." Thus Voltaire turns primitive socialism enforced by primitive punishments into an example of priestly presumption and rapacity.

There are many excuses that can be offered for such tactics. If he sometimes fought with dirty weapons, so did his opponents, who had the support of church and state and who blackened his name, tried to smoke him out of his refuges, stole and disfigured his writings. His attack on the Jews, with all its ferocity, was really an attack on the Christians, their heirs—a kind of Nietzschean tactic before Nietzsche. The war in which he was engaged was a deadly conflict in which positions must be simplified and enemies caricatured; this is how wars are fought: to pity your enemy is to paralyze yourself. In that war, he was scattering his shots, trying to hit dozens of targets, and inevitably some went astray. Finally, Voltaire was fighting a good fight, for humanity, decency, rationality, the rule of law, and against caprice, superstition, fanaticism, cruelty—must we not forgive such a gallant warrior a great deal?

Surely we must. These circumstances do justify much of what he did. Voltaire was not a bad man fighting a good fight; fortunately we are spared the painful decision whether his foul methods corrupted his good ends: after all, not all his methods were crooked, not all his blows were unfair, not all his motives were questionable, not all his prejudices were petty. But troublesome reservations remain. Subterfuges to deceive censors or arbitrary authority are part of a grim game: a state that compels its writers to be liars has only itself to blame if its writers lie. Again, institutions that have been solidly entrenched for centuries and resent, or even punish, dissent inevitably invite irony and other techniques of oblique attack. But a distortion remains a distortion, and a lie designed to harm those who, like the Jews, were themselves victims rather than powers, remains a pernicious lie. No doctrine of "higher truth" can change that. Indeed, the *philosophes*, with Voltaire at their head, would have vehemently repudiated the doctrine that all methods are justified.

No. It is best to see Voltaire as he really was, a complex and fallible human being. He was a humanitarian who would run a fever on the anniversary of the St. Bartholomew's Day massacre; we have independent corroboration for this improbable claim. He was a reformer who spent years of his life battling for obscure victims. He was a great clarifier who sought the truth and tried to spread it abroad. He was an irrepressible wit who (at least on second thought) preferred his independence to gilded dependence on the great. He was a generous patron and a loyal friend. But he could also be vicious, as in his unrelenting slander of the Jews; ignorant, as in his contempt for Egyptian culture; ungrateful, as in his treatment of Calmet; and obtuse, as in his blindness before medieval civilization. And like its author, the *Philosophical Dictionary* is a complex mixture: it is the great rubbish-clearer with some rubbish of its own, the unsparing enemy of cant that is not free from cant. The book taught generations to be critical, but when we read and enjoy it today, we should remember that its critical acid can be applied to it as well. This, I suppose, is the final irony of Voltaire's masterpiece.

PETER GAY

PHILOSOPHICAL
DICTIONARY

VOLTAIRE'S PREFACE
to the Seventh Edition

THERE have already been six editions of this Dictionary, but all of them incomplete and imperfect; we were unable to supervise any of them. Now we offer the present one, which is superior to all the others in authenticity, order, and number of articles. For all of them, we have drawn upon the best authors in Europe, and sometimes have not hesitated to copy out a page from a well-known book, when that page was necessary to our collection. There are complete articles by persons still living, including learned pastors. These pieces have long been familiar to learned men—for instance, the articles on APOCALYPSE, CHRISTIANITY, MESSIAH, MOSES, MIRACLES, etc. But in the article on MIRACLES we have added an entire page by the celebrated Doctor Middleton, librarian of Cambridge.

You will also find several passages by the learned bishop of Gloucester, Warburton. We have also been greatly helped by the manuscripts of M. Dumarsais; though we have unanimously thrown out everything that seemed to favor Epicureanism. The dogma of Providence is so sacred, so necessary to the happiness of mankind, that no honest man should expose his readers to doubting a truth which can do no harm in any case, and which can always do much good.

We do not regard the doctrine of a universal Providence as a system, but as a matter demonstrated to all reasonable minds; on the other hand, the various systems concerning the nature of the soul, grace, and metaphysics, which divide all persuasions, can be subjected to examination: for, since they have been argued over for seventeen hundred years, it is obvious that they do not bear the stamp of certainty; they are enigmas which everyone can guess at according to the capacity of his intelligence.

The article on GENESIS is by a very clever man, honored by the esteem and confidence of a great prince: we ask his pardon for shortening it. The limits we prescribed ourselves did not permit our printing it in its entirety; it would have filled almost half a volume.

As for matters of pure literature, you will easily recognize the sources from which we have drawn. We have tried to join the agreeable to the useful, having no other share in this work but the selection, and deserving no other credit. Persons of every estate will find here something that will instruct, while it amuses, them. The book does not demand a continuous reading; but at whatever place you open it, you will find something to think about. Those books are most useful in which the readers do half the work themselves; they develop the thought whose germ has been presented to them; they correct what seems defective, and with their own reflections strengthen what appears weak.

This book will be read by enlightened persons alone; the common herd are not made for such knowledge; philosophy will never be their portion. Those who say there are truths that should be hidden from the people need not feel any alarm; the common people do not read; they work six days a week and go to the tavern on the seventh. In a word, the works of philosophy are made for philosophers alone, and every honest man should strive to be a philosopher without priding himself on being one.

We conclude by offering our humble apologies to persons of importance who favored us with several new articles: we could not use them as we should have wished; they came too late. But we are no less grateful for their kindness and their praiseworthy zeal.

ABBÉ

"Where are you going, *Monsieur l'Abbé?*" etc. Do you know that the word Abbé means *Father?* If you become a father you do a service to the state; surely you do the best work a man can do: you cause the birth of a thinking being. There is something divine in this act. But if you are *Monsieur l'Abbé* merely because you like your head shaved, wear a small collar, a short cloak, and to wait for a benefice, you don't deserve the name of Abbé.

The ancient monks gave this name to the superior they elected. The Abbé was their spiritual father. What different things do the same names mean at different times! The spiritual Abbé was a poor man at the head of several other poor men: but the poor spiritual fathers have since got incomes of two hundred, four hundred thousand francs, and today there are poor fathers in Germany who have a regiment of guards.

A poor man taking a vow of poverty and consequently becoming a sovereign! I have already said it; I must say it again a thousand times: this is intolerable. The laws protest against this abuse, religion is indignant at it, and the really poor who lack food and clothing cry to heaven at the door of *Monsieur l'Abbé.*

But I hear the abbés of Italy, Germany, Flanders, and Burgundy say: "Why shouldn't we accumulate wealth and honors, why shouldn't we become princes? After all, the bishops are. They were once poor like us; they have enriched themselves, they have elevated themselves; one of them has even become superior to kings; let us imitate them as much as we can."

Gentlemen, you are right. Overrun the land; it belongs to the strong man, or the clever who seize it. You have profited from times of ignorance, superstition, and insanity to despoil us of our inheritance and trample us under your feet, that you might fatten on the substance of the unfortunate. But tremble, lest the day of reason arrive.

ABRAHAM

Abraham is one of the names famous in Asia Minor and Arabia, as was Thout among the Egyptians, the first Zoroaster in Persia, Hercules in Greece, Orpheus in Thrace, Odin among the northern nations, and so many others known better through their fame than through any authentic history. I speak here only of profane history; as for that of the Jews, our masters and our enemies, whom we believe in and detest: since the history of that people was evidently written by the Holy Spirit, we feel about it as we should. I speak here, then, only about the Arabs. They boast that they descend from Abraham through Ishmael; they believe that this patriarch built Mecca and died in that city.

In fact, the race of Ishmael was infinitely more favored by God than the race of Jacob. It is true that both races have produced thieves; but the Arabian thieves have been vastly superior to the Jewish thieves. The descendants of Jacob conquered only a very small country, which they have lost, while the descendants of Ishmael conquered parts of Asia, Europe, and Africa, established an empire greater than that of the Romans, and drove the Jews from their caverns, which they called the Promised Land.

Judging matters only by examples found in our modern histories, it would be hard to believe that Abraham was the father of two such different nations; we are told that he was born in Chaldaea and that he was the son of a poor potter who earned his living making little earthen idols. It is hardly likely that the son of this potter should have founded the city of Mecca, a thousand miles away in the tropics, after traversing impassable deserts. If he was a conqueror, he doubtless aimed at the beautiful country of Assyria, and if he was only a poor man, as he is depicted, he did not found kingdoms far away from home.

Genesis relates that he was seventy-five years old when he left the land of Haran after the death of his father, Terah the potter: but the same Genesis also says that Terah, having begotten Abraham at the age of seventy, lived to be two hundred and five, and that Abraham did not depart from Haran until after the death of his father. On this calculation it is clear from Genesis itself that Abraham was a hundred and thirty-five when he left Mesopotamia. He went from a country that is called idolatrous to another idolatrous country called Shechem, in Palestine. Why did he go there? Why did he leave the fertile banks of the Euphrates for a place so remote, so barren, and so stony as Shechem? The Chaldaean language must have been very different from that of Shechem, which was not a place of trade; Shechem is more than two hundred and fifty miles from Chaldaea; one must pass through deserts to get there. It was God who wanted Abraham to make this journey; he wanted to show him the land which his descendants were to occupy several centuries after him. The human mind has difficulty understanding the reasons for such a journey.

Hardly had he arrived in the little mountainous country of Shechem than famine made him leave it. He went into Egypt with his wife to find sustenance. It is five

hundred miles from Shechem to Memphis—is it natural
to go so far to ask for grain, to a country whose
language you don't understand? Strange journey indeed,
undertaken at the age of nearly a hundred and forty.

He brought his wife Sarah along to Memphis; she
was extremely young and almost a child compared to
him, for she was only sixty-five. Since she was very
beautiful, he resolved to turn her beauty to account.
"Say you are my sister, that it may go well with me
because of you." Rather he should have said to her,
"Claim to be my daughter." The king fell in love with
young Sarah and gave the alleged brother "many sheep,
oxen, asses, she-asses, camels, servants, and maids":
which proves that Egypt was then a very powerful and
highly civilized and consequently very ancient kingdom,
and that brothers who came and offered their sisters to
the kings of Memphis were rewarded munificently.

Young Sarah was ninety years old when God promised her that Abraham, who was then a hundred and
sixty, would give her a child within a year.

Abraham, who loved to travel, went into the dreadful desert of Kadesh with his pregnant wife, who was
still young and pretty. Naturally, a king of this desert
would fall in love with Sarah, as the king of Egypt had
done. The father of the faithful told the same lie he had
told in Egypt; he passed off his wife as his sister, and got
from this business more sheep, oxen, servants, and maids.
We might say that this Abraham grew rich chiefly
through his wife. Commentators have written a prodigious number of volumes to justify Abraham's conduct and to reconcile the chronology. We must therefore refer the reader to these commentaries; they are all
composed by subtle and exquisite minds, excellent metaphysicians, men free from prejudices, and not at all
pedantic.

This name Bram, Abram, was also famous in India and Persia: several learned men even claim that he was the same legislator whom the Greeks called Zoroaster. Others say that he was the Brahma of the Indians: this is not demonstrated.

But what seems extremely reasonable to many scholars is that this Abraham was a Chaldaean or a Persian; in the course of time the Jews boasted that they had descended from him, as the Franks claim to be descended from Hector and the Bretons from Tubal. It is an established fact that the Jewish nation was a quite modern horde; that it did not settle on the borders of Phoenicia until very late; that it was surrounded by ancient nations; that it adopted their language; that it took from them even the name of Israel, which is Chaldaean, according to the testimony of the Jew Flavius Josephus himself. We know that it took even the names of the angels from the Babylonians; that, finally, it called God by the names of Eloi or Eloa, Adonai, Jehovah or Hiao, after the Phoenician usage. It probably learned the name of Abraham or Ibrahim only from the Babylonians; for the ancient religion of all the countries from the Euphrates to the Oxus was called *Kish-Ibrahim, Milat-Ibrahim*. This is confirmed by all the investigations done on the spot by the learned Hyde.

The Jews, then, treat their history and ancient fables as their peddlers treat their old clothes: they turn them and sell them for new as dearly as possible.

It is a strange example of human stupidity that we should have so long regarded the Jews as a nation which taught everything to others, while their historian Josephus himself admits the contrary.

It is hard to penetrate the shadows of antiquity; but it is evident that all the kingdoms of Asia had been flourishing mightily, long before the vagabond horde of

Arabs, called Jews, had a small spot of earth that was
their own, before they had a town, laws, or a settled religion. Therefore, when we see an ancient rite, an ancient
opinion, established in Egypt or Asia and among the
Jews, it is natural to suppose that this small, new, ignorant, crude people, still destitute of the arts, copied the
ancient, flourishing, and industrious nation as best it
could.

It is on this principle that we must judge Judaea, Biscay, Cornwall, Bergamo the land of Harlequin, etc.:
surely triumphant Rome didn't imitate Biscay, Cornwall, or Bergamo in anything; and a man must be either
a great ignoramus or a great rascal to say that the Jews
taught the Greeks.

(*Article taken from M. Fréret*)

ADAM

Pious madame de Bourignon was sure that Adam
was a hermaphrodite, like the divine Plato's first men.
God had revealed this great secret to her; but since I
have not had the same revelation, I won't say anything
more about it. The Jewish rabbis have read the books of
Adam; they know the names of his teacher and his
second wife: but since I have not read our first parent's
book, I won't say a word. Some acute minds, very
learned, are quite astonished, when they read the Vedas
of the ancient Brahmins, to find that the first man was
created in India; that he was called Adimo, which signifies begetter; and that his wife was called Pocriti, which
signifies life. They say that the sect of the Brahmins is
incontestably more ancient than that of the Jews; that
the Jews could not write in the Canaanite language un-

til very late, since they didn't settle in the little country of Canaan until very late; they say that the Indians were always inventors and the Jews always imitators, the Indians always ingenious and the Jews always coarse; they say that it is hard to understand how Adam, ruddy with red hair, should be the father of the Negroes, who are black as ink and have black wool on their polls. What don't they say? As for me, I don't say a word; I leave this research to the Reverend Father Berruyer of the Society of Jesus; he is the greatest innocent I have ever known. His book was burned as the work of a man who wanted to make the Bible ridiculous: but I can testify that he intended no such malicious enterprise.

(Taken from a letter of the chevalier de R* * *)

ÂME · SOUL

It would be a fine thing to see our soul. *Know thyself* is an excellent precept, but it remains for God alone to put it into practice: who but he alone can know his own essence?

We call soul that which animates. Since our intelligence is limited, we know hardly anything more about the subject. Three-fourths of mankind go no further and don't worry about this thinking being; the other fourth look for it; no one has found it or will find it.

Poor pedant, you see a plant that vegetates, and you say *vegetation*, or even *vegetative soul*. You notice that bodies have and produce motion, and you say *force;* you see your hunting dog learn his craft from you, and you exclaim *instinct, sensitive soul;* you have complex ideas, and you say *spirit*.

But, please, what do you understand by these words?

This flower vegetates, but is there any real being called *vegetation?* This body pushes another, but does it possess within itself a distinct being called *force?* This dog brings you a partridge, but is there a being called *instinct?* Wouldn't you laugh at a logician (had he been teacher to Alexander) who told you: "All animals live, therefore there is in them a being, a substantial form, which is life"?

If a tulip could talk and were to tell you: "My vegetation and I are two beings evidently joined together," wouldn't you laugh at the tulip?

Let's see first of all what you know and what you are sure of: that you walk with your feet, that you digest with your stomach, that you feel with your whole body, and that you think with your head. Let's see if your reason could have given you enough insight by itself to conclude, without supernatural aid, that you have a soul.

The first philosophers, whether Chaldaeans or Egyptians, said: "There must be something within us which produces our thoughts; that something must be very subtle; it is a breath, it is fire, it is ether, it is a quintessence, it is a faint image, it is an entelechy, it is a number, it is a harmony." Finally, according to the divine Plato, it is a compound of the *same* and the *other.* "It is atoms which think in us," said Epicurus, following Democritus. But, my friend, how does an atom think? Admit that you have no idea.

The opinion we should doubtless adopt is that the soul is an immaterial being; but certainly you can't imagine what that immaterial being is. "No," the scholars reply, "but we know that its nature is to think." And how do you know that? "We know it because it thinks." Oh, scholars! I'm afraid that you are as ignorant as

Epicurus: the nature of the stone is to fall, because it falls; but I ask you what makes it fall.

"We know," they go on, "that a stone has no soul." Granted, I believe that too. "We know that a negation and an affirmation are not divisible, are not parts of matter." I am of your opinion. But matter, too, otherwise unknown to us, possesses qualities which are not material, which are not divisible; it has gravitation toward a center, which God has given it. Now, this gravitation has no parts; it is not divisible. The moving force of bodies is not a being composed of parts. Nor is the vegetation of organized bodies, their life, their instincts. These are not beings apart, divisible beings; you can no more cut in two the vegetation of a rose, the life of a horse, the instinct of a dog, than you can cut in two a sensation, a negation, an affirmation. Therefore your fine argument, drawn from the indivisibility of thought, proves nothing at all.

What, then, do you call your soul? What notion do you have of it? You cannot by yourself, without revelation, admit anything more within you than a power of feeling, of thinking, unknown to you.

Now tell me honestly, is this power of feeling and thinking the same as the one that makes you digest and walk? You'll admit to me that it is not, for your understanding would say in vain to your stomach: *Digest*— it won't do it if it is sick; in vain would your immaterial being order your feet to walk—they won't move if they have gout.

The Greeks clearly perceived that thought often has nothing to do with the play of our organs; they held that these organs had an animal soul and that thoughts had a finer, subtler soul, a *nous*.

Here is this soul of thought, which has the ascendancy

over the animal soul on a thousand occasions. The
thinking soul commands its hands to take, and they take.
But it does not tell its heart to beat, its blood to flow,
its chyle to form; all this is done without it. Here are
two souls deeply enmeshed, and hardly master in their
own house.

Now, this animal soul certainly does not exist; it is
nothing more than the movement of our organs. Take
care, O man! Your feeble reason may have no more
proof that the other soul exists. You cannot know it except through faith. You are born, you live, you act,
you think, you wake, you sleep, without knowing how.
God has given you the faculty of thinking, as he has
given you all the rest; and if he had not come at the
time appointed by his providence to teach you that you
have an immaterial and immortal soul, you would have
no proof of it whatever.

Let's look at the fine systems about souls your philosophy has fabricated.

One says that the soul of man is part of the substance of God himself; another, that it is part of the
great whole; a third, that it is created from all eternity;
a fourth, that it is made, and not created; others assert
that God makes souls as they are needed, and that they
arrive at the moment of copulation. "They are lodged
in the seminal animalcules," exclaims one. "No," says
another, "they inhabit the Fallopian tubes." "You are
wrong," says a bystander; "the soul waits for six weeks,
until the foetus is formed, and then it takes possession
of the pineal gland; but if it finds a stunted embryo, it
turns back and waits for a better opportunity." The
latest opinion is that its dwelling is in the *corpus callosum;* this is the position assigned to it by La Peyronie;
a man would have to be first surgeon to the king of
France to dispose of the soul's lodging in this way.

Still, the *corpus callosum* didn't make the same hit the surgeon did.

St. Thomas, in his question 75 and following, says that the soul is a form *subsistante per se;* that it is all in all; that its essence differs from its power; that there are three *vegetative* souls, namely, the *nutritive,* the *augmentative,* the *generative;* that the memory of spiritual things is spiritual and the memory of corporeal things is corporeal; that the rational soul is a form "immaterial as to operations and material as to being." St. Thomas wrote two thousand pages as forceful and clear as this; besides, he is the angel of the schoolmen.

Nor have there been fewer systems about the manner in which this soul will feel when it has left the body it feels with; how it will hear without ears, smell without a nose, and touch without hands; what body it will resume afterwards, the one it had at the age of two or of eighty; how the *I,* the identity of the same person, will subsist; how the soul of a man who went mad at the age of fifteen, and died mad at the age of seventy, will resume the thread of the ideas it had at the age of puberty; by what contrivance a soul, whose leg was cut off in Europe and which lost an arm in America, will recover this leg and this arm, which will have passed into the blood of some other animal after being transformed into vegetables. We should never be done if we tried to report all the extravagances this poor human soul has imagined about itself.

What is quite remarkable is that the laws of God's people don't say one word about the spirituality and immortality of the soul: nothing in the Decalogue, nothing in Leviticus, or in Deuteronomy.

It is quite certain, it is beyond doubt, that Moses nowhere offers the Jews rewards and punishments in another life, that he never speaks to them of the immortality of their souls, that he never gives them hopes of heaven, nor threatens them with hells: all is temporal.

He told them before he died, in his Deuteronomy:

"When you beget children and children's children, and have grown old in the land, if you act corruptly, you will soon utterly perish from the land; and you will be left few in number among the nations where the Lord will drive you.

"I the Lord your God am a jealous God, visiting the iniquity of the fathers upon the children to the third and fourth generation.

"Honor your father and your mother, that your days may be prolonged.

"You shall eat and be full.

"If you serve other gods and worship them, you will perish quickly. . . .

"If you will obey my commandments, the Lord will give the rain for your land in its season, the early rain and the later rain, that you may gather in your grain and your wine and your oil. And he will give grass in your fields for your cattle, and you shall eat and be full.

"Lay up these words of mine in your heart and in your soul; and you shall bind them as a sign upon your hand, and they shall be as frontlets between your eyes. And you shall write them upon the doorposts of your houses, that your days may be multiplied.

"You shall destroy all the peoples that the Lord your God will give over to you; your eye shall not pity them.

"You shall not eat impure birds, the eagle, the griffin, the ixion, etc.

"Of animals that chew the cud or have the hoof cloven you shall not eat these: the camel, the hare, the porcupine, etc.

"And because you keep and do all these ordinances, the Lord your God will bless you and multiply you; he will also bless the fruit of your body and the fruit of your ground, the increase of your cattle . . .

"But if you do not keep all these ordinances or be careful to do all his statutes, you shall be cursed in the city and cursed in the field . . . you will suffer famine, poverty; you will die of misery, of cold, of poverty, of fever; you will have the itch, the scurvy, the ulcers . . . the Lord will smite you on the knees and on the legs with grievous boils.

"To a foreigner you may lend upon interest, but to your brother you shall not lend upon interest; that the Lord your God may bless you . . .

"And you shall eat the offspring of your own body, the flesh of your sons and daughters, etc."

It is evident that in all these promises and all these threats there is nothing but the temporal, and that we don't find a word about the immortality of the soul or the future life.

Several illustrious commentators have believed that Moses was perfectly aware of these two great dogmas; and they prove it by the words of Jacob, who, when he believed that his son had been devoured by wild beasts, said in his grief: "I shall descend with my son into the grave, *in infernum*, into hell"; that is, I shall die, since my son is dead.

They prove it further by passages in Isaiah and Ezekiel; but the Hebrews to whom Moses spoke could not have read either Ezekiel or Isaiah, who came only several centuries later.

It is quite useless to argue about the private feelings of Moses. The fact is that in his public laws he never spoke of a life to come, that he limited all punishments and all rewards to the present. If he knew of a future

life, why didn't he set forth that dogma explicitly?
And if he did not know of it, what were the object
and extent of his mission? This is a question several
great personages are asking; they reply that the Master
of Moses and of all men reserved to himself the right
to explain, at his convenience, a doctrine to the Jews
which they were in no condition to understand while
they were in the desert.

If Moses had proclaimed the dogma of the immortality of the soul, a great school among the Jews would
not have persistently combated it; the great school of
the Sadducees would not have been permitted in the
state; the Sadducees would not have filled the highest
offices; and great pontiffs would not have been chosen
from among them.

It appears that it was not until after the founding of
Alexandria that the Jews split into three sects: The
Pharisees, the Sadducees, and the Essenes. The historian
Josephus, who was a Pharisee, informs us in book XIII
of his *Antiquities* that the Pharisees believed in metempsychosis; the Sadducees believed that the soul perishes
with the body; the Essenes, Josephus continues, held
that souls were immortal. According to them, souls
descended into bodies in aerial form from the highest
region of the air; they were carried back there by a
violent attraction, and after death those which had belonged to good men dwelt beyond the Ocean, in a
country where there was neither heat nor cold, neither
wind nor rain. The souls of the wicked passed into the
opposite kind of climate. This was the theology of the
Jews.

He who alone was to instruct all men, came and condemned these three sects; without him we should never
have known anything about our soul, since the philosophers never had a settled idea of it, while Moses,

the world's only true lawgiver before our own, Moses, who spoke with God face to face, left men in profound ignorance on this great matter. It is, then, only for seventeen hundred years that we have been certain of the existence and immortality of the soul.

Cicero had nothing but doubts; his grandson and granddaughter might have learned the truth from the first Galileans who came to Rome.

But before that time, and since then, in all the rest of the world where the apostles did not penetrate, everyone must have said to his soul: "What are you? Where do you come from? What are you doing? Whither do you go? You are I know not what; you think and feel, and were you to feel and think for a hundred thousand million years, you would never know any more about it by your own intelligence, without the assistance of a God."

O man! God has given you understanding to conduct yourself well, and not to penetrate into the essence of the things he has created.

This is what Locke thought, and before Locke, Gassendi, and before Gassendi, a multitude of sages; but we have bachelors of arts who know everything those great men didn't know.

Cruel enemies of reason have dared to rise up against these truths acknowledged by all the sages. They have carried bad faith and impudence so far as to charge the authors of this Dictionary with affirming that the soul is matter. You know perfectly well that at the bottom of page 64, there are these very words against Epicurus, Democritus, and Lucretius: "My friend, how does an atom think? Acknowledge that you know nothing about it." Obviously, then, you are slanderers.

No one knows the nature of that being called *spirit*, to which even you give this material name of *spirit*,

which signifies *wind*. All the first Fathers of the Church
thought the soul was corporeal. It is impossible for us
other limited beings to know whether our intelligence
is substance or faculty: we cannot fully know either
the extended substance, nor the thinking being, nor the
mechanism of thought.

We declare to you, with the respectable Gassendi
and Locke, that we know nothing by ourselves of the
secrets of the Creator. Are you gods who know everything? We repeat to you that we can know the nature
and destiny of the soul by revelation alone. Well! Isn't
this revelation enough for you? You must surely be
enemies of this revelation, since you persecute those
who expect everything from it and who believe in it
alone.

We tell you that we call upon the word of God;
and you, enemies of reason and God, you, who blas-
pheme the one and the other, you treat the humble
doubt and humble submission of the philosopher as the
wolf treated the lamb in Aesop's fables; you say to
him: "You spoke ill of me last year; I must suck your
blood." Philosophy takes no revenge; she smiles in peace
at your vain endeavors; she gently enlightens mankind,
whom you would brutalize so as to make them in your
image.

AMITIÉ · FRIENDSHIP

This is the marriage of souls; it is a tacit contract between two impressionable and virtuous persons. I say
impressionable, for a monk or a hermit may not be
wicked at all and yet live without knowing friendship.
I say *virtuous*, for the wicked have only accomplices,

the voluptuous have companions in debauchery, the interested have associates, politicians assemble factions, the mass of idle men have connections, princes have courtiers; virtuous men alone have friends. Cethegus was the accomplice of Catiline, and Maecenas the courtier of Octavius; but Cicero was the friend of Atticus.

What does this contract between two tender and honest minds produce? Its obligations are stronger or weaker according to their degree of sensibility and the number of services rendered, etc.

The enthusiasm of friendship was stronger among the Greeks and Arabs than among us. The tales about friendship these nations have invented are admirable; we have none like them; we are a little cold in everything.

Friendship was a matter of religion and legislation among the Greeks. The Thebans had a regiment of lovers: a fine regiment! Some have taken it for a regiment of Sodomites; they are wrong; that is to mistake the accidental for the essence. Among the Greeks, friendship was prescribed by law and religion. Unfortunately, pederasty was tolerated by the mores; we should not impute shameful abuses to the law. I shall say more about this later.

AMOUR · LOVE

Amor omnibus idem. Here we must have recourse to bodily things; it is the cloth of nature embroidered by imagination. If you want a notion of love, look at the sparrows in your garden; look at your pigeons; regard the bull being introduced to your heifer; look at that spirited horse which its two grooms are leading toward the quietly waiting mare that lifts its tail to receive him; see how his eyes glitter; hear his neighings; regard the leaps, the bows, the ears erect, the mouth opening with little convulsions, the flaring nostrils, the fiery breath streaming out of them, the mane raised and waving, the imperious movement with which he rushes toward the object that nature has destined for him. But don't be jealous of him, and think about the advantages the human species enjoys: love compensates for all those advantages which nature has conferred on animals— strength, beauty, lightness, rapidity.

There are even animals that know no sexual enjoyment. Scaly fishes are deprived of this pleasure: the female drops millions of eggs in the ooze, and the male, swimming along, passes over them and fertilizes them with his semen without caring to which female they belong.

Most of the animals that copulate taste pleasure only through a single sense; and when that appetite is satisfied, all is extinguished. No animal, besides yourself, knows embraces; your whole body is susceptible; your lips especially enjoy a pleasure that nothing wearies, and this pleasure belongs to your species alone; finally, you can give yourself to love at all times, while animals have only a definite period. If you reflect on these advantages, you will say, with the Earl of Rochester: "Love would make a nation of atheists worship the Divinity."

Since men have received the gift of perfecting whatever nature has granted them, they have perfected love. Cleanliness, personal care, increase the pleasure of touch by making the skin more delicate, and attention to your health makes the organs of voluptuousness more sensitive.

All the other sentiments subsequently enter into that of love, like metals which amalgamate with gold: friend-

ship, esteem, come to its aid; talents of body and mind
are yet other bonds.

Nam facit ipsa suis interdum femina factis,
Morigerisque modis, et munde corpore culto,
Ut facile insuescat secum degere vitam.

Lucretius, Book V

[Sometimes the woman herself takes a hand—
With her obliging ways and neat care of her body
She accustoms him to share his life with her.

De rerum natura, IV, 1280-1282]

Pride, above all, tightens all these ties. Men congratulate themselves on their choice, and a crowd of illusions are the ornament of the work whose foundation
has been laid by nature.

All this makes you superior to the animals; but while
you taste so many pleasures they don't know, on the
other hand how many vexations of which they have no
notion! What is dreadful for you is that in three-quarters
of the world nature has poisoned the pleasures of love
and the sources of life with a terrible disease, to which
man alone is subject and which infects only his organs
of generation.

This pestilence is not like so many other maladies that
are the consequences of our excesses. It was not introduced into the world by debauchery. The Phrynes, the
Laises, the Floras, the Messalinas were never attacked
by it; it was born in islands where men lived in innocence, and has spread from there throughout the Old
World.

If one could ever accuse nature of despising its work,
thwarting its plan, acting against its design, it would be
in this instance. Is this the best of all possible worlds?
Very well! If Caesar, Antony, Octavius, never had this
disease, wasn't it possible to prevent Francis I from

dying of it? No, people say, things were so ordained for the best: I want to believe it, but it is sad for those to whom Rabelais dedicated his book.

AMOUR NOMMÉ SOCRATIQUE
SO-CALLED SOCRATIC LOVE

How did it come about that a vice which would destroy mankind if it were general, that a sordid outrage against nature, is still so natural? It seems the highest degree of deliberate corruption, and yet it is the ordinary lot of those who have not yet had time to be corrupted. It enters hearts that are wholly inexperienced, which have not yet known ambition, fraud, or thirst for wealth; blind youth whose instincts are not sorted out throws itself into this disorder upon leaving childhood.

The inclination of the two sexes toward one another announces itself early; but, whatever people have said about Africans and women of southern Asia, this inclination is generally much stronger in the man than in the woman; this is a law nature has established for all the animals. It is always the male who assaults the female.

When the young males of our species, brought up together, feel the force which nature begins to unfold in them, and fail to find the natural object of their instinct, they fall back on what resembles it. Often, for two or three years, a young man resembles a beautiful girl, with the freshness of his complexion, the brilliance of his coloring, and the sweetness of his eyes; if he is loved, it's because nature makes a mistake; homage is paid to the fair sex by attachment to one who owns its beauties, and when the years have made this resemblance disappear, the mistake ends.

Citraque juventam
Aetatis breve ver et primos carpere flores.

[*And this is the way:*
Pluck the brief Spring, the first flowers of youth.
Ovid, *Metamorphoses*, X, 84-85]

It is well known that this mistake of nature is much more common in mild climates than in the icy north, because the blood is more inflamed there and opportunity more frequent: also, what seems only a weakness in young Alcibiades is a disgusting abomination in a Dutch sailor or a Muscovite sutler.

I cannot bear to hear people say that the Greeks authorized this license. They quote the legislator Solon, because he said in two bad verses:

Tu chériras un beau garçon
Tant qu'il n'aura barbe au menton.

[*Until the handsome boy must shave,*
You'll cherish him and be his slave.]

But really, was Solon a legislator when he wrote these two ridiculous lines? He was a youth then; but when the debauchee turned into a sage, he didn't enact such infamy into the laws of his republic; it's like accusing Théodore de Beza of preaching pederasty in his church because in his youth he made verses for the young Candide, writing:

Amplector hunc et illam.

[*Cherish both him and her.*]

People misuse that text of Plutarch's, who in his garrulity makes one of his interlocutors say in the *Dialogue on Love* that women are not worthy of real love; but another interlocutor rightly upholds the women's part.

It is certain, as certain as knowledge of antiquity can be, that Socratic love was not a sordid love: this word *love* has deluded us. Those who were called *the lovers of a young man* were precisely those who are the minions of our princes today, those who were the children of honor, young men assisting in the education of a distinguished child, sharing the same studies, the same military labors: a martial and saintly institution which was wrongly turned into nocturnal feasts and orgies.

The troop of lovers established by Laius were an invincible body of young warriors bound by oath to give their lives for one another; ancient discipline never had anything finer than that.

In vain have Sextus Empiricus and others claimed that pederasty was recommended by the laws of Persia. Let them cite the text of that law; let them show the code of the Persians, and if they show it, I still shan't believe it, I shall say that the thing isn't true, because it is impossible. No, it is not in human nature to make a law that contradicts and outrages nature, a law that would annihilate mankind if it were observed to the letter. How men have taken the shameful and merely tolerated customs of a country for the laws of that country! Sextus Empiricus, who doubted everything, might well have had doubts about these statutes. If he had lived in our time, and seen two or three young Jesuits seduce some school-boys, would he have the right to say they were permitted this game by the constitutions of Ignatius de Loyola?

The love of boys was so common in Rome that they did not dare to punish this nonsense into which everyone fell heedlessly. Octavius-Augustus, that debauched murderer and coward, who dared to exile Ovid, approved of Vergil's singing Alexis and of Horace writing

little odes for Ligurinus; but the ancient law *Scantinia,*
which prohibited pederasty, always remained in force:
Emperor Philip revived it and chased out of Rome the
young men who practiced it as a profession. Finally, I
don't believe that there has ever been a civilized nation
which made laws against morals.*

AMOUR-PROPRE · EGOTISM

A beggar of the vicinity of Madrid grandly asked
for alms; a passerby said to him: "Aren't you ashamed
to carry on this sordid trade, when you could work?"
"Sir," replied the mendicant, "I asked you for money,
not for advice"; and turned his back on him, preserving
all his Castilian dignity. This gentleman was a proud
beggar; very little was needed to wound his vanity. He

---

*We should condemn messieurs the * * * for presenting the po-
lice every year with a child of their own making. The abbé Desfon-
taines was on the point of being roasted on the place de Grève, for
seducing little Savoyards who were sweeping his chimney; protectors
saved him. A victim was needed: they roasted Deschaufours in his
place. That is too much; *est modus in rebus:* we should proportion
punishments to crime; what would Caesar, Alcibiades, Nicomedes,
king of Bithynia, Henri III, king of France, and so many other kings
have said?

When they burned Deschaufours they based themselves on the
Etablissements de St. Louis, put into French in the fifteenth century. "If anyone is suspected of . . . , he should be taken to the bishop;
and if it should be proved, he should be burned, and all his personal
property shall belong to the baron," etc. But St. Louis does not say
what one should do to the baron if the baron is suspected of . . .
"and if it should be proved." I might observe that by the word . . .
St. Louis understood the heretics, who were at that time called by no
other name. An ambiguity got Deschaufours, gentleman from Lorraine, burned in Paris. Despréaux had good reason to write a satire
against ambiguity; it has caused far more harm than people think.

asked for alms out of self-love and couldn't bear the reprimand he got from another self-love.

A missionary traveling in India met a fakir loaded with chains, naked as a monkey, lying on his stomach, and having himself lashed for the sins of his compatriots, who gave him a few pennies. "What self-renunciation!" said one of the spectators. "Self-renunciation!" replied the fakir. "Let me inform you that I only have myself lashed in this world to pay you back in the next, when you will be the horse and I shall be the rider."

Those who say that love of ourselves is the basis of all our feelings and all our actions are therefore quite right about India, Spain, and all the habitable world: and just as people don't write to prove to men that they have a face, there is no need to prove to them that they are egotistical. This egotism is the instrument of our preservation; it resembles the instrument for the perpetuation of the species: we need it, we cherish it, it gives us pleasure, and we must hide it.

ANGE · ANGEL

Angel, in Greek, *sent;* you won't be much better informed when you know that the Persians had *Peris,* the Hebrews *Malakim,* the Greeks their *Daimonoi.*

But what will perhaps teach us more is that one of man's first ideas has always been to place intermediate beings between the Divinity and us; such were the demons, the genii, conceived by antiquity; man always made the gods in his own image. People saw princes communicate their orders by messengers, therefore the Divinity also sent his couriers: Mercury, Isis, were couriers, messengers.

The Jews, the only people guided by the Divinity himself, did not at first give names to the angels whom God finally deigned to send to them; they borrowed the names from the Chaldaeans during the time when the Jewish nation was captive in Babylon; Michael and Gabriel are mentioned for the first time by Daniel, who was a slave in that nation. The Jew Tobit, who lived at Nineveh, knew the angel Raphael, who traveled with Tobit's son to help him recover the money which the Jew Gabael owed him.

The laws of the Jews, that is, Leviticus and Deuteronomy, don't make the slightest mention of the existence of angels, nor of their worship: the Sadducees didn't believe in angels either.

But in the histories of the Jews they are talked about a great deal. These angels were corporeal; they had wings on their backs, as the Gentiles imagined Mercury had wings on his heels; sometimes they hid their wings under their clothes. How could they be without bodies, since they ate and drank, and since the inhabitants of Sodom wanted to commit the sin of pederasty with the angels who came to Lot's house?

The ancient Jewish tradition, according to Ben Maimon, acknowledged ten degrees, ten orders, of angels: 1. The *chaios acodesh*, pure, holy. 2. The *ofanin*, swift. 3. The *oralim*, strong. 4. The *chasmalim*, the flames. 5. The *seraphim*, sparks. 6. The *malakim*, angels, messengers, deputies. 7. The *eloim*, the gods or judges. 8. The *ben eloim*, sons of the gods. 9. *Cherubim*, images. 10. *Ychim*, the animated.

The story of the fall of the angels is not in the book of Moses; the first evidence we have of it is from the prophet Isaiah, who exclaims as he apostrophizes the king of Babylon: "What has become of the extorter of tributes? The pines and the cedars rejoice in his fall.

How you are fallen from heaven, O Hellel, star of the morning." This *Hellel* has been translated by the Latin word *Lucifer;* and later, by an allegorical interpretation, the name of *Lucifer* was given to the prince of the angels who made war in heaven; and finally this word, which signifies *phosphorus* and *aurora*, has become the name of the Devil.

The Christian religion is founded on the fall of the angels. Those who rebelled were hurled from the spheres they inhabited into hell, in the center of the earth, and became devils. A devil in the shape of a serpent tempted Eve and damned mankind. Jesus came to redeem mankind and to triumph over the Devil, who tempts us still. Nevertheless, this fundamental tradition is found only in the apocryphal Book of Enoch, and even there it is in a form quite different from the accepted tradition.

St. Augustine, in his 109th letter, doesn't hesitate to attribute slender and agile bodies to the angels, good and bad. Pope Gregory II has reduced to nine choirs, nine hierarchies or orders, the ten choirs of angels accepted by the Jews: they are the seraphim, the cherubim, the thrones, the dominations, the virtues, the powers, the principalities, the archangels, and finally the angels, who give their name to the eight other hierarchies.

In their temple the Jews had two cherubim with two heads each—one head of an ox, the other of an eagle with six wings. Today we paint them in the form of a flying head, with two small wings below their ears. We paint the angels and archangels in the form of young men, with two wings at the back. As for the thrones and dominations, no one has yet thought of painting them.

St. Thomas, at question 108, article 2, says that the thrones are as close to God as the cherubim and the seraphim, because it is upon them that God sits. Scotus has counted a thousand million angels. After the ancient mythology of the good and bad demons passed from the East to Greece and Rome, we sanctified this opinion in admitting for each person a good and a bad angel, one of whom helps him and the other hurts him, from his birth to his death; but it is not yet known whether these good and bad angels are continually passing from one post to another, or if they are relieved by others. On this matter, consult the *Summa* of St. Thomas.

It is not known precisely where the angels dwell, whether in the air, in the void, or on the planets: God has not wished us to be informed about it.

ANTITRINITAIRES · UNITARIANS

To reveal their sentiments, it is enough to say:

That they maintain that nothing is more contrary to reason than what is taught among Christians about the trinity of persons in a single divine essence, of whom the second is begotten by the first, and the third proceeds from the other two.

That this unintelligible doctrine is not found anywhere in Scripture.

That no passage can be produced authorizing it, or to which we cannot give a sense clearer, more natural, or more consistent with usual notions and first and immutable truths, without departing from the spirit of the text in any way.

That to maintain, as their adversaries do, that there are several distinct *persons* in the divine essence, and that the Eternal is not the only true God, but that the Son and the Holy Spirit must be joined to him, is to introduce into the Church of Jesus Christ the crudest and

most dangerous error, since it openly promotes polytheism.

That it implies a contradiction to say that there is but
one God and that nevertheless there are three *persons*,
each of which is truly God.

That this distinction of one in essence and three in person was never in Scripture.

That it is manifestly false, since it is certain that there
are no fewer *essences* than *persons*, nor *persons* than
essences.

That the three persons of the Trinity are either three
different substances, or accidents of the divine essence,
or that essence itself without division.

That in the first case, you have three Gods.

That in the second case, you have God composed of
accidents, you worship accidents, and metamorphose accidents into persons.

That in the third case, you needlessly and ground-
lessly divide an indivisible subject, and distinguish into
three that which is not distinguished within itself.

That if you say that the three *personalities* are neither
different substances in the divine essence, nor accidents
of that essence, you will have trouble persuading yourself that they are anything at all.

That it must not be believed that the most rigid and
decided *Trinitarians* have themselves any clear idea of
the way in which the three *hypostases* subsist in God,
without dividing his substance, and consequently without multiplying it.

That after he advanced a thousand arguments on this
subject, as false as they are obscure, St. Augustine himself was forced to concede that nothing intelligible
could be said about the matter.

Then they repeat a passage by this Father, which is
indeed very odd: "When it is asked," he says, "what are

the three, the language of man fails, and there are no terms to express them: however, people have said *three persons*, not in order to say anything, but because we must speak and not remain silent." *Dictum est tamen tres personae, non ut aliquid diceretur, sed ne taceretur.* (*De Trinit.* book V, chap. 9.)

That modern theologians have not cleared up this matter any better.

That when they are asked what they understand by this word *person*, they explain it only by saying that it is a certain incomprehensible distinction which causes us to distinguish a Father, a Son, and a Holy Spirit in a nature single in number.

That the explanation they give of the terms *begetting* and *proceeding* is no more satisfactory, since it comes down to saying that these terms indicate certain incomprehensible relationships among the three persons of the Trinity.

That hence we may gather that at this point the controversy between the anti-Trinitarians and the orthodox is over whether there are in God three distinctions, of which we have no idea, and among which there are certain relations of which we have no more idea.

They conclude from all this that it would be wiser to stick to the authority of the apostles, who never spoke of the Trinity, and to banish from religion forever all terms which are not in the Scriptures, such as *Trinity, person, essence, hypostatic and personal union, incarnation, generation, proceeding,* and many others like them, which are absolutely meaningless, since they are not represented in nature by a real being, and can excite in the understanding nothing but false, vague, obscure, and undefinable notions.

(*Taken from the article* UNITAIRES *of the* Encyclopédie, *which article is by the abbé de Bragelogue*)

To this article let me add what dom Calmet says in his dissertation on the following passage from the Epistle of John the Evangelist: "There are three that bear witness on the earth, the spirit, the water, and the blood; and these three are one. There are three that bear witness in heaven, the Father, the Word, and the Spirit, and these three are one." Dom Calmet acknowledges that these two passages are not in any ancient Bible; indeed, it would be very strange if St. John had spoken of the Trinity in a letter, and said not a single word about it in his Gospel. We find no trace of this dogma either in the canonical or in the apocryphal gospels. All these reasons and many others might excuse the anti-Trinitarians, if the councils had not decided against them. But since the heretics make light of councils, we no longer know what to do to confound them.

ANTROPOFAGES · CANNIBALS

I have spoken of love. It is hard to move from people who kiss one another to people who eat one another. It is only too true that there have been cannibals; we have found them in America; perhaps they still exist; and the cyclops were not the only ones in antiquity who sometimes fed on human flesh. Juvenal reports that among the Egyptians, so wise a nation, so renowned for its laws, a people so pious that they worshiped crocodiles and onions, the Tentyrites ate one of their enemies who had fallen into their hands. He does not tell this tale on hearsay; the crime was committed almost before his eyes; he was then in Egypt, and a short distance from Tentyra. On this occasion he cites the Gascons and the Saguntines, who formerly fed on the flesh of their compatriots.

In 1725 four savages were brought from the Mississippi to Fontainebleau; I had the honor of talking with them; among them was a lady whom I asked if she had eaten men; she replied, with great simplicity, that she had. I appeared a little shocked; she excused herself by saying that it was better to eat one's dead enemy than leave him to be devoured by wild beasts, and that the victors deserved to exercise the preference. We kill our neighbors in battles pitched or unpitched; and for the most paltry pay provide meals for the crows and the worms. That is the horror, that's the crime; what does it matter, when a man has been killed, if a soldier eats him, or a crow and a dog?

We respect the dead more than the living. We should respect both the one and the other. The nations we call civilized have done right not to put their vanquished enemies on the spit; for if we were allowed to eat our neighbors, we would soon eat our compatriots, which would have grave consequences for the social virtues. But civilized nations have not always been civilized; all had long been savage; and in the infinite number of revolutions which this globe has undergone, mankind has been sometimes numerous and sometimes sparse. What is happening today to elephants, lions, tigers, whose numbers have much decreased, once happened to human beings. In times when a country was thinly inhabited by men, these had few skills and were hunters. The habit of nourishing themselves on what they killed easily led them to treat their enemies like their stags and their boars. It was superstition that caused human victims to be immolated; it was necessity that caused them to be eaten.

Which is the greater crime, to assemble piously to plunge a knife into the heart of a girl adorned with fillets, in honor of the Divinity, or to eat a worthless man whom we killed in self-defense?

Yet we have many more instances of girls and boys being sacrificed than of girls and boys being eaten: almost all nations we know anything about have sacrificed boys and girls. The Jews immolated them. This was called the *anathema;* it was a true sacrifice, and it is ordained in the twenty-seventh chapter of Leviticus not to spare the living souls which shall be consecrated; but it is nowhere prescribed that they shall be eaten: they are only threatened with it: Moses, as we have seen, tells the Jews that if they do not observe his ceremonies they will not only have the itch, but the mothers will eat their children. It is true that in the time of Ezekiel the Jews must have been in the habit of eating human flesh, for in chapter 39 he predicts to them that God will make them eat, not only the horses of their enemies, but even the horsemen and the other warriors. That is established. And, indeed, why shouldn't the Jews have been cannibals? It was the only thing that was needed to make the people of God the most abominable on earth.

I have read in anecdotes of the history of England in Cromwell's time that a female tallow chandler in Dublin sold excellent candles made of the fat of Englishmen. After some time one of her customers complained that the candles were no longer so good. "Alas!" she said. "It's because we were short of Englishmen this month." I ask who were the guiltiest, those who assassinated the English, or the woman who made candles of their tallow?

APIS

Was the ox Apis worshiped at Memphis as a god, as a symbol, or as an ox? It is to be presumed that the fanatics regarded him as a god, the wise as a mere symbol, and that the stupid mob worshiped the ox. Did Cambyses, when he conquered Egypt, do right to kill this ox with his own hand? Why not? He showed the imbeciles that their God could be put on the spit without nature's arming herself to avenge the sacrilege. The Egyptians have been much praised. I hardly know of a more despicable people; there must always have been some radical vice in their character and government which perpetually made them into vile slaves. I grant that they conquered the earth in times almost unknown; but in historical times they have been subjugated by all who cared to take the trouble—by the Assyrians, by the Greeks, by the Romans, by the Arabs, by the Mamelukes, by the Turks—in short by everybody except our crusaders, who were even more imprudent than the Egyptians were cowardly. It was the Mameluke militia that beat the French. There are perhaps only two tolerable things about this nation: first, that those who worshiped an ox never tried to coerce those who worshiped an ape to change their religion; second, that they have always hatched chickens in ovens.

People praise their pyramids; but they are monuments of an enslaved people. The whole nation must have been made to work on them, or those ugly masses could never have been raised. What were they good for? To preserve in a small chamber the mummy of some prince, or some governor, or some intendant, which his soul was to reanimate at the end of a thousand years.

But if they hoped for this resurrection of bodies, why did they take out the brain before they embalmed them? Were the Egyptians to be resuscitated without a brain?

APOCALYPSE

Justin Martyr, who wrote around the year 270 of our era, was the first to mention the Apocalypse; he attributes it to the apostle John the Evangelist. In Justin's dialogue with Tryphon, that Jew asks him if he does not believe that Jerusalem will be re-established one day. Justin answers that he believes it, with all right-thinking Christians. "There was among us," he says, "a certain personage named John, one of the twelve apostles of Jesus; he predicted that the faithful will spend a thousand years in Jerusalem."

A belief in the millennium was long accepted among the Christians. This time period had a high repute among the Gentiles. The souls of the Egyptians recovered their bodies at the end of a thousand years; in Vergil, the souls in purgatory were trained for the same space of time, *et mille per annos*. The New Jerusalem of a thousand years was to have twelve gates, in memory of the twelve apostles; its form was to be square; its length, breadth, and height were each to be a thousand stadia, that is, one thousand two hundred and fifty miles, so that the houses would also be one thousand two hundred and fifty miles high. It would be rather disagreeable to live on the highest floor; but we find all this in chapter 21 of the Apocalypse.

Although Justin was the first to attribute the Apocalypse to St. John, some persons have rejected his testimony, since in the same dialogue with the Jew Tryphon he says that, according to the apostles' story, Jesus Christ, when he went into the Jordan, made the waters of that river boil; but this is not to be found in any of the apostles' writings.

The same St. Justin confidently cites the oracles of the sybils; what is more, he claims to have seen the remains of the madhouses in which the seventy-two interpreters were confined on the Pharos in Egypt, in the time of Herod. The testimony of the man who had the misfortune of seeing these madhouses seems to indicate that the author should have been shut up there himself.

St. Irenaeus, who comes later, and who also believed in the millennium, says that he learned from an old man that St. John wrote the Apocalypse. But St. Irenaeus has been reproached for writing that there should be only four gospels, because there are only four quarters of the world, and four principal winds, and because Ezekiel saw only four animals. He calls this reasoning demonstrative. It must be admitted that the way Irenaeus demonstrates is just as good as the way Justin sees.

In his *Electa*, Clement of Alexandria only mentions an Apocalypse of St. Peter, of which a great deal was made. Tertullian, one of the great partisans of the millennium, not only assures us that St. John predicted the resurrection and the millennium in the city of Jerusalem, but claims that this Jerusalem was already beginning to form itself in the air; all the Christians of Palestine, and even the pagans, had seen it for forty consecutive days toward the end of the night, but unfortunately the city disappeared as soon as it was daylight.

Origen, in his preface to the Gospel of St. John, and in his *Homilies*, quotes the oracles of the Apocalypse; but he also quotes the oracles of the sybils. Yet St. Dionysius of Alexandria, who wrote about the middle of the third century, says, in one of the fragments preserved by Eusebius, that nearly all the scholars rejected the Apocalypse as a book devoid of reason; and that this book was not composed by St. John, but by one Cerinthus, who used a great name to lend his reveries more weight.

The Council of Laodicea, held in 360, did not count the Apocalypse among the canonical books. It's rather odd that Laodicea, which was one of the churches to whom the Apocalypse was addressed, should have rejected a treasure destined for it; and that the bishop of Ephesus, who attended the council, should have also rejected this work by St. John, who was buried at Ephesus.

It was plain to all eyes that St. John was still turning in his grave, continually making the earth rise and fall. Yet the same people who were sure that St. John was not quite dead were also sure that he hadn't written the Apocalypse. But those who held to the millennium were unshakable in their opinion. Sulpicius Severus, in his *Sacred History*, calls those who do not accept the Apocalypse mad and impious. Finally, after many doubts, after clashes of council with council, the opinion of Sulpicius Severus prevailed. The matter once cleared up, the Church decided that the Apocalypse was incontestably by St. John; thus there is no appeal.

Every Christian persuasion has applied the prophecies contained in this book to itself; the English have found the revolutions of Great Britain in it; the Lutherans, the troubles of Germany; the French Protestants, the reign of Charles IX and the regency of Catherine de Medici: they are all equally right. Bossuet and Newton both commented on the Apocalypse; yet, considering everything, the eloquent declamations of the one and the sublime discoveries of the other have done them greater honor than their commentaries.

ARIUS

Here is an incomprehensible question that has aroused curiosity, sophistic subtlety, bitterness, the spirit of cabal, the passion for domination, the rage to persecute, blind and bloody fanaticism, and barbarous credulity for more than sixteen hundred years, and has produced more horrors than the ambitions of princes, which surely have produced a great deal. Is Jesus Word? If he is Word, did he emanate from God in time or before time? If he emanated from God, is he coeternal and consubstantial with him, or is he of a similar substance? Is he distinct from him, or is he not? Is he made or begotten? Can he beget in his turn? Has he paternity or productive virtue without paternity? Is the Holy Spirit made, or begotten, or produced, or does he proceed from the Father, or proceed from the Son, or proceed from the two of them? Can he beget, can he produce? Is his hypostasis consubstantial with the hypostasis of the Father and the Son? And how is it that, having precisely the same nature, the same essence, as the Father and the Son, he cannot do the same things as these two persons who are himself?

Certainly I don't understand any of this; nobody has ever understood any of this, and this is why people have cut one another's throats!

Among the Christians before the time of Arius and Athanasius, they subtilized, they quibbled, they hated and they excommunicated one another because of some of these dogmas inaccessible to the human mind. The Egyptian Greeks were clever people; they split a hair in four, but this time they split it only in three. Alexandros, bishop of Alexandria, took it into his head to

preach that since God is necessarily individual, single,
a monad in the strictest sense of the word, this monad
is triune.

The priest Arios or Arious, whom we call Arius,
was quite shocked by Alexandros's monad; he explained
the matter differently: he quibbled partly like the priest
Sabellius, who had quibbled like the Phrygian Praxeas,
a great quibbler. Alexandros quickly assembled a small
council of persons who agreed with him, and excommunicated his priest. Eusebius, bishop of Nicomedia,
took the side of Arios: the whole Church was in flames.

The Emperor Constantine was a scoundrel, I confess
it; a parricide who smothered his wife in a bath,
butchered his son, assassinated his father-in-law, his
brother-in-law, and his nephew, I don't deny it; a man
bloated with pride and immersed in pleasures, I concede
it; a detestable tyrant, like his children, *transeat;* but he
had good sense. One does not get an empire, one does
not subdue all one's rivals, without reasoning closely.

When he saw civil war kindled in scholastic brains,
he dispatched the celebrated Bishop Hosius with dissuad-
ing letters to the two belligerent parties. "You are great
madmen," he tells them in so many words in this letter,
"to quarrel about things you don't understand. It is unworthy of the gravity of your ministries to make so much
noise about such a trifling matter."

By "such a trifling matter" Constantine did not mean
that which concerns the Divinity, but the incomprehensible manner in which they were straining to explain the
nature of the Divinity. The Arabian patriarch who
wrote the *History of the Church of Alexandria* has
Hosius say, when he presents the emperor's letter:

"My brethren, Christianity is scarcely beginning to
enjoy peace, and you wish to plunge it into eternal discord. The emperor is only too right to tell you that you
are *quarreling about a very trifling matter.* Surely, if

the object of the dispute were essential, Jesus Christ, whom we all acknowledge as our legislator, would have mentioned it; God would not have sent his son to earth in order not to teach us our catechism. Whatever he has not expressly told us is the work of men, and their destiny is to err. Jesus has commanded you to love one another, and you start out by disobeying him in hating one another, stirring up discord in the empire. Pride alone gives birth to disputes, and Jesus, your master, has commanded you to be humble. Not one of you can know whether Jesus is made or begotten. And what does his nature matter to you, provided yours is to be just and reasonable? What has a frivolous science of words in common with the morality that should guide your actions? You encumber doctrine with mysteries— you, who were made only to strengthen religion by virtue. Do you want the Christian religion to be nothing but a mass of sophistries? Is it for this that Christ came? Cease arguing; worship, edify, humble yourselves, feed the poor, make up family quarrels, instead of shocking the whole empire with your dissensions."

Hosius spoke to obstinate men. They assembled the Council of Nicaea and a civil war rent the Roman Empire. This war led to others, and there has been mutual persecution through the centuries, down to our own time.

ATHÉE, ATHÉISME
ATHEIST, ATHEISM

FIRST SECTION

Formerly, anyone who had a trade secret ran the risk of being considered a sorcerer; every new sect was accused of butchering infants in its mysteries; and every philosopher who departed from the jargon of the schools was accused of atheism by fanatics and knaves, and was condemned by fools.

Does Anaxagoras dare to assert that the sun is not guided by Apollo mounted in a quadriga?—he is called atheist and compelled to flee.

Aristotle is accused of atheism by a priest, and unable to have his accuser punished, he retired to Chalcis. But it is the death of Socrates that is the most odious thing in Greek history.

Aristophanes (the man whom commentators admire because he was a Greek, forgetting that Socrates was a Greek too)—Aristophanes was the first to accustom the Athenians to think of Socrates as an atheist.

We wouldn't have permitted this comic poet, who is neither comic nor a poet, to give his farces at the fair of Saint-Laurent. He seems to me viler and more despicable than Plutarch portrays him. Here is what the wise Plutarch says of this humbug: "The language of Aristophanes reeks of his miserable quackery: it is made up of the lowest and most disgusting puns; he doesn't even please the people, and to men of judgment and honor he is intolerable; his arrogance is insufferable, and all honest men detest his malice."

This, then, just by the way, is the buffoon whom madame Dacier, an admirer of Socrates, dares to admire: this was the man who from afar prepared the poison with which infamous judges put the most virtuous man in Greece to death.

The tanners, cobblers, and seamstresses of Athens applauded a farce that showed Socrates hoisted up in the air in a basket, announcing that there was no God and boasting of having stolen a coat while teaching philosophy. A nation whose bad government authorized such infamous license thoroughly deserved what happened to it, to become slaves of the Romans and, today, of the Turks.

Let us leap over the time between the Roman republic and us. The Romans, much wiser than the Greeks, never persecuted any philosopher for his opinions. But this was not the way among the barbarous nations which succeeded the Roman Empire. As soon as emperor Frederick II quarreled with the popes, he was accused of being an atheist and of being the author of the book *The Three Impostors* jointly with his chancellor De Vineis.

Does our chancellor, de l'Hôpital, declare himself against persecution?—he is immediately accused of atheism. *Homo doctus, sed verus atheos.** A Jesuit, as inferior to Aristophanes as Aristophanes is to Homer, a wretch whose name has become ridiculous even among fanatics, in a word the Jesuit Garasse, found *atheists* everywhere; that is what he calls all those with whom he loses his temper. He calls Thédore de Beza an atheist; it was he who misled the public about Vanini.

Vanini's unhappy end does not arouse our indignation and pity because Vanini was nothing but a foreign pedant without merit; but still, Vanini was not an atheist as people claimed; he was the very opposite.

He was a poor Neapolitan priest, a preacher and a theologian by trade, who wrangled to the death about quiddities and universals, *et utrum chimaera bombinans in vacuo possit comedere secundas intentiones.* But in any case there wasn't an ounce of anything like atheism in him. His notion of God conformed with the soundest and most correct theology: "God is the beginning and the end, father of one and the other, without need of either one or the other; eternal without being in time, present everywhere without being in any place. Neither

* *Commentarium rerum Gallicorum*, Book 28.

past nor future exists for him; he is everywhere and outside everything, governing everything and, having created everything, immutable, infinite, without parts; his
power is his will, etc."

Vanini plumed himself on reviving Plato's fine notion, adopted by Averroes, that God had created a
chain of beings from the smallest to the greatest, whose
last link was attached to his eternal throne; an idea, to
be sure, more sublime than true, but as far from atheism
as being is from non-being.

He traveled to make his fortune and to argue; but
unfortunately, disputation is the road that leads away
from fortune; a man makes himself as many sworn enemies as he finds scholars or pedants to argue against.
Vanini's misfortune had no other source; his heat and
rudeness in disputation earned him the hatred of several
theologians; and having quarreled with one Francon,
or Franconi, this Francon, the friend of his enemies,
naturally accused him of being an atheist, of teaching
atheism.

At the confrontation, Francon, or Franconi, aided by
some witnesses, had the barbarity to insist on what he
had asserted. Vanini, on the stand, interrogated about
what he thought of the existence of God, answered
that he worshiped, with the Church, a God in three persons. Taking a straw from the ground, he said, "This
wisp is sufficient to prove there is a creator." He then
delivered a fine discourse on vegetation and motion and
the necessity for a supreme being, without whom there
would be neither motion nor vegetation.

Président Grammont, who was then at Toulouse, reports this discourse in his *Histoire de France*, now so
neglected; and the same Grammont, by some unac-
countable prejudice, asserts that Vanini said all this from
"vanity, or from fear, rather than from inner convic-
tion."

On what could the *président* base this rash and dreadful judgment? It is obvious that on the basis of Vanini's answer he had to be acquitted of the charge of atheism. But what happened? This unfortunate foreign priest also dabbled in medicine: they found a big live toad which he kept at home in a vessel filled with water; they naturally accused him of being a sorcerer. They maintained that the toad was the god he worshiped; they gave an impious sense to several passages in his books, which is quite easy and quite common, by taking objections for answers, maliciously interpreting some equivocal phrase and poisoning an innocent expression. Finally, the faction persecuting him extorted from his judges the sentence that condemned the poor fellow to death.

In order to justify his death it was necessary to accuse the unfortunate man of the most terrible things. Minim —the very minim!—Mersenne pushed idiocy so far as to print that "Vanini set out from Naples with twelve of his apostles to convert all the nations to atheism." What a pitiful story! How could a poor priest have twelve men in his pay? How could he persuade twelve Neapolitans to travel at great expense, at the peril of their lives, to spread abroad this abominable and revolting doctrine? Is there a king powerful enough to pay twelve preachers of atheism? No one before Father Mersenne had put forward so enormous an absurdity. But after him, it was repeated; the journals, the historical dictionaries, were infected; and the world, which loves the extraordinary, has believed the fable without examination.

Even Bayle, in his *Pensées diverses*, speaks of Vanini as an atheist: he uses this example to support his paradox that *a society of atheists could exist;* he assures us that Vanini was a man of extremely regular morals and that he was martyr to his philosophical opinions. He is equally wrong on both points. Vanini informs us in his *Dialogues*, written in imitation of Erasmus, that he had a mistress named Isabel. He was as free in his writings as in his conduct; but he was not an atheist.

A century after his death, the learned La Croze, and the man who took the name of *Philaletus*, tried to vindicate him; but since nobody takes any interest in the memory of an unfortunate Neapolitan who was a very bad writer, almost nobody has read these apologies.

In his book entitled *Athei detecti*, the Jesuit Hardouin, more learned than Garasse and no less rash, charges Descartes, Arnauld, Pascal, Malebranche, with atheism: fortunately, they did not suffer Vanini's fate.

From all these facts I pass on to the question of ethics raised by Bayle, namely, *whether a society of atheists could exist.* Let us first observe on this score how men contradict themselves in the dispute: those who have stood against the opinion of Bayle with the greatest vehemence, those who have denied, with the greatest insults, the possibility of a society of atheists, have since maintained, with the same fearlessness, that atheism is the religion of the state of China.

They are most certainly wrong about the Chinese state; they needed only to read the edicts of the emperors of that vast country to see that those same edicts are sermons, which everywhere mention a supreme Being, governing, avenging, and rewarding.

And, at the same time, they are no less wrong about the impossibility of there being a society of atheists; and I don't know how M. Bayle could have overlooked a striking example that would have made his cause victorious.

In what way does a society of atheists seem impossible? It is thought that men who have no check upon them could never live together; that laws can do noth-

ing against secret crimes; that there is need of an avenging God who punishes, in this world or the next, the
evildoers who escape human justice.

To be sure, the laws of Moses did not teach a life to
come, did not threaten punishments after death, did not
teach the primitive Jews the immortality of the soul;
but the Jews, far from being atheists, far from believing
that they could escape the divine vengeance, were the
most religious of all men. They believed not only in the
existence of an eternal God, but they believed that he
was always present among them; they trembled lest
they be punished in themselves, in their wives, in their
children, in their posterity, to the fourth generation: this
check was very powerful.

But among the gentiles several sects had no such
check: the Skeptics doubted everything; the Academics
suspended their judgment on everything; the Epicureans
were persuaded that the Divinity could not meddle in
human affairs, and at bottom acknowledged no Divinity.
They were convinced that the soul is not a substance,
but a faculty which is born and perishes with the body;
consequently they bore no yoke but that of morality
and honor. The Roman senators and knights were true
atheists, for the gods did not exist for men who neither
feared them nor hoped for anything from them. The
Roman senate, then, in Caesar's and Cicero's time, was
really an assembly of atheists.

In his harangue for Cluentius, the great orator says
to the whole assembled senate: "What harm does death
do him? We reject all the silly fables about hell: what,
then, can death take from him: nothing but the feeling
of pain."

Doesn't Caesar, Catiline's friend, wishing to save the
life of his friend from the same Cicero, object that to
put a criminal to death is not to punish him; that death

is nothing, that it is but the end of our ills, that it is
more a happy than a dreadful moment? Did not Cicero
and the whole senate yield to these arguments? The
conquerors and legislators of the known world thus
evidently formed a society of men who feared nothing
from the gods; they were real atheists.

Bayle next examines whether idolatry is more dangerous than atheism; whether it is a greater crime not to
believe in the Divinity than to have unworthy ideas
about him. In this he holds Plutarch's view: he believes
that it is better to have no opinion than a bad one; but,
without offense to Plutarch, it is evident that it was
infinitely better for the Greeks to fear Ceres, Neptune,
and Jupiter than to fear nothing at all. It is clear that
the sanctity of oaths is necessary, and that we should
rather trust those who think a false oath will be punished
than those who think they may swear a false oath with
impunity. It cannot be doubted that in a civilized society
it is infinitely more useful to have a religion, even a bad
one, than to have none at all.

It appears, then, that Bayle should rather have examined which is more dangerous, fanaticism or atheism.
Fanaticism is surely a thousand times more disastrous,
for atheism inspires no sanguinary passion, as fanaticism
does; atheism does not inhibit crimes, but fanaticism sees
that they are committed. Let us suppose, with the author
of the *Commentarium rerum Gallicorum*, that the chancellor de l'Hôpital was an atheist; yet he made none but
wise laws, and counseled only moderation and concord:
it was fanatics who committed the massacres of St.
Bartholomew. Hobbes was considered an atheist; he led
a tranquil and innocent life: the fanatics of his time deluged England, Scotland, and Ireland with blood. Spi-
noza was not only an atheist, but taught atheism: surely
he had no part in the judicial assassination of Barne-

veldt; he didn't tear the two brothers De Witt to pieces and didn't eat them from the grill.

Atheists are for the most part bold and misguided scholars who reason badly and, unable to comprehend the creation, the origin of evil, and other difficulties, have recourse to the hypothesis of the eternity of things and of necessity.

The ambitious, the voluptuous, hardly have the time to reason and to espouse a bad system; they have something else to do than to compare Lucretius with Socrates. This is the way things are with us.

But it was not so in the Roman senate, which was composed almost entirely of theoretical and practical atheists, that is, of men who believed neither in Providence nor in a future life; this senate was an assembly of philosophers, voluptuaries, and ambitious men, all very dangerous, who ruined the republic. Epicureanism persisted under the emperors: the atheists of the senate had been factious in the times of Sulla and Caesar; under Augustus and Tiberius they were atheist slaves.

I should want no dealings with an atheist prince, whose interest it would be to have me pounded in a mortar: I am quite sure that I would be pounded. If I were sovereign, I should want no dealing with atheist courtiers, whose interest it would be to poison me: I should need to take an antidote every day at random. Hence it is absolutely necessary for princes and people to have profoundly engraved on their minds the idea of a supreme Being, creator, governor, rewarder, and avenger.

There are nations of atheists, says Bayle in his *Pensées sur les comètes*. The Kaffirs, the Hottentots, the Topinambus, and many other small nations have no God. They neither deny nor affirm him; they have never heard of him. Tell them there is one, and they will easily believe it; tell them that all is done by the nature of things, and they will believe you too. To maintain that they are atheists is like saying that they are anti-Cartesians: they are neither for nor against Descartes. They are really children; a child is neither atheist nor deist—he is nothing.

What conclusion shall we draw from all this? That atheism is a most monstrous evil in those who govern; that it is the same in councilors, even though their lives be innocent, since they may influence men who hold office; that even though it is less disastrous than fanaticism, it is almost always fatal to virtue. Above all, let us add that there are fewer atheists today than ever, since philosophers have recognized that there is no vegetative being without germ, no germ without design, etc., and that pure grain does not come from rottenness.

Unphilosophical geometers have rejected final causes, but true philosophers accept them; and, as a well-known author has said, a catechist announces God to children, and Newton demonstrates him to the wise.

ATHÉE, ATHÉISME
ATHEIST, ATHEISM

SECOND SECTION

If there are atheists, who is responsible but the mercenary tyrants of souls who, as they provoke us against themselves with their impostures, compel some feeble spirits to deny the God whom these monsters dishonor? How often have the people's bloodsuckers driven the overburdened citizens even to revolt against the king! (See FRAUDE.)

Men fattened on our substance cry out to us, "Be convinced that a she-ass spoke; believe that a fish swallowed a man and threw him up three days later safe and sound on the shore; don't doubt that the God of the universe ordered one Jewish prophet to eat shit (Ezekiel) and another prophet to buy two prostitutes and have children by them (Hosea)." These are the very words which they have the God of purity and truth pronounce: "Believe a hundred things either manifestly abominable or mathematically impossible: otherwise the God of mercy will burn you in the fires of hell, not only for millions of billions of centuries, but for all eternity, whether you have a body or whether you don't."

These unbelievable stupidities are revolting to feeble and rash minds as well as to firm and wise ones. The former say: "If our teachers portray God to us as the most senseless and the most barbarous of all beings, there is no God"; but they should say: "Since our teachers attribute to God their absurdities and rages, therefore God is the opposite of what they proclaim, therefore God is as wise and as good as they say he is mad and evil." That is what the wise conclude. But if a fanatic hears them, he denounces them to a magistrate, a sergeant of priests, and this sergeant has them burned on a slow fire, thinking that he is avenging and imitating the Divine Majesty, which he insults.

BABEL

Vanity has always raised great monuments. It was out of vanity that men built the beautiful tower of Babel. "Let us go and raise a tower with its top in the heavens, and render our name famous before we are scattered through the earth." The enterprise was undertaken in the time of one Phaleg, who reckoned good old Noah as his great-great-great-grandfather. You can see that architecture and all the arts which accompany it had made great progress in five generations. St. Jerome, the very man who saw fauns and satyrs, didn't see the tower of Babel any more than I; but he assures us that it was twenty thousand feet high. That's not much. The ancient book *Yalkut*, written by one of the most learned of Jews, demonstrates that its height was eighty-one thousand Jewish feet, and there's no one who doesn't know that the Jewish foot was nearly as long as the Greek. This size is much more likely than Jerome's. The tower still exists; but it is no longer quite so high. Several quite truthful travelers have seen it; I, who haven't seen it, will talk about it as little as about my grandfather Adam, with whom I never had the honor of conversing. But consult the Reverend Father dom Calmet; he is a man of fine intellect and profound philosophy; he will explain the thing to you. I don't know why it is said in Genesis that Babel signifies confusion, for *Ba* signifies father in the oriental languages, and *Bel* signifies God; Babel signifies the city of God, the holy city. The ancients gave this name to all their capitals. But it is incontestable that Babel means confusion, whether because the architects were confounded after they raised their work to eighty-one thousand

Jewish feet, or whether because the languages were confounded; evidently from that time on the Germans no longer understood the Chinese; although it is clear, according to the learned Bochart, that Chinese was originally the same language as High German.

BATÊME · BAPTISM

Baptism, Greek word signifying immersion. Men, who are always guided by their senses, easily imagined that what washes the body also washes the soul. There were great vats in the caverns under the Egyptian temples for the priests and the initiates. From time immemorial, the Indians purified themselves in the water of the Ganges, and that ceremony is still in great vogue. It spread to the Hebrews: they baptized all the strangers who embraced the Jewish law and who didn't wish to submit to circumcision; above all, the women (on whom they did not impose this surgery and who underwent it only in Ethiopia) were baptized; it was a regeneration: it gave a new soul, just as in Egypt. See, on this, Epiphanius, Maimonides, and the Gomara.

John baptized in the Jordan, and he even baptized Jesus, who, however, never baptized anybody but who deigned to hallow this ancient ceremony. Every sign is unimportant in itself, and God attaches his grace to the sign it pleases him to choose. Baptism soon became the first rite and the mark of the Christian religion. Nevertheless, the first fifteen bishops were all circumcised; it is not certain they were baptized.

The sacrament was misused in the first centuries of Christianity; nothing was more common than to wait till one was at death's door to receive baptism. The

examples of the emperor Constantine is sufficient proof
of that. This is how he reasoned: Baptism purifies
everything; I can therefore kill my wife, my son, and all
my relatives; after that I'll have myself baptized and
I'll go to heaven; and in fact that's just what he did. It
was a dangerous example; the custom of waiting for
death before immersing oneself in the sacred bath was
gradually abolished.

The Greeks always retained baptism by immersion.
About the end of the eighth century, after the Latins
had extended their religion into Gaul and Germany, and
seen that immersion might be fatal to infants in cold
countries, they substituted simple sprinkling, which
brought down on them frequent anathemas from the
Greek Church.

St. Cyprian, bishop of Carthage, was asked if those
who had their bodies only sprinkled were really baptized. He answers, in his seventy-sixth letter, that "several churches do not believe that those so sprinkled are
Christians; that, as for himself, he believes that they are
Christians, but that they have an infinitely smaller grace
than those who have been dipped three times, according to custom."

With the Christians a man was initiated as soon as he
had been dipped; before that moment he was only a
catechumen. To be initiated one had to have sponsors,
guarantors, who were called by a name corresponding
to *Godfathers*, so that the Church could be sure that the
new Christians would be faithful and that the mysteries
would not be divulged. This is why the gentiles, in the
first centuries, were generally as ill-informed of the
mysteries of the Christians as the latter were of the mysteries of Isis and the Eleusine.

Cyril of Alexandria, in his polemic against the emperor Julian, expresses himself as follows: "I would

speak of baptism if I did not fear that my words would reach those who are not initiated."

In the second century they began to baptize infants; it was natural that the Christians should want this sacrament for their children, who would have been damned without it. Finally, it was decided that it must be administered to them at the end of eight days, because that was the age at which Jews were circumcised. In the Greek Church this is still the custom. Nevertheless, in the third century the custom of having oneself baptized only at death's door got the upper hand.

Those who died in the first week were, according to the most rigorous Fathers of the Church, damned. But Peter Chrysologos, in the fifth century, invented *limbo*, a sort of mitigated hell, or properly the brink of hell, the suburb of hell; all infants dying without baptism go there; the patriarchs stayed there until Jesus Christ's descent into hell; so the view that Jesus descended into limbo, and not into hell, has prevailed since then.

It has been debated whether a Christian in the deserts of Arabia might be baptized with sand: the reply was No; it has been debated whether one could baptize with rose water: it was decided that pure water was necessary; however, muddy water might be employed. It is obvious that all this discipline depended on the prudence of the first pastors who established it.

Ideas of the Rigid Unitarians About Baptism

"It is evident to whomsoever is willing to reason without prejudice that baptism is neither a mark of grace conferred nor a seal of alliance, but a simple sign of profession of faith;

That baptism is unnecessary, either by necessity of precept, or by necessity of means;

That it was not instituted by Jesus Christ, and that the Christian may dispense with it without inconvenience.

That one should baptize neither children, nor adults, nor, in general, anyone.

That baptism might have been useful at the birth of Christianity to those who left paganism, in order to make their profession of faith public, and be its authentic sign; but that at present it is absolutely useless and altogether unimportant."

(Taken from the Dictionnaire Encyclopédique,
from the article UNITAIRES)

IMPORTANT ADDITION

In his immortal satire on the Caesars, emperor Julian, the philosopher, puts these words into the mouth of Constantius, son of Constantine: "Whosoever feels himself guilty of rape, murder, plunder, sacrilege, and all the most abominable crimes, as soon as I have washed him with this water, he shall be clean and pure."

It was in fact this fatal doctrine that induced the Christian emperors and the magnates of the empire to defer their baptism until near death. They thought they had discovered the secret of living criminally and dying virtuously.

(Taken from M. Boulanger)

ANOTHER ADDITION

What a strange idea, that a pot of water should wash away all crimes—as though you were cleaning clothes! Today all children are baptized because an idea no less absurd supposes them all to be criminals; here they are, all saved until they reach the age of reason and can become guilty. Cut their throats, then,

as quickly as possible to assure them paradise. This is so
just a conclusion that there was once a devout sect
that went about poisoning and killing all newly baptized infants. These pietists reasoned perfectly. They
said: "We do these little innocents the greatest possible
favor; we prevent them from being wicked and unhappy in this life, and we give them eternal life."

(*From M. l'abbé Nicaise*)

BEAUTÉ · BEAUTY

Ask a toad what beauty is, the supreme beauty, the
to kalon. He will tell you it is his lady toad with her two
big round eyes coming out of her little head, her large
flat snout, yellow belly, brown back. Interrogate a
Negro from Guinea; for him beauty is a black, oily
skin, sunken eyes, and flat nose.

Interrogate the Devil; he will tell you that the beautiful is a pair of horns, four claws, and a tail. Then consult the philosophers; they will answer you with jargon;
they must have something conforming to the archetype
of the beautiful in essence, to the *to kalon*.

I once attended a tragedy sitting next to a philosopher. "How beautiful it is!" he said. "What do you find
beautiful in it?" I asked. He said, "The author has attained his goal." The next day he took medicine, which
did him good. "It has attained its goal," I told him;
"there's a beautiful medicine!" He understood that one
can't say a medicine is beautiful, and that before we
give anything the name *beautiful* it must make one feel
admiration and pleasure. He admitted that the tragedy
had inspired him with these two sentiments, and that
the *to kalon*, the beautiful, lay there.

We took a trip to England; the same piece was

played there, perfectly translated; it made all the spectators yawn. "Oh, oh!" he said. "The *to kalon* is not the same for the English as for the French." He concluded after much reflection that the beautiful is often quite relative, so that what is decent in Japan is indecent in Rome, and what is fashionable in Paris is not so in Peking, and he thus saved himself the trouble of composing a long treatise on the beautiful.

BÊTES · BEASTS

How absurd, how platitudinous, to say that beasts are machines, devoid of knowledge and feeling, which perform all their operations in the same manner, which learn nothing, which perfect nothing, etc.!

What? This bird which makes a semicircular nest when it builds against a wall, which builds in a quarter-circle in a corner, and in a full circle on a tree—this bird does everything in the same fashion? Doesn't the hound you have disciplined for three months know more at the end of that time than it did before your lessons? Does the canary you teach an air repeat it immediately? Don't you employ considerable time to teach it? Haven't you seen it making mistakes and correcting itself?

Is it because I speak to you that you decide I have feeling, memory, ideas? Well, suppose I don't speak to you; let's say you see me enter my house with a distressed air, look uneasily for a paper, open the bureau in which I remember putting it, find it, and read it with joy. You decide that I have experienced feelings of distress and pleasure, that I have memory and knowledge.

Then extend the same view to the dog who has lost his master, who has looked for him all over with piteous cries, who enters the house agitated and restless, who goes upstairs and down, from room to room, and at last finds the master he loves in his study, and shows his joy by the gentleness of his cries, by his leaps, and his caresses.

Barbarians seize this dog, who surpasses man so greatly in his capacity for friendship; they nail him to a table and dissect him alive to show you the mesenteric veins. You discover in him the same organs of feeling that are in yourself. Answer me, mechanist, has nature arranged all the springs of feeling in this animal in order that he should not feel? Has he nerves in order to be unmoved? Don't suppose such a pointless contradiction in nature.

But the masters of this school ask, What is the soul of beasts? I don't understand this question. A tree has the faculty of receiving in its fibers the sap that circulates in it, of displaying the buds of its leaves and its fruits; will you ask me what is the soul of this tree? It has received these gifts; the animal has received those of feeling, of memory, of a certain number of ideas. Who has bestowed all these gifts? Who has given all these faculties? He who made the grass of the field to grow, and who makes the earth gravitate toward the sun.

"The souls of beasts are substantial forms," Aristotle said; and after Aristotle, the Arab school; and after the Arab school, the angelic school; and after the angelic school, the Sorbonne; and after the Sorbonne, nobody in the world.

"The souls of beasts are material," other philosophers explain. These have not had a greater success. They are asked in vain what a material soul is; they must admit that it is matter which has sensation: but who gave it this sensation? The answer is: a material soul, that is, it is matter which gives sensation to matter; they don't get out of this circle.

Listen to other beasts reasoning about beasts: the soul is a spiritual being which dies with the body; but what proof do you have of that? What idea do you have of this spiritual being which, in fact, has feeling, memory, and its share of ideas and associations, but which can never know what a child of six knows? On what ground do you imagine that this being, which is not body, perishes with the body? The greatest beasts are those who have suggested that this soul is neither body nor spirit. There's a fine system! By spirit we can only understand something unknown which is not body: thus the system of these gentlemen amounts to this, that the soul of beasts is a substance which is neither body nor not body.

Whence come so many contradictory errors? From the habit men have always had of examining what a thing is before they know whether it exists. They call a valve—the valve of a bellows—the soul of the bellows. What is this soul? It is a name I have given to this valve which falls, lets the air in, rises again, and pushes it through a nozzle when I move the bellows.

There is no soul here, distinct from the machine. But what moves the bellows of animals? I have already told you, he who moves the stars. The philosopher who said, *Deus est anima brutorum*, was right; but he should have gone further.

BIEN, SOUVERAIN BIEN · GOOD, SUPREME GOOD

Antiquity debated a good deal about the supreme good. It would have been just as well to ask, What is the supreme blue, or the supreme stew, the supreme walk, the supreme reading, etc.

Everyone finds his good where he can, and has as much of it as he can, in his own fashion.

> *Quid dem? quid non dem? renuis tu, quod iubet alter*
>
> [*What should I give, what not give? You refuse what another commands*
>
> Horace, *Epistles*, II, ii, 63]
>
> *Castor gaudet equis; ovo prognatus eodem Pugnis*
>
> [*Castor delights in horses; he, born from the same egg, Likes fighting*
>
> Horace, *Satires*, II, i, 25-26]

The greatest good is something that pleases you so strongly that you are completely unable to feel anything else, just as the greatest evil is something that deprives us of all feeling. These are the two extremes of human nature; and these two moments are short.

Neither extreme delight nor extreme torture can last a lifetime: the supreme good and the supreme evil are chimeras.

We have the beautiful fable of Crantor: Wealth, Pleasure, Health, Virtue, compete at the Olympic games; each claims the apple. Wealth says: "I am the supreme good, for with me all goods are purchased." Pleasure says: "The apple belongs to me, for men desire wealth only to have me." Health asserts that without her there can be no pleasure, and wealth is useless. Finally, Virtue announces that she is superior to all three because with gold, pleasures, and health, a man may make himself quite miserable if he behaves badly. Virtue wins the apple.

The fable is quite ingenious, but it doesn't resolve the absurd question of the supreme good. Virtue is not a good, it is a duty; it is of a different nature, of a superior order. It has nothing to do with painful or agreeable sensations. The virtuous man with the stone and the gout, without help, without friends, destitute of necessities, persecuted, chained by a voluptuous tyrant who enjoys good health, is miserable; and his insolent persecutor, caressing a new mistress on his bed of purple, is happy. Say that the persecuted sage is preferable to his insolent persecutor; say that you like the one and detest the other; but confess that the sage in chains is beside himself with rage. If the sage will not admit this, he deceives you, he is a charlatan.

TOUT EST BIEN · ALL IS GOOD

There was a fine clamor raised in the schools, and even among men who think, when Leibnitz, paraphrasing Plato, built his edifice of the best of all possible worlds and imagined that all was for the best in it. He asserted, in the north of Germany, that God could make but a single world. Plato at least had left him the liberty of making five, because there are only five solid regular bodies: the tetrahedron, or pyramid with three faces, with uniform base, the cube, the hexahedron, the dodecahedron, the icosahedron. But since our world is not shaped like any of Plato's five bodies, he had to allow God a sixth method.

Let us leave the divine Plato to one side. Leibnitz, then, who was surely a better geometer than he, and a more profound metaphysician, did mankind the service of persuading us that we should be quite content, and that God could do no more for us; that indisputably, he necessarily chose, among all the possible choices, the best one.

"What will become of original sin?" they shouted at him. "Let it become what it may," said Leibnitz and his

friends; but in public he wrote that original sin necessarily was a part of the best of worlds.

What! To be chased out of a place of delights, where
we would have lived forever if we hadn't eaten an
apple! What! To produce in misery miserable children,
who will suffer everything, who will make others
suffer everything! What! To undergo all illnesses, feel
all sorrows, die in pain, and for refreshment to be
burned in the eternity of centuries! Is this really the
best of available lots? It is not too *good* for us; in what
way can it be good for God?

Leibnitz sensed that he had no reply to this: so he
made fat books in which he disagreed with himself.

To deny there is evil—that can be done laughingly by
a Lucullus who is in good health and who has a good
dinner with his friends and his mistress in the salon of
Apollo; but let him stick his head out the window, he
will see unhappy people enough; let him catch a fever,
he will be unhappy himself.

I don't like to quote; that's usually thorny work: you
neglect what precedes and what follows the passage you
quote, and expose yourself to a thousand quarrels. Nevertheless I must quote Lactantius, Church Father, who in
chapter 13 of *The Wrath of God* has Epicurus say this:
"Either God wishes to expunge the evil from this world
and cannot; or he can and does not wish to; or he neither
can nor wishes to; or finally he wishes to and can. If he
wishes to and cannot, that is impotence, which is contrary to the nature of God; if he can and does not wish
to, that is wickedness, and that is no less contrary to
his nature; if he neither wishes to nor can, that is wickedness and impotence at the same time; if he wishes to
and can (which is the only one among these choices
appropriate to God), where does the evil in this world
come from?"

The argument is serious; and, indeed, Lactantius replies to it very feebly, by saying that God wishes evil, but has given us the wisdom with which to choose the good. It must be admitted that this reply is rather weak in comparison with the objection; for it supposes that God grants wisdom only through creating evil; and anyhow, our wisdom is a laughable one!

The origin of evil has always been an abyss whose bottom nobody has been able to see. It is this that reduced so many ancient philosophers and legislators to supposing two principles, one good, the other bad. Among the Egyptians, Typhon was the bad principle; among the Persians, it was Arimane. It is well known that the Manicheans adopted this theology; but since these gentlemen never had conversation either with the good principle or the bad, we needn't believe every word they said.

Among the absurdities with which this world overflows, and which may be numbered among our evils, it is not a trifling one to have imagined two all-powerful beings fighting to see which of them would put more of himself into the world, and making a treaty like the two doctors in Molière: Pass me the emetic, and I'll pass you the bleeding cup.

Following the Platonists, Basilides maintained, as early as the first century of the Church, that God has assigned the creation of our world to his lowest angels, and that these, lacking skill, made things as we see them now. This theological fable collapses before the powerful objection that it is not in the nature of an all-powerful and all-wise God to have a world built by architects who know nothing about their job.

Simon, who felt the force of this objection, attempted to forestall it by saying that the angel who superintended the workshop was damned for botching his work; but burning the angel does not cure us.

Pandora's adventure among the Greeks does not answer the objection any better. The box holding all the evils, and at whose bottom hope remains, is admittedly a charming allegory; but this Pandora was made by Vulcan only to revenge himself on Prometheus, who had fashioned a man from mud.

The Indians did no better: after God created man, he gave him a drug which assured him everlasting health; man loaded his donkey with the drug; the donkey was thirsty; the serpent showed him a fountain, and while the donkey drank the serpent took the drug for himself.

The Syrians imagined that after man and woman had been created in the fourth sky, they took it into their heads to eat a pancake instead of the ambrosia which was their natural food. The ambrosia was exhaled through the pores; but after they had eaten the pancake, they had to go to the toilet. The man and woman asked an angel to show them where the bathroom was. "Do you see," the angel asked them, "that little planet, a mere nothing in size, which is some fifty million miles from here? There's the privy of the universe; go there as fast as you can." They went there; they were left there; and from that time on our world has been what it is.

We may still ask the Syrians why God permitted man to eat the pancake and why a host of such appalling evils should descend on us.

I move quickly from that fourth sky to Lord Bolingbroke, lest I grow bored. That man, who undoubtedly possessed great talent, provided the celebrated Pope with his plan for his *All is good*, which in fact we find word for word in Lord Bolingbroke's posthumous works, and which Lord Shaftesbury had earlier inserted into his *Characteristics*. Read in Shaftesbury the chapter on the moralists and there you will see these words:

"Much is alleged in answer to show why Nature errs, and how she came thus impotent and erring from an unerring hand. But I deny she errs. . . . 'Tis from this order of inferior and superior things that we admire the world's beauty, founded thus on contrarieties, whilst from such various and disagreeing principles a universal concord is established. . . . The vegetables by their death sustain the animals, and animal bodies dissolved enrich the earth, and raise again the vegetable world. . . . The central powers, which hold the lasting orbs in their just poise and movement, must not be controlled to save a fleeting form, and rescue from the precipice a puny animal, whose brittle frame, however protected, must of itself so soon dissolve."

Bolingbroke, Shaftesbury, and Pope, their promoter, didn't resolve the question any better than the others: their *All is good* means nothing more than that everything is directed by immutable laws; who does not know that? You teach us nothing when you observe, with all the little children, that flies are born to be eaten by spiders, spiders by swallows, swallows by shrikes, shrikes by eagles, eagles to be killed by men, men to kill one another and to be eaten by worms and then—excepting one in a thousand—by devils.

Here's a clear and constant order among the animals of all species; here is order throughout. When a stone is formed in my bladder, it is by an admirable piece of machinery: gravelly juices pass little by little into my blood, filter into the kidneys, pass through the urethras, deposit themselves in my bladder, assemble there by an excellent Newtonian attraction; the stone is formed, grows larger; I suffer evils a thousand times worse than death, by the most beautiful arrangement in the world; a surgeon, having perfected the art invented by Tubal-cain, comes to thrust a sharp and pointed iron into the perineum and seizes my stone with his pincers. It breaks under his efforts by a necessary mechanism; and, by the same mechanism, I die in horrible torments. *All this is good*, all this is the evident consequence of unchangeable physical principles; I agree, and I know it as well as you do.

If we were without feeling, there would be no objection to this natural philosophy. But that is not the issue; we ask you if there are not perceptible evils, and where they come from. "There are no evils," says Pope in his fourth epistle on the *All is good;* "or, if there are particular evils, they compose the general good."

Here's a strange general good, composed of the stone, the gout, all crimes, all sufferings, death, and damnation.

The fall of man is the ointment we put on all the specific maladies of body and soul, which you call the *general health;* but Shaftesbury and Bolingbroke jeered at original sin; Pope doesn't talk about it; it is clear that their system saps the Christian religion at its foundations, and explains nothing at all.

Nevertheless, this system has recently been approved by several theologians who are perfectly willing to put up with agreeable contradictions; we shouldn't begrudge anyone the consolation of reasoning as best he can about the deluge of evils that inundates us. It is right to let desperately sick men eat what they want. They have gone so far as to claim that this system is comforting.

"God," says Pope,

> . . . *sees with equal eye, as God of all,*
> *A hero perish, or a sparrow fall,*
> *Atoms or systems into ruin hurled,*
> *And now a bubble burst, and now a world.*
> [*Essay on Man*, I, 87-90]

That's a pleasant consolation, I admit; don't you find a great relief in the ordinance of Lord Shaftesbury which says that God will not upset his eternal laws for the sake of an animal as puny as man? We must at least admit that this puny animal is right to cry out humbly and, crying out, to seek to understand why these eternal laws are not made for the well-being of every individual.

The system of *All is good* merely represents the author of nature as a powerful and malicious king, who does not care if it should cost the lives of four or five hundred thousand men, and if the others drag out their days in want and tears, provided that he accomplishes his work.

So then, far from consoling them, the notion of the best of possible worlds drives the philosophers who adopt it to despair. The question of good and evil remains an inexplicable chaos for those who search honestly; it is a witticism for those who argue: they are galley-slaves who jingle their chains. As for the unthinking, they closely resemble fish who have been brought from a river to a reservoir; they don't suspect that they are to be eaten during Lent. Similarly, on our own none of us knows a thing about the causes of our destiny.

Let us put at the end of almost all the chapters of metaphysics the two letters the Roman judges set down when they could not understand a cause: *N. L., non liquet*, it is not clear.

BORNES DE L'ESPRIT HUMAINE
LIMITS OF THE HUMAN MIND

They are everywhere, poor doctor. Do you want to know why your arm and foot obey your will, and why your liver doesn't? Do you seek to know how thought forms itself in your puny understanding, and the infant in the uterus of that woman? I give you time to answer me. What is matter? Your colleagues have written ten thousand volumes on the subject; they have discovered some of the substance's qualities: children know them as well as you do. But what is that substance at bottom? And what is this thing you've called *spirit*, from the Latin word meaning *breath*, unable to do better because you knew nothing about it?

Look at the grain of wheat I drop in the earth and tell me how it rises to produce a stalk loaded with an ear. Teach me how the same earth produces an apple high up in this tree and a chestnut in the neighboring tree. I could make you a folio of questions, to which you could reply with only four words: *I have no idea*.

And yet you have taken your degrees and you are covered with fur, and your cap is too, and they call you *master*. And this proud imbecile, invested with a little job in a little town, believes he has purchased the right to judge and condemn what he does not understand!

Montaigne's motto was: *What do I know?* and yours is: *What don't I know?*

CARACTÈRE · CHARACTER

From the Greek word *impression, engraving.* It is what nature has engraved in us. Can we efface it? Great question. If I have a twisted nose and two cat's eyes, I can hide them behind a mask—do I have more power over the character nature has given me? A man born violent, hot-headed, presents himself before Francis I, king of France, to complain against a trespass; the countenance of the prince, the respectful behavior of the courtiers, the very place he is in, make a powerful impression on him; he instinctively lowers his eyes, his rude voice becomes gentle, he presents his petition humbly; one would think him as gentle as the courtiers are (at least at that moment); he is even disconcerted in their midst; but if Francis I knows his physiognomies, he will easily discover in his eyes, lowered but alight with a somber fire, in the taut muscles of his face, in his lips, tightly pressed against each other, that the man is not so gentle as he is obliged to appear. This man follows him to Pavia, is taken prisoner along with him and thrown into prison with him in Madrid; the majesty of Francis I no longer makes the same impression on him; he becomes familiar with the object of his respect. One day, while he is pulling off the king's boots, and pulling them off badly, the king, embittered by his misfortune, grows angry: my man sends the king packing and throws his boots out of the window.

Sixtus V was born petulant, obstinate, haughty, impetuous, vindictive, arrogant: this character seems to have been curbed during the trials of his novitiate. As he begins to enjoy some influence in his order he loses his temper with a caretaker and beats him with his fist;

once inquisitor at Venice, he exercises his office with insolence; behold him cardinal, he is possessed *della rabbia papale:* his rage subdues his nature; he buries his person and his character in obscurity; he apes the humble and the dying; he is elected pope: in this moment all the long-restrained resiliency of the spring, which policy had kept under control, is restored; he is the proudest and most despotic of sovereigns.

Naturam expellas furca, tamen usque recurret.

[*Drive out nature with a pitchfork, she'll always return.*
Horace, *Epistles*, I, x, 24]

Religion, ethics, put a curb on nature's strength; they cannot destroy it. The drunkard in a cloister, reduced to a gallon of cider each meal, will not get drunk any more, but he will always love wine.

Age weakens the character; it is a tree which no longer produces anything but degenerate fruits, but they are always of the same nature; it is covered with knots and moss, becomes worm-eaten, but it is always an oak or pear tree. If we could change our character, if we could give ourselves one, we would be the master of nature. Can we give ourselves anything? Don't we receive everything? Try to arouse the indolent man with regular activity, to freeze with apathy the boiling soul of the impetuous, to inspire the man who lacks taste or ear with a taste for music and poetry: you would succeed no better than if you undertook to give sight to a man born blind. We perfect, we smoothe down, we hide what nature has placed in us, but we put nothing there ourselves.

A farmer is told: "You have too many fish in this pond, they won't thrive; there are too many sheep in your meadows; grass is lacking, they will grow lean." After this exhortation it happens that the pikes eat half

my man's carp, and the wolves half his sheep: the rest
fatten. Will he applaud his economy? This rustic is you;
one of your passions devours the rest and you think you
have triumphed over yourself. Don't we almost all resemble that old general of ninety who, when he encountered
young officers who were making a disturbance with some
girls, said to them in great anger: "Gentlemen, is this the
example I set you?"

CARÊME · LENT
Questions about Lent

Did the first men to think of fasting put themselves on
this regimen on their physician's order, because they had
indigestion?

Is the lack of appetite we feel when we are melancholy
the origin of the fast days prescribed in melancholy religions?

Did the Jews adopt the custom of fasting from the
Egyptians, all of whose rites they imitated, including
flagellation and the scapegoat?

Why did Jesus fast for forty days in the desert, where
he was carried off by the devil, by the *Knathbull?* St.
Matthew remarks that after his fast *he was hungry;* was
he then not hungry during his fast?

Why, in the days of abstinence, does the Roman
Church consider it a crime to eat terrestrial animals and
a good work to be served with sole and salmon? The
rich papist who has five hundred francs' worth of fish
on his table will be saved, and the poor man, dying of
hunger, who eats four sous' worth of salt pork will be
damned!

Why must we ask our bishop's permission to eat eggs?
If a king commanded his people never to eat eggs,

wouldn't he be considered the most ridiculous of tyrants? What strange aversion do bishops have for omelets?

Can we believe that among papists there have been tribunals imbecile enough, mean enough, barbarous enough, to condemn to death poor citizens who had committed no other crime than to eat horseflesh during Lent? The fact is only too true: I have a sentence of this kind in my hands. What makes it strange is that the judges who imposed such sentences thought themselves superior to the Iroquois.

Idiotic and cruel priests! To whom do you prescribe Lent? Is it to the rich? They take good care not to observe it. Is it to the poor? They keep Lent all year round. The unhappy farmer hardly ever eats meat, and has no cash to buy fish. Madmen that you are, when will you correct your absurd laws?

CATÉCHISME CHINOIS
CHINESE CATECHISM
OR

Conversation of CU-SU, *Disciple of* CONFUCIUS, *with Prince* KOU, *son of the King of Lou, Tributary of the Chinese Emperor* GNENVAN, *417 years before our Common Era.*

> *Translated into Latin by Father Foucquet, former Jesuit.*
> *The manuscript is in the Vatican library, n. 42759.*

FIRST CONVERSATION

KOU. What should I understand when I'm told to worship heaven (Chang-ti)?

CU-SU. Not the material heaven we see; for that

heaven is nothing but the air, and that air is composed of all the exhalations of the earth: it would be an absurd madness to worship vapors.

KOU. Still, I wouldn't be surprised at it. It seems to me that men have committed greater follies than that.

CU-SU. That's true; but you are destined to govern; you must be wise.

KOU. There are so many nations who worship heaven and the planets!

CU-SU. Planets are nothing but earths like our own. The moon, for instance, might just as well worship our sand and our mud, as for us to kneel before the sand and the mud of the moon.

KOU. What do people mean when they say: heaven and earth, rising to heaven, to be worthy of heaven?

CU-SU. They talk tremendous nonsense.* There is no heaven; every planet is surrounded by its atmosphere, as by a shell, and rolls in space around its sun. Each sun is the center of several planets which travel continuously around it: there is neither high nor low, neither ascent nor descent. If the inhabitants of the moon were to say that one rises to the earth, that one must become worthy of the earth, you would know that they are talking extravagantly. In the same way we speak meaningless words when we say that we must make ourselves worthy of heaven; it is as though we had said: we must make ourselves worthy of the air, worthy of the constellation of the dragon, worthy of space.

KOU. I think I understand you; we must worship only the God who has made the heaven and the earth.

CU-SU. To be sure; we must worship God alone. But when we say that he has made the heaven and the earth, we are piously pronouncing a great platitude. For if by heaven we understand the prodigious space in which

* See the article CIEL.

God lighted up so many suns and made so many worlds revolve, it is much more ridiculous to say "heaven and earth" than to say "mountains and a grain of sand." Our globe is infinitely less than a grain of sand in comparison to the millions of billions of universes before which we vanish into insignificance. All we can do is to join our feeble voice to the voices of the innumerable beings in the abyss of space who render homage to God.

KOU. Then we were badly deceived when we were told that Fo descended among us from the fourth heaven and appeared as a white elephant.

CU-SU. Those are tales the bonzes tell children and old men: we must worship only the eternal author of all beings.

KOU. But how could one being make the others?

CU-SU. Look at this star; it is fifteen hundred thousand million *lis* from our little globe: rays from it form two angles, equal at the apex, in your eyes; they form the same angles in the eyes of all animals: isn't that a fixed plan? Isn't that an admirable law? Now who does a piece of work, if not a workman? Who makes laws, if not a legislator? There is a workman, then, an eternal legislator.

KOU. But who made that workman? And how is he made?

CU-SU. My prince, yesterday I strolled past the vast palace built by the king, your father. I heard two crickets, and one said to the other: "Here is an awe-inspiring edifice." "Yes," said the other, "glorious as I am, I admit that it was someone more powerful than crickets who made this marvel; but I have no notion of that being; I see that it is, but I do not know what it is."

KOU. I tell you that you are a better educated cricket than I am; and what pleases me about you is that you don't pretend to know what you don't know.

SECOND CONVERSATION

CU-SU. You agree, then, that there is an all-powerful being, existing of himself, supreme artisan of all nature?

KOU. Yes; but if he exists of himself, then nothing can limit him, he is therefore everywhere; he exists, then, in all matter, in all parts of me?

CU-SU. Why not?

KOU. I myself would then be a part of Divinity?

CU-SU. That perhaps does not follow. This piece of glass is pervaded by light in all its parts; still, is it light itself? It is only sand, and nothing more. All is in God, to be sure; that which animates everything must be everywhere. God is not like the emperor of China, who lives in his palace and who sends his orders through colaos. Since he exists, it necessarily follows that his existence fills all space and all his works; and since he is in you, that is a continual admonition not to do anything for which you might blush before him.

KOU. What must we do to dare look at ourselves in this way, without repugnance and without shame before the supreme Being?

CU-SU. Be just.

KOU. And what else?

CU-SU. Be just.

KOU. But the sect of Laokium says that there is neither right nor wrong, neither vice nor virtue.

CU-SU. Does the sect of Laokium say that there is neither health nor sickness?

KOU. No, it doesn't make so great a blunder.

CU-SU. The blunder of thinking that there is neither health of the soul nor sickness of the soul, neither virtue nor vice, is as great and more disastrous. Those who have said that all is the same are monsters: is it the same thing to nourish one's son or to crush him on a stone, to aid one's mother or to plunge a knife into her heart?

KOU. You make me shudder; I detest the sect of Laokium; but justice has so many shades. Who knows precisely what is permitted or what is forbidden? Who can confidently place the limits that separate good and evil? What rules will you give me to discriminate between them?

CU-SU. Those of Confucius, my master: "Live as in dying you would wish to have lived; treat your neighbor as you want him to treat you."

KOU. I admit these maxims ought to be the code of mankind; but what will it matter to me when I am dying to have lived well? What will I get out of it? Will that clock, when it has been destroyed, be happy that it sounded the hours well?

CU-SU. That clock doesn't feel; it doesn't think; it cannot feel remorse; but you feel it when you feel guilty.

KOU. But if I come to have no remorse after I have committed a number of crimes?

CU-SU. Then you would have to be smothered to death; and be sure that among men who don't like to be oppressed some will be found who will see to it that you do not commit new crimes.

KOU. Thus God, who is in them, will permit them to be evildoers after having permitted me to be one?

CU-SU. God has given you reason, let neither you nor them abuse it. Not only will you be unhappy in this life, but who has told you that you won't be unhappy in another?

KOU. And who has told you that there is another life?

CU-SU. If in doubt you should conduct yourself as if there were one.

KOU. But if I am sure that there isn't one?

CU-SU. I challenge you.

THIRD CONVERSATION

KOU. You are pressing me, Cu-su. In order for me to be rewarded or punished when I am gone, there must subsist something in me that goes on feeling and thinking after my death. Now, since nothing of me possessed either feeling or thought before my birth, why should there be any such thing after my death? What could this incomprehensible part of me be? Will the buzzing of this bee remain when the bee is gone? Does the vegetation of this plant continue to exist after the plant has been uprooted? Is not vegetation a word that men use to signify the inexplicable manner in which the supreme Being has wished the plant to draw its sap from the ground? In the same way, soul is a word invented to express, feebly and obscurely, the springs of our life. All animals move; and that power of moving is called *active force;* but there is no distinct being that is this force. We have passions, memory, reason; they are not distinct things; they are not little persons who have a separate existence; they are generic words, invented to fix our ideas. Hence the soul, which signifies our memory, our reason, our passions, is itself only a word. Who makes movement in nature? it is God. Who makes all the plants vegetate? it is God. Who makes movement in the animals? it is God. Who makes the thought of man? it is God.

If the human soul* were a little person shut up in our body, directing its movements and ideas, wouldn't that be an unworthy contrivance for the eternal artisan of the world, and a sign of impotence in him? Was he, then, incapable of making automatons having the gift of movement and of thought in themselves? You taught me Greek, you made me read Homer; I find Vulcan a

---

* See the article ÂME.

divine blacksmith when he makes tripods of gold that
march to the council of the gods by themselves: but
this Vulcan would seem a miserable charlatan to me
if he had hidden one of his journeymen in the body of
these tripods to make them move without our noticing it.

There are frigid dreamers who think that the planets
revolve because of genii who push them ceaselessly; a
beautiful invention, but God was not reduced to this
pitiful expedient: in a word, why postulate two springs
for a mechanism when one will do? You dare not deny
that God has the power to animate the little-known
being we call *matter;* why then should he avail himself
of another agent?

And much more: what would this soul be that you
confer so generously on our body? Where would it
come from? When would it come? Would the Creator
of the universe need to lie continually in wait for men
and women to couple, note the exact moment the seed
leaves the body of the man and enters that of the woman,
and then quickly dispatch a soul into that seed? And if
that seed dies, what would become of the soul? It would
then have been created unnecessarily, or would have to
wait for another opportunity.

Here, let me say, is a strange occupation for the
master of the world; and not only must he keep continual watch over the copulations of the human species,
but he must do the same with all the animals; for they all
have, like us, memory, ideas, passions; and if a soul is
required to form them, God must labor perpetually to
forge souls for elephants and pigs, owls, fish, and bonzes.

What would you make of the architect of so many
millions of worlds who would have to keep on mending
his construction with invisible cement to keep it going!

These are only a few of the reasons that might make me
doubt the existence of the soul.

CU-SU. You argue honestly, and this virtuous inclination would be agreeable to the supreme Being, even if it erred. You may deceive yourself, but you don't try to deceive yourself, and consequently you may be pardoned. But consider: you have only proposed doubts to me, and these doubts are sad ones. Admit more consoling probabilities: it is painful to be annihilated; hope to live. You know that a thought is not matter; why then is it so difficult for you to believe that God has endowed you with a divine principle which cannot be subject to death since it cannot be dissolved? Dare you say that it is impossible for you to have a soul? Certainly not, and if it is possible, isn't it highly probable that you have one? Could you reject so noble a system, so necessary to mankind? What are the difficulties that repel you?

KOU. I'd like to accept the system, but I'd like to have it proved first. I'm not at liberty to believe something I don't have the evidence for. I am forever struck with this great idea that God has made everything, that he is everywhere, that he pervades everything, that he gives movement and life to all; and if he is in all parts of my being, as he is in all parts of nature, I don't see what I need a soul for. What do I need that little subordinate being for, since I am animated by God himself? What good is that soul to me? We are not responsible for our own ideas, for we have them almost always in spite of ourselves; we have them when we are asleep; everything happens within us without our having a hand in it. In vain would the soul tell the blood and the animal spirits, "Flow, I beg you, in this fashion, to give me pleasure"; they will always circulate in the manner God prescribed for them. I prefer being the machine of a God who is demonstrated to me to being the machine of a soul about which I have doubts.

cu-su. Well! If God himself animates you, never sully with crimes the God who is within you; and if he has given you a soul, let that soul never offend him. By either system you have a will; you are free; that is, you have the power to do what you will: avail yourself of that power to serve the God who gave it to you. It is good that you are a philosopher, but it is necessary that you be just. You will be so even more when you believe that you have an immortal soul.

Deign to answer me: isn't it true that God is sovereign justice?

kou. Certainly; and if it were ever possible for him to cease to be (which is a blasphemy), I, for one, should still like to act justly.

cu-su. Isn't it true that it will be your duty, when you are on the throne, to reward virtuous actions and to punish criminal ones? Would you want God not to do what you yourself are bound to do? You know that in this life there are and will always be instances of unrewarded virtue and unpunished crime; it is therefore necessary that good and evil should be judged in another life. It is this idea—so simple, so natural, so general—which has led to the establishment, in so many nations, of the belief in the immortality of our souls and in a divine justice that judges them when they have sloughed off their mortal skin. Is there a system more reasonable, more agreeable to the Divinity, and more useful to mankind?

kou. Why then have several nations not adopted this system? You know that we have in our province about two hundred families of the ancient Sinous,* who lived at one time in a part of Arabia Petraea: neither they nor their ancestors have ever believed in an immortal soul;

* These are the Jews of the ten tribes who in their dispersion got as far as China; they are there called *Sinous*.

they have their *five Books*, as we have our *five Kings;*
I have read them in translation; their laws, inevitably
similar to those of all other nations, command them to
respect their parents, neither to steal nor lie, to be
neither adulterers nor murderers; but these same laws
say nothing about either rewards or punishments in another life.

CU-SU. If that idea hasn't yet developed in that poor
nation, it will doubtless do so one day. But what do we
care about one unfortunate little nation when the Babylonians, the Eyptians, the Indians, and all civilized nations have accepted this salutary dogma? If you were ill,
would you reject a remedy approved by all the Chinese
on the pretext that a few barbarians from the mountains
did not wish to make use of it? God has given you
reason; it tells you that the soul must be immortal; it is
thus God himself who tells you so.

KOU. But how could I be rewarded or punished when
I'll no longer be myself, when I'll no longer be anything
of that which has constituted my person? It is only
through my memory that I am always myself; I lose
my memory in my last illness; would it therefore require
a miracle to restore it to me after my death, to make me
return the existence I have lost?

CU-SU. That is to say that if a prince butchers his
family in order to reign, if he tyrannizes over his subjects, he can get off by saying to God: "That wasn't
me, I lost my memory, you're mistaken, I'm no longer
the same person." Do you think that God would be
satisfied with such a sophism?

KOU. All right, agreed, I give up;* I wish to do good

* Well! Wretched enemies of reason and truth, will you still say
that this work teaches the mortality of the soul? This piece was
printed in all the editions. How dare you slander it, then, with such
impudence? Alas! If your souls kept their character through eternity,

on my own account; I shall also do it to please the supreme Being; I thought it was enough if, in this life, my soul is just; I hope it will be happy in another. I can see that this view is good for peoples and princes, but the worship of God troubles me.

FOURTH CONVERSATION

CU-SU. What is it that shocks you in our *Chu-King*, that first canonical book, so respected by all the Chinese emperors? You cultivate a field with your royal hands to set an example to the people, and you offer its first fruits to Chang-Ti, to Tien, to the supreme Being; you sacrifice to him four times a year; you are king and pontiff; you promise God to do all the good that will be in your power; is there anything in this that repels you?

KOU. I'm far from seeing anything wrong in it; I know that God doesn't need our sacrifices or our prayers; but we need to make them to him; his cult was not estab-

---

they would be foolish and unjust souls forever. No, the authors of this reasonable and useful work do not tell you that the soul dies with the body: they only tell you that you are ignorant men. Don't blush for it; all the sages have confessed their ignorance: none of them was impertinent enough to profess to know the nature of the soul. Gassendi, summarizing all that antiquity has said about it, speaks to you as follows: "You know what you think, but you don't know what species of substance you are, you who think: you resemble a blind man who, feeling the heat of the sun, thinks he has a distinct notion of that star." Read the rest of this admirable letter to Descartes; read Locke; reread this work attentively, and you will see that it is impossible for us to have the smallest notion of the nature of the soul, because it is impossible for the creature to know the hidden ways of the Creator; you will see that we must try to think exactly and justly without knowing the principle of our thoughts; that we must be everything that you are not: modest, gentle, beneficent, indulgent; resemble Cu-Su and Kou, and not Thomas Aquinas or Scotus, whose souls were extremely obscure, or Calvin and Luther, whose souls were harsh and fervid. Try to make your souls resemble ours a little, then you will have a tremendous laugh at your own expense.

lished for him, but for us. I greatly enjoy saying prayers, but I don't want to be ridiculous; for, when I have shouted that *the mountain of Chang-ti is a rich mountain,* and that *we ought not to look at rich mountains;* when I have made the sun run away and the moon dry up, will this gibberish be agreeable to the supreme Being, useful to my subjects and to me?

Above all I cannot stand the lunacy of the sects that surround us: on one side I see Lao Tse, whom his mother conceived through the union of heaven and earth, and with whom she was pregnant for eighty years. I have no more faith in his doctrine of annihilation and universal spoliation than in the white hair with which he was born and the black cow on which he mounted to go preach his doctrine.

Nor does the god Fo impress me, even though he had a white elephant for his father and promises eternal life.

What displeases me above all is that these fantasies are continually preached by the bonzes who mislead the people in order to govern them; they make themselves respectable by mortifications that terrify nature. Some deprive themselves of the most salutary nourishments all their lives long, as though one could please God only by a bad diet; others put an iron collar around their neck which they sometimes deserve; they drive nails into their thighs as though their thighs were boards; the people follow them in crowds. If a king issues some edict that displeases them, they coldly tell you that the edict cannot be found in the commentary of the god Fo, and that it is better to obey God than men. How can we remedy a popular malady that is so extravagant and dangerous? You know that toleration is the principle of the government of China, and of all those of Asia; but isn't that toleration fatal when it exposes an empire to being overthrown by fanatical opinions?

CU-SU. Chang-ti preserve me from wishing to extinguish the spirit of toleration in you, that respectable virtue which is to souls what the permission to eat is to bodies! Natural law permits everyone to believe what he wishes and to eat what he wants. A physician has no right to kill his patients because they fail to observe the diet he has prescribed for them. A prince has no right to hang those subjects who do not think as he does. But he does have the right to prevent disturbances; and if he is wise, it will be quite easy for him to uproot superstitions. Do you know what happened to Daon, sixth king of Chaldea, about four thousand years ago?

KOU. No, I have no idea; you would give me pleasure if you told me about it.

CU-SU. The Chaldean priests had hit on the idea of worshiping the pikes in the Euphrates; they claimed that a famous pike named *Oannès* had at one time taught them theology, that this pike was immortal, that it was three feet long and had a little crescent on its tail. It was out of respect for this *Oannès* that the eating of pike was prohibited. A great dispute arose among the theologians whether the pike *Oannès* was soft-roed or hard-roed. The parties excommunicated one another, and several times they came to blows. Now here's what king Daon did to put an end to this commotion.

He imposed a rigorous fast of three days on both parties, and then he had the partisans of the hard-roed pike come to dinner with him. He had a three-foot pike brought in; a little crescent had been put on its tail. "Is this your god?" he asked the savants. "Yes, Sire," they replied, "for it has a crescent on its tail." The king ordered the pike to be opened, and it had the finest milt in the world. "You can see," he said, "that this is not your god, for it is soft-roed." And the pike was eaten by the king and his satraps, to the great satisfaction of the theologians of the hard-roed pike, who saw that the God of their adversaries had been fried.

Then he sent for the savants of the opposing party: they were shown a three-foot god who had spawn and a crescent on its tail; they claimed that this was the god *Oannès* and that it was soft-roed: it was fried like the other and seen to be hard-roed. Thus the two parties were equally foolish; since they had had no lunch, the good king Daon told them that he had nothing but pike to give them for dinner; they ate it greedily, be it hard-roed or soft-roed. The civil war came to an end; everyone blessed good king Daon; and from that time on the citizens served as much pike at dinner as they liked.

KOU. I like king Daon very much, and I firmly promise to imitate him at the first opportunity. I will always do the best I can (without doing violence to anyone) to keep people from adoring Fos and pikes.

I know that in Pegu and in Tonking there are little gods and little monkeys who make the moon go down when it is waning, and who make definite predictions about the future, that is, who see clearly what is not, for the future is not. As far as I am able, I will stop the monkeys from appearing before me to mistake the future for the present and make the moon go down.

What a pity there should be sects going from town to town retailing their fantasies, like charlatans selling drugs! What a disgrace for the human mind that small nations should think that they alone possess the truth, and that the vast empire of China is consigned to error! Is the eternal Being merely the God of the island of Formosa or of Borneo? Would he abandon the rest of the universe? My dear Cu-Su, he is the father of all men; he permits everyone to eat pike; the worthiest homage we can offer him is to be virtuous; a pure heart is the finest of all his temples, as the great emperor Hiao said.

FIFTH CONVERSATION

CU-SU. Since you love virtue, how will you practice it when you are king?

KOU. By being unjust neither to my neighbors nor to my people.

CU-SU. It is not enough to do no evil; you must also do good; you must feed the poor by employing them at useful labors, and not by rewarding idleness; you must improve the highways; you must dig canals; you must erect public buildings; you must encourage all the arts; you must reward merit in all pursuits; you must pardon involuntary errors.

KOU. That is what I meant by not being unjust; these things are so many duties.

CU-SU. You think like a true king; but there is the king and the man, public life and private life. You must marry soon: how many wives do you plan to have?

KOU. Well, I think a dozen will be enough for me; a larger number might deprive me of time for business. I don't approve of the kings who have three hundred wives, seven hundred concubines, and thousands of eunuchs to serve them. Above all, the mania for eunuchs seems to me too great an outrage against human nature. I can forgive the caponizing of cocks; it makes them better eating; but so far eunuchs haven't been put on the spit. What purpose does their mutilation serve? The Dalai-Lama has fifty of them to sing in his pagoda. I'd like to know how pleased Chang-ti is to hear the clear voices of these fifty geldings.

I also think it's ridiculous that there should be bonzes who don't marry. They boast of being wiser than other Chinese: all right! Then let them produce wise children. That's a fine way of honoring Chang-ti—by depriving him of worshipers! That's a remarkable way of serving mankind—by setting an example of destroying mankind!

The nice little lama called *Stelca ed isant Errepi** was pleased to say that *every priest* should have as many children as he can; he practiced what he preached and was highly useful in his time. As far as I'm concerned, I will marry off all the lamas and bonzes and lamaesses and bonzesses who have a vocation for this holy work; they will surely be better citizens for it, and I think I shall be doing the kingdom of Lou a great favor.

CU-SU. Oh! What a good prince we have here! You make me weep with joy. But you won't be content with having only wives and subjects; for after all you cannot spend the whole day making edicts and children: surely you'll have friends?

KOU. I already have them, and good ones, who admonish me for my faults; I give myself the liberty of reproving theirs; they console me, I console them. Friendship is the balm of life; it is worth more than the balm of the chemist Erueil, and even than the sachets of the great Ranoud. I'm surprised that friendship has not been made a precept of religion; I have a mind to insert it into our ritual.

CU-SU. Beware of that; friendship is sacred enough by itself; don't ever command it; the heart must be free; besides, if you make friendship a precept, a mystery, a rite, a ceremony, there will be a thousand bonzes who will make friendship ridiculous by preaching and writing their fantasies; it must not be exposed to this profanation.

But how will you treat your enemies? There are twenty places where Confucius recommends that we should love them; doesn't that seem a little difficult to you?

KOU. Love one's enemies! My God! Nothing is more common.

* *Stelca ed isant Errepi* signifies, in Chinese, *the abbé Castel de Saint-Pierre.*

CU-SU. What do you mean?

KOU. As one should mean it, I think. I served my apprenticeship of war under the prince of Décon against the prince of Vis-Brunck:* when one of our enemies was wounded and fell into our hands, we took care of him as if he were our brother: we often gave our own bed to our captive wounded, and we slept next to them on tiger skins spread on the ground; we served them ourselves: what more do you want? That we should love them as we love our mistress?

CU-SU. Everything you tell me is highly edifying, and I wish all the nations in the world might hear you; for I am told that there are nations impertinent enough to dare to say that we do not know true virtue, that our good actions are nothing but splendid sins, that we need lessons from their monkeys to acquire good principles. Alas! Those wretches! They've only known how to read and write since yesterday, and they try to teach their masters!

SIXTH CONVERSATION

CU-SU. I won't repeat to you all the commonplaces retailed among us for five or six thousand years about the moral virtues. There are those which are good only for ourselves, like prudence to guide our souls, temperance to govern our bodies; these are precepts of policy and health. The true virtues are those which are useful to society, like fidelity, magnanimity, beneficence, tolerance, etc. Thank heaven, there isn't an old woman among us who doesn't teach all these virtues to her grandchildren; that is rudimentary for our youth in the

---

* It is a remarkable thing that in turning round *Décon* and *Vis-Brunck*, which are Chinese names, one discovers *Condé* and *Brunswick*, so much are great men celebrated throughout the world!

villages as well as in the town: but there is one great virtue which, I am displeased to see, is beginning to go out of practice.

KOU. Which one is that? Quick, tell me; I'll try to revive it.

CU-SU. It's hospitality; that social virtue, that sacred bond between men, has begun to slacken since we introduced taverns. This pernicious institution, I understand, came to us from certain savages of the Occident. Those miserable fellows apparently don't have a house in which to welcome travelers. What a pleasure it is, in the great town of Lou, in my house Ki, on the lovely place Honchan, to receive a generous stranger just arrived from Samarkand, for whom at that moment I become a sacred man, and who is obligated in turn, by all the laws divine and human, to welcome me into his house when I travel in Tartary, and to be my intimate friend!

The savages I speak of receive strangers in disgusting huts for money only; they sell this sordid reception dearly, and I understand that these miserable people think they are superior to us, that they boast of having a purer morality. They claim their preachers preach better than Confucius—in short, that it's up to them to teach us justice because they sell bad wine on the highways and because their females walk in the streets like madwomen and dance while ours cultivate silkworms.

KOU. I find hospitality a very good thing; I practice it with pleasure, but I fear its abuse. There are people near Great Tibet whose houses are wretched and who like to roam about—they would travel from one end of the world to the other free of charge; if you were to go to Great Tibet to enjoy their hospitality, you would find neither bed nor dinner for yourself; that sort of thing could make people averse to politeness.

CU-SU. The inconvenience is small; it is easy to remedy

by receiving only highly recommended persons. There are no virtues that don't have their dangers; and it is noble to adopt them for just that reason.

How wise and holy was our Confucius! There isn't a virtue he doesn't inspire. Each one of his sentences is related to the happiness of men; here's one that comes to mind, it's the fifty-third:

"Acknowledge kindnesses with kindnesses, and never avenge injuries."

What maxim, what law, could the people of the Occident match against a morality so pure? In how many places Confucius recommends humility! If people practiced this virtue, there would never be a quarrel in the world.

KOU. I have read everything Confucius and the sages of earlier centuries have written about humility; but it seems to me that they never gave a sufficiently precise definition: there's perhaps little humility in daring to find fault with them, but at least I have the humility of admitting that I have not understood them. Tell me what you think of it.

CU-SU. I shall obey humbly. I believe that humility is the modesty of the soul; for external modesty is nothing but civility. Humility cannot consist of denying yourself the superiority that you may have acquired over someone else. A good physician cannot conceal from himself that he knows more than his delirious patient; the man who teaches astronomy must admit to himself that he knows more than his students; he cannot stop himself from believing it, but he shouldn't get conceited about it. Humility is not abjectness; it is the corrective of egotism, as modesty is the corrective of pride.

KOU. All right! It is in the practice of all these virtues and the cult of a single universal God that I wish to live, far from the chimeras of sophists and the illusions of false prophets. Love of my neighbor will be my virtue on the throne, and love of God my religion. I shall despise the god Fo, and Lao Tse, and Vishnu who has incarnated himself so many times among the Indians, and Sammonocodom who descended from heaven to fly kites among the Siamese, and the Camis who arrived in Japan from the moon.

How unhappy is the nation so idiotic and barbarous as to think that there is a God for its province alone! That is blasphemy. What! The light of the sun illuminates all eyes, and the light of God illuminates only a small and puny nation in a corner of the globe! How horrible and how stupid! Divinity speaks to the heart of all men, and the bonds of charity ought to unite them from one end of the universe to the other.

CU-SU. O wise Kou! you have spoken like a man inspired by Chang-ti himself; you shall be a worthy prince. I have been your teacher, and you have become mine.

CATÉCHISME DU CURÉ
THE PRIEST'S CATECHISM

ARISTON. Well, my dear Téotime, so you're going to be a country priest?

TÉOTIME. Yes, they're giving me a little parish, and I like that better than a large one. I have only a limited amount of intelligence and energy; I certainly couldn't guide seventy thousand souls; that is, assuming I have one myself. I've always admired the self-confidence of those who take charge of these immense districts, but I don't feel myself capable of it; a large flock frightens

me, but I may be able to do some good in a small one.
I've studied enough law to stop my poor parishioners, as
much as I can, from ruining themselves with lawsuits. I
know enough medicine to show them simple remedies
when they are ill. I have enough knowledge of agriculture to give them useful advice from time to time. The
squire of the place and his wife are decent people;
they're not devout, and they will help me to do good. I
expect that I'll live happily enough, and that they won't
be unhappy with me.

ARISTON. Aren't you displeased at having no wife? It
would be a great consolation; after preaching, chanting,
confessing, communicating, baptizing, burying, it would
be pleasant to find a sweet, agreeable, and decent wife
in your lodgings who would take care of your linen and
your person, who would cheer you up in health, who
would care for you in sickness, and who would bear
you pretty children who, properly educated, would be
useful to the state. I pity you: you who serve men are
deprived of a consolation so necessary to men.

TÉOTIME. The Greek Church takes great care to encourage its priests to marry; the Anglican Church and
the Protestants show the same wisdom; the Latin Church
shows a contrary wisdom: I must submit myself to it.
Perhaps today, when the philosophic spirit has made so
much progress, a council will make rules more favorable
to humanity than the Council of Trent. But while I wait
I must conform to existing laws; it costs a great deal, I
know; but so many people better than I am have submitted to them, I must not grumble.

ARISTON. You are learned, furnished with wise eloquence; in what way do you expect to preach to country
folk?

TÉOTIME. As I would preach to kings. I shall always
speak of morality and never of controversy; God pre-

serve me from digging into concomitant grace, efficacious grace which you can resist, sufficient grace which
does not suffice; from examining whether the angels who
ate with Abraham and with Lot had a body, or whether
they pretended to eat. There are a thousand things my
audience wouldn't understand—nor would I. I shall try
to make honest men and to be one myself; but I won't
make theologians, and I'll be one as little as possible.

ARISTON. Oh, good priest! I'd like to buy a country
house in your parish. Tell me, please, what you will do
in confession.

TÉOTIME. Confession is an excellent thing, a curb on
crime, invented in remote antiquity; confession was a
part of the celebration of all the ancient mysteries; we
have imitated and sanctified that wise practice; it is very
useful for persuading hearts cankered by hatred to forgive, and to make petty thieves return what they may
have stolen from their neighbor. It has some drawbacks.
There are many indiscreet confessors, chiefly among the
monks, who sometimes teach more nonsense to young
girls than all the young men of a village can practice
with them. No details in confession: it's not a judicial
interrogation, it is the avowal of faults which a sinner
makes to the supreme Being under the guidance of another sinner who will accuse himself in turn. This salutary avowal was not devised to satisfy the curiosity of a
man.

ARISTON. And excommunications—will you use them?

TÉOTIME. No; there are rituals for excommunicating
locusts, sorcerers, and actors; I won't forbid locusts to
enter the church, since they'll never come there; I won't
excommunicate sorcerers because there aren't any; and
as for actors, since they are pensioned by the king and
authorized by the government, I'll take care not to slander them. I will even confess to you, as my friend, that

I enjoy the theatre when it doesn't offend against good morals. I passionately love *Le Misanthrope, Athalie*, and other pieces which seem to me schools of virtue and decency. The squire of my village has some of these pieces performed in his *château* by young people with talent: these representations inspire virtue by the attraction of pleasure; they form taste; they teach good speech and good pronunciation. I see in this something quite innocent and even quite useful; I certainly plan to attend these performances for my instruction—but in an enclosed box, in order not to shock the delicate.

ARISTON. The more you disclose your sentiments to me, the more anxious I am to become your parishioner. There's a very important matter that troubles me. What will you do to prevent peasants from getting drunk on holidays? That is their favorite method of celebrating. You see some of them overpowered by liquid poison, head between their knees, hands dangling, seeing nothing, hearing nothing, reduced to a state far beneath that of brute beasts, taken home, staggering, by their weeping wives, unable to work the next day, often sick and brutalized for the rest of their lives. You see others driven mad by wine, starting bloody quarrels, beating and being beaten, and sometimes concluding these terrible scenes, which are the disgrace of mankind, with a murder. We must acknowledge that the state loses more subjects through feasts than through battles; how will you reduce such a detestable abuse in your parish?

TÉOTIME. My mind is made up; I shall permit them, I shall even urge them, to cultivate their fields on holidays after divine services, which I will hold very early. It is the idleness of the holiday that drives them into the tavern. Work days are not days of debauchery and murder. Moderate labor is conducive to health of body and soul; more, this work is necessary to the state. Let us suppose five million men who each produce ten *sous'* worth of labor every day—and that estimate is very moderate; you make these five million men useless thirty days a year: that's thirty times five million ten-*sou* pieces which the state loses in manual labor. Now surely God never ordained either the loss or the drunkenness.

ARISTON. So you will reconcile prayer and work; God ordains one and the other. You will serve God and your neighbor. But what side will you take in ecclesiastical disputes?

TÉOTIME. None. There are never any disputes over virtue, since it comes from God: people quarrel over opinions, which come from men.

ARISTON. Oh! Good priest! Good priest!

CATÉCHISME DU JAPONAIS
JAPANESE CATECHISM

THE INDIAN. Is it true that in the old days the Japanese couldn't cook, that they submitted their kingdom to the grand lama, that this grand lama had sovereign power over their drinking and eating, that from time to time he sent a little lama to you to collect tribute, and that in exchange he gave you a sign of protection, made with the thumb and first two fingers?

THE JAPANESE. Alas! It's only too true. Imagine, all the posts of the Canusi,* who are the grand cooks of our island, were given out by the lama, and not for the love of God. More: each of our lay households paid an ounce of silver a year to this grand cook of Tibet. In return he gave us nothing but little bad-tasting dishes which are called *relics*. And when he was possessed by some new

* The Canusi are the ancient priests of Japan.

fantasy, like making war on the people of Tangut, he levied new subsidies on us. Our nation often complained, but without result; indeed, every complaint ended up with our paying a little more. At last love, which does all for the best, delivered us from this servitude. One of our emperors quarreled with the grand lama over a woman: but it must be admitted that those who served us best in that business were our Canusi, or Pauxcospie;* it is to them that we are obliged for having thrown off the yoke; and here's how.

The grand lama had a pleasant mania: he thought he was always right; our dairi and our Canusi wanted to be right at least sometimes. The grand lama found this claim absurd; our Canusi wouldn't yield—and broke with him forever.

THE INDIAN. Well! Surely from that time on you have been happy and peaceful?

THE JAPANESE. Not at all; we persecuted, lacerated, devoured one another, for two centuries. Our Canusi wanted in their turn to be always right; they have been reasonable for only a hundred years. Since that time we may dare consider ourselves one of the happiest nations of the world.

THE INDIAN. How can you enjoy such happiness if it is true, as they tell me, that you have a dozen cooking factions in your empire? You should have a dozen civil wars a year.

THE JAPANESE. Why? If there are a dozen restaurateurs each of whom has a different recipe, need we cut each others' throats over that, instead of dining? Quite the contrary; everybody lives well in his own fashion with the cook whom he finds most agreeable.

THE INDIAN. It's true that people should not argue about tastes; but they do argue about them, and the quarrels get heated.

* *Pauxcospie*, anagram of *Episcopaux*.

THE JAPANESE. After people have argued for a very long time, and have seen that all the quarrels teach men only how to hurt themselves, they decide at last to tolerate one another, and beyond doubt that's the best thing to do.

THE INDIAN. And, please, who are these restaurateurs who divide your nation in the art of drinking and eating?

THE JAPANESE. First there are the *Breuxeh*,* who never give you either blood pudding or lard; they are attached to the ancient cuisine; they would rather die than lard a chicken: besides, they are great schemers, and if there's an ounce of silver to be divided among them and the eleven other cooks, they will first take half for themselves and the rest is for those who can count best.

THE INDIAN. I imagine that you don't eat with these people.

THE JAPANESE. No. Then there are the *Pispates*, who on certain days of every week, and even during a considerable part of the year, would a hundred times rather eat turbot, trout, sole, salmon, sturgeon, for a hundred *écus*, than feed themselves with a veal stew that wouldn't come to more than four *sous*.

As for our other Canusi, they greatly enjoy beef and a certain pastry called *pudding* in Japanese. Everybody agrees that they are infinitely more learned than those of the *Pispates*. No one has studied the *garum* of the Romans more profoundly than we, no one knows better the onions of ancient Egypt, the locust paste of the early Arabs, the horse meat of the Tartars; and there is always something to learn in the books of the Canusi, who are generally called *Pauxcospie*.

I won't tell you about those who only eat *à la Terluh*, nor about those who hold to the diet of *Vincal*, nor about the *Batistapanes*, nor about the others; but the

---

* It is easy to see that the *Breuxeh* are the *Hebrews, et sic de ceteris.*

Quekars deserve special attention. They are the only table companions whom I've never seen get drunk and swear. They are very hard to deceive; and they will never deceive you. It seems as though the law, love your neighbor as yourself, was made for these people alone; for, in truth, how can a good Japanese boast of loving his neighbor as himself, when he goes to the front lines to put a bullet in his head or stab him with a four-inch knife—all for a little money? He exposes himself to being stabbed and to receiving bullets: thus we may say with much more truth that he hates his neighbor as himself. The *Quekars* have never had this frenzy; they say that poor humans are clay pitchers made to last a little while, and that there's no point going out and gleefully breaking one against the other.

I admit to you that if I were not a Canusi, I wouldn't mind being a *Quekar*. And you'll admit to me that there's no way of quarreling with such pacific cooks.

There are others, in great numbers, who are called *Diestes;* they give dinner to everybody without distinction, and at their house you are free to eat as you like, with lard, with bacon, without lard, without bacon, eggs, oil, partridge, salmon, rosé wine, red wine; all that makes no difference to them: provided you say some prayer to God before or after dinner, or even simply before breakfast, and are a decent fellow, they will laugh with you at the expense of the grand lama, to whom this will do no harm, and at the expense of Ter-luh, of Vincal, and of Memnon, etc. Only, it would be useful if our *Diestes* admitted that our Canusi are very clever at cooking, and above all, if they didn't ever talk of curtailing our revenues; then we would live together quite peaceably.

THE INDIAN. But still there must be a dominant cuisine, the cuisine of the king.

THE JAPANESE. I admit it; but when the king of Japan

lives well, he should be in a good mood, and he must not prevent his good subjects from digesting.

THE INDIAN. But if obstinate men want to eat sausages, for which the king had an aversion, right under the king's nose, if they assemble four or five thousand strong, armed with gridirons to cook their sausages, and if they insult those who won't eat them?

THE JAPANESE. Then they must be punished like drunkards who disturb the public peace. We have provided against this danger. Only those who eat in the king's manner are eligible for the dignities of the State: all the others can dine in accordance with their fancy, but they are excluded from office. Riotous assemblies are prohibited by the sovereign and punished on the spot without pardon; all quarrels at table are carefully curbed, in accordance with the precept of our great Japanese cook, SUTI RAHO, CUS FLAC, who wrote in the sacred language,

> *Natis in usum laetitiae scyphis*
> *Pugnare Thracum est . . .*
> [Horace, *Odes*, I, xxvii, 1-2]

which is to say, "Dinner was made for collective and decent joy, and we must not throw glasses at each others' heads."

With these maxims we live happily in our country; our liberty is established under our *Taicosema*, our wealth grows, we have two hundred junks of the line, and we are the terror of our neighbors.

THE INDIAN. Why then did the fine versifier Recina, son of that Indian poet Recina,* so tender, so precise, so harmonious, so eloquent, say in a didactic work in rhyme, entitled *la Grâce*, and not *les Grâces:*

---

* Racine; probably Louis Racine, son of the admirable Racine.

Le Japon, où jadis brilla tant de lumière,
N'est plus qu'un triste amas de folles visions.

[*Japan, where once the light so brightly shone.*
Is now a sorry heap of crazy visions.]

THE JAPANESE. The Recina you're talking about is himself a great visionary. Doesn't this poor Indian know that we taught him what light is; that if they know the true course of the planets in India today, it's because of us; that we alone taught mankind the first laws of nature and the infinitesimal calculus; that, if we must descend to things of more general use, the people of his country learned how to make mathematically proportioned junks from us alone; that they owe us even those breeches called *bas au métier,* with which they cover their legs? Is it possible that, having invented so many admirable and useful things, we are nothing but madmen, and that a man who has put the dreams of others into verse is the only sage? Let him leave us to our cooking, and find more poetic subjects to make verses about, if he wants to.*

THE INDIAN. What do you expect! He has the prejudices of his country, of his party, and his own.

THE JAPANESE. Oh! Too many prejudices here.

* N.B. That Indian Recina, taking the word of the dreamers of his country, believed that men could make good sauces only when Brahma himself taught that sauce to his favorites, as a private whim; that there was an infinite number of cooks who couldn't possibly make a ragout, for all their serious intentions, and that Brahma deprived them of this power from sheer malice. Such an impertinence found no credence in Japan, and this Japanese sentence is considered an incontestable truth: *God never acts by partial will, but by general laws.*

CATÉCHISME DU JARDINIER
THE GARDENER'S CATECHISM
OR
Conversation of the Pasha TUCTAN
with the Gardener KARPOS

TUCTAN. Well, Karpos, my friend, you are selling vegetables dearly; but they are good . . . What religion are you now?

KARPOS. Really, pasha, I'd find it hard to tell you. When our little island of Samos belonged to the Greeks, I remember they made me say that the *agion pneuma* was produced by the *tou patrou* alone; they made me pray to God upright on my two legs, hands crossed: they didn't let me touch milk in Lent. The Venetians came; then my Venetian priest made me say that the *agion pneuma* came from the *tou patrou* and the *tou you*, permitted me to touch milk, and made me pray to God on my knees. The Greeks came back and chased the Venetians out; then I had to give up the *tou you* and cream. Finally you chased out the Greeks; and I hear you shouting *Allah il Allah* with all your might. I no longer know very clearly what I am; I love God with all my heart, and I sell my vegetables reasonably.

TUCTAN. You've got some beautiful figs there.

KARPOS. Pasha, they are entirely at your disposal.

TUCTAN. I understand that you also have a beautiful daughter.

KARPOS. Yes, pasha, but she is not at your disposal.

TUCTAN. Why not, wretch?

KARPOS. Because I'm an honest man: I'm allowed to sell my figs, but not to sell my daughter.

TUCTAN. By what law aren't you allowed to sell *that* fruit?

KARPOS. By the law of all honest gardeners; the honor of my daughter does not belong to me, it belongs to her; it is not merchandise.

TUCTAN. Then you're not faithful to your pasha?

KARPOS. Completely faithful in just matters, as long as you are my master.

TUCTAN. But if your Greek pope started a conspiracy against me, and ordered you by *tou patrou* and *tou you* to join his plot, wouldn't you have the devotion to do so?

KARPOS. Me? Not at all; I'd take care not to.

TUCTAN. And why would you refuse to obey your Greek pope on such a fine occasion?

KARPOS. Because I've taken an oath of obedience to you, and because I know very well that the *tou patrou* doesn't order conspiracies.

TUCTAN. I'm reassured; but if unhappily the Greeks recaptured the island and chased me out, would you be faithful to me?

KARPOS. Eh! How could I be faithful to you then, when you'd no longer be my pasha?

TUCTAN. And what will become of the oath you took to me?

KARPOS. It will be like my figs; you'll no longer taste it. Isn't it true (with all due respect) that if you were to die right now, while we're talking, I'd no longer owe you anything?

TUCTAN. The supposition is impolite, but the fact is true.

KARPOS. Well, if you were chased out, that would be the same as if you were dead; for you would have a successor to whom I'd have to swear another oath. Could you exact from me a loyalty that would do you no good? That would be as though, unable to eat my figs, you would want to prevent me from selling them to others.

TUCTAN. You are a logician: do you have any principles?

KARPOS. Yes, in my fashion: they are few in number, but they are enough for me; and if I had more of them, they would encumber me.

TUCTAN. I'd be curious to know your principles.

KARPOS. Well, for instance, to be a good husband, good father, good neighbor, good subject, and good gardener; I don't go beyond that, and I hope that God will have mercy on me.

TUCTAN. And do you think that he will have mercy on me. the governor of your island?

KARPOS. And how can you expect me to know that? Is it up to me to guess what God does with pashas? That business is between you and him; I have no part in it whatever. All I imagine is that if you are as decent a pasha as I am a decent gardener, God will treat you well enough.

TUCTAN. By Mahomet! I am very pleased with that idolator. Goodby, my friend; may Allah have you in his holy safekeeping!

KARPOS. Many thanks. May Theos have pity on you, my pasha!

CERTAIN, CERTITUDE
CERTAIN, CERTAINTY

"How old is your friend Christopher?" "Twenty-eight; I have seen his marriage contract, his baptismal certificate; I have known him since his childhood; he is twenty-eight, I am certain, absolutely certain of it."

I have hardly heard the reply of this man who is so sure of what he says, and the replies of twenty others saying the same thing, when I learn that for secret reasons, and by a strange trick, Christopher's baptismal certificate had been antedated. Those I talked to don't know anything about it yet; nevertheless they continue to be certain about something that is not so.

If you had asked the whole world before the time of Copernicus: "Did the sun rise today? Did it set?" all men would have answered you: "We are absolutely certain of it." They were certain, and they were wrong.

Witchcraft, divinations, possessions, were for a long time the most certain things in the world in the eyes of all nations. What an innumerable crowd of people who saw all these fine things, who were certain of them! Today that certainty has diminished a little.

A young man beginning to study geometry sought me out; he had only reached the definition of triangles. "Aren't you certain," I asked him, "that the three angles of a triangle are equal to two right angles?" He answered me that he was not only uncertain of it, but that he didn't even have a clear idea of the proposition. I demonstrated it to him; he then became quite certain of it, and will be so all his life.

This is a certainty very different from the others: they were nothing but probabilities, and, once examined, became errors; but mathematical certainty is immutable and eternal.

I exist, I think, I feel pain; is all this as certain as a geometric truth? Yes. Why? Because these truths are proved by the same principle that a thing cannot be and not be at the same time. I can't exist and not exist, feel and not feel, at the same time. A triangle can't have a hundred and eighty degrees, which is the sum of two right angles, and at the same time not have them.

The physical certainty of my existence and of my feeling are thus of the same value as mathematical certainty, although they are different in kind.

The same is not true of certainty founded on appearances, or on unanimous reports that men draw up for us.

"But look!" you say to me, "aren't you certain that Peking exists? Don't you have cloth from Peking in your house? Haven't men of different countries, different opinions, who wrote violently against each other while they were all preaching the truth in Peking— haven't they all assured you of the existence of that town?" I reply that it seems extremely probable to me that there was a city of Peking at that time; but I wouldn't want to bet my life that the town exists; and I would bet my life at any time that the three angles of a triangle are equal to two right angles.

The *Dictionnaire Encyclopédique* has printed a very amusing thing; it is argued there that a man should be as sure, as certain, that the Marshal de Saxe had been resurrected if all Paris told him so, as he is sure that the Marshal de Saxe won the battle of Fontenoy, when all Paris tells him so. Please look how admirable this argument is: "I believe all Paris when it tells me something that is morally possible; therefore I should believe all Paris when it tells me something that is morally and physically impossible."

Apparently the author of this article wanted to laugh; and the other author who goes into raptures at the end of this article, and wrote against himself, wanted to laugh too.*

* See the article CERTITUDE, *Dictionnaire Encyclopédique.*

CHAINE DES ÊTRES CRÉÉS
GREAT CHAIN OF BEING

The first time I read Plato and came across that gradation of beings which ascends from the littlest atom to
the supreme Being, that ladder struck me with wonder;
but once I looked at it attentively, the great phantom
vanished, as in the old days all the apparitions used to
flee in the morning at the crowing of the cock.

At first, the imagination delights to see the imperceptible transition from brute matter to organized matter,
from plants to zoophytes, from these zoophytes to
animals, from these to man, from man to spirits, from
these spirits, equipped with a little aerial body, to immaterial substances, and finally to a thousand different orders of these substances which, through degrees of
beauty and perfection, ascend up to God himself. This
hierarchy greatly pleases all those good people who like
to see the pope and his cardinals followed by arch-
bishops, then by bishops; after which come rectors, vic-
ars, simple priests, deacons, sub-deacons; then appear the
monks, and the parade ends with capuchin friars.

But there is somewhat more distance between God
and his most perfect creatures than between the holy
father and the dean of the sacred college: this dean
could become pope, but the most perfect of the spirits
created by the supreme Being cannot become God; there
is an infinity between God and him.

This chain, this so-called gradation, no more exists
among vegetables than it does among animals; the proof
for this is that there are species of plants and animals
which have been utterly destroyed. There are no longer
any murexes. Jews were forbidden to eat the griffin and

the ixion; these two species have disappeared from the world, no matter what Bochart says about them: where then is the chain?

Even if we had not lost several species, it is evident that they could be destroyed. Lions and rhinoceroses are becoming very scarce.

It is highly probable that there were races of men which are no longer to be found. But I wish that they had all survived—like the whites, Negroes, the Caffirs, whom nature has given an apron in their skin, hanging from the belly half-way down the thigh; the Samoyedes, whose women have a nipple of beautiful ebony, etc.

Isn't there obviously a void between a monkey and a man? Isn't it easy to imagine a two-footed animal without feathers, intelligent without either the use of words or our shape, which we could tame, which would answer our signals, and which would serve us? And, between this new species and that of man, couldn't we imagine others?

Beyond man, O divine Plato, you lodge in the heavens a row of celestial substances; we too believe in some of these substances, because our faith teaches us to. But you, what reason did you have for believing in them? Apparently you didn't talk to Socrates' demon; and good old Er, who came back to life expressly to teach you the secrets of the other world, didn't teach you anything about these substances.

The so-called chain is no less interrupted in the visible universe.

Look, what gradation is there among your planets? The moon is forty times smaller than our globe. When you have traveled from the moon into the void, you find Venus: it is about as big as the earth. From there you go to Mercury; it revolves in an ellipse which is very different from the circle Venus describes; it is twenty-seven times smaller than we are, the Sun a million times bigger, Mars five times smaller; the last makes its revolution in two years; Jupiter, its neighbor, in twelve; Saturn in thirty; and finally Saturn, the most distant of all, is not as large as Jupiter. Where is the so-called gradation?

And then, how could you have, in the great empty spaces, a chain that linked everything? If there is one, it is surely the one that Newton discovered; the one that makes all the globes of the planetary world gravitate toward one another in the immense void.

O much-admired Plato! You have told nothing but fables, and there has come from the island of the Cassiterides, where in your time men went stark naked, a philosopher who taught the world truths as great as your fancies were puerile.

CHAINE DES ÉVÉNEMENS
CHAIN OF EVENTS

For a long time people have asserted that all events are linked one to the other by an invincible fatality: Destiny, which in Homer is superior to Jupiter himself. The master of gods and men frankly declared that he could not prevent Sarpedon, his son, from dying at the appointed time. Sarpedon was born at the fated moment, and could not have been born at another; he could not die anywhere but before Troy; he could not be buried anywhere but in Lycia, at the appointed time; his body had to produce vegetables which had to change into the substance of some Lycians; his heirs had to establish a new order in his state; this new order had to influence neighboring kingdoms; there resulted from this a new arrangement concerning war and peace with the neighbors of the neighbors of Lycia; thus, gradually, the destiny of the whole world came to depend on Sarpedon's death, which depended on another event, which was linked by others to the origin of things.

If a single one of these facts had been arranged differently, a different universe would have resulted; now, it is not possible for the actual universe not to exist: therefore it was not possible for Jupiter to save his son's life, Jupiter though he was.

This system of necessity and fatality was invented in our time by Leibnitz (according to him) under the name of *sufficient reason*. Nevertheless, it is very old: it is no news to say that there can be no effect without a cause, and that often the smallest cause produces the greatest effects.

Lord Bolingbroke admits that the petty quarrels between the duchess of Marlborough and Lady Masham gave him his opportunity for making the private treaty between Queen Anne and Louis XIV: this treaty led to the peace of Utrecht; the peace of Utrecht confirmed Philip V on the throne of Spain. Philip V took Naples and Sicily from the house of Austria; the Spanish prince who is today king of Naples clearly owes his kingdom to Lady Masham; and he wouldn't have had it, perhaps he wouldn't even have been born, if the duchess of Marlborough had been more civil to the queen of England. His existence in Naples depended on a piece of nonsense, more or less, at the court of London. Examine the situations of all the nations in the universe: they are thus founded on a sequence of facts which seem to have no connection and which are connected in everything. In this immense machine, all is wheels, pulleys, cords, springs.

The same is true in the physical order. A wind that blows from the heart of Africa and the Australian seas carries with it part of the African atmosphere, which falls as rain in the valleys of the Alps; these rains fertilize our lands; our north wind in turn transmits our mists to the Negroes; we do Guinea good, and Guinea does the same for us in return. The chain extends from one end of the universe to the other.

But it seems to me that the truth of this principle is oddly misused. People conclude from it that there is no atom so small that its movement doesn't influence the actual arrangement of the entire world; that there is no accident so small, be it among men, be it among animals, that is not an essential link in the great chain of destiny.

Let's understand each other: every effect obviously has its cause, rising from cause to cause in the abyss of eternity; but every cause doesn't have its effect that descends to the end of the ages. All events are produced one by the other, I admit it; if the past is big with the present, the present is big with the future; everything has a father—but everything doesn't always have a child. In this, the world is exactly like a genealogical tree: every house, as we know, goes back to Adam, but in that family there are plenty of people who died without leaving descendants.

There is a genealogical tree of the events in this world. It is incontestable that the inhabitants of Gaul and Spain are descended from Gomer, and the Russians from Magog, his younger brother: we find this genealogy in so many fat books! On that basis, it can't be denied that we are indebted to Magog for the sixty thousand Russians who are today in arms somewhere around Pomerania and the sixty thousand Frenchmen who are near Frankfurt. But whether Magog spat to the right or the left near Mount Caucasus, whether he made two or three circles in a well, whether he slept on his left side or on his right side—I don't see how that had much influence on the resolution taken by Elizabeth, empress of Russia, to send an army to the aid of Maria Theresa, empress of the Romans. A dog may dream or not dream while he sleeps. I don't perceive what relation this momentous event can have to the affairs of the Grand Mogul.

It must be remembered that nature is not a plenum and that every movement does not communicate itself until it has gone round the world. Throw a body of a certain density into the water; you can easily calculate that at the end of some time the movement of that body and the movement it communicated to the water will be gone; movement is lost and restored; hence the movement Magog could produce by spitting into a well cannot have influenced what is happening today in Russia and in Prussia. Hence present events are not the children of all past events; they are their direct descendants; but a thousand little collateral descendants are of no use to them. Once again, every being has its father, but every being does not have children: we will perhaps say more about this when we discuss destiny.

DE LA CHINE · OF CHINA

We go to China seeking clay as though we had none of our own; cloth, as though we lacked cloth; a small herb to steep in water, as though we didn't have medicinal plants in our own parts. In repayment, we should like to convert the Chinese; that's very praiseworthy zeal, but we should not question their antiquity, nor tell them they are idolators. Really, would people like it if a capuchin friar, having been well received in a *château* of the Montmorencys, tried to persuade them that they were recent nobility, like the secretaries of the king, and accused them of being idolators because he had found in the *château* two or three statues of High Constables, for whom they have profound respect?

The celebrated Wolff, professor of mathematics at the university of Halle, one day delivered a fine oration in praise of Chinese philosophy; he praised that ancient species of men who differ from us in their beard, their eyes, their nose, their ears, and their arguments; he praised, I say, the Chinese for worshiping a supreme God and loving virtue; he did the emperors of China, the *Kalao*, the tribunals, the men of letters, full justice. The justice he did the bonzes was of a different kind.

Wolff, I must tell you, attracted to Halle a thousand students from every nation. There was in the same university a professor of theology named Lange, who attracted nobody; in despair at freezing to death alone in his lecture hall, he quite reasonably decided to ruin the professor of mathematics; following the custom of his kind, he promptly accused him of not believing in God.

Some European writers who had never been to China had claimed that the government of Peking was atheistic; Wolff had praised the philosophers of Peking, hence Wolff was an atheist. Envy and hatred never constructed a better syllogism. This argument of Lange's, supported by a cabal and a protector, was considered conclusive by the king of the land, who presented the mathematician with this formal dilemma: leave Halle in twenty-four hours or be hanged. And, excellent reasoner that he was, Wolff promptly left; his departure deprived the king of two or three hundred thousand *écus* per year which the philosopher had brought to the kingdom through the affluence of his disciples.

This example ought to impress sovereigns that they

shouldn't always listen to calumny and sacrifice a great man to the insanity of a fool. But let's return to China.

Why do we presume, on this side of the world, to argue bitterly, amid torrents of insults, over whether there were or were not fourteen princes before Fo-hi, emperor of China, and whether this Fo-hi lived three thousand or two thousand nine hundred years before our common era? I'd like to see two Irishmen take it into their heads to quarrel in Dublin over who, in the twelfth century, was the owner of the lands I occupy today: isn't it obvious that they must refer to me, who has the archives in his hands? In my opinion, the same thing is true of the first emperors of China: we must refer to the tribunals of the country.

Argue as much as you like about the fourteen princes who ruled before Fo-hi, your fine argument will only end by proving that China was very populous at that time, and lived under the rule of law. Now I ask you whether a united nation, with laws and princes, does not suggest prodigious antiquity. Think how much time is needed before an extraordinary conjunction of circumstances leads to the discovery of iron in mines, before it is used in agriculture, before the shuttle and all the other skills are invented.

Those who make children with a stroke of the pen have thought up a very odd calculation. Through a pretty computation, the Jesuit Pétau calculates that two hundred and eighty-five years after the deluge, the world had a hundred times as many inhabitants as we dare estimate it has today. The Cumberlands and the Whistons have made equally comical calculations; these gentlemen need only have consulted the registers of our colonies in America; they would have been greatly astonished: they would have learned how slowly mankind multiplies, and that it often diminishes instead of increasing.

Let us then, men merely of yesterday, descendants of the Celts who have barely cleared the forests of our savage lands—let us leave the Chinese and Indians to enjoy their lovely climate and their antiquity in peace. Above all let us stop calling the emperor of China and the soubab of Decan idolators. We should not be fanatical about the merits of the Chinese: the constitution of their empire is in fact the best in the world, the only one founded entirely on paternal power (which doesn't prevent the mandarins from caning their children); the only one in which the governor of a province is punished when he fails to win the acclamation of the people upon leaving office; the only one that has instituted prizes for virtue, while everywhere else the laws are restricted to punishing crime; the only one that has made its conquerors adopt its laws, while we are still subject to the customs of the Burgundians, the Franks, and the Goths, who subjugated us. But I must admit that the common people, governed by bonzes, are as rascally as ours; that they sell everything to foreigners very expensively, just as we do; that in the sciences the Chinese are still at the point we were at two hundred years ago; that they have a thousand ridiculous prejudices, as we do; that they believe in talismans and in judicial astrology, as we used to believe for a long time.

Let me admit also that they were amazed at our thermometer, at our manner of freezing liquids with saltpeter, and at all the experiments of Torricelli and Otto von Guericke, just as we were when we saw these scientific amusements for the first time; let me add that their doctors cure mortal illnesses no better than ours do, and that nature cures minor ailments by herself in China, as it does here. Still, four thousand years ago, when we couldn't even read, the Chinese knew all the absolutely useful things we boast about today.

Once again, the religion of the men of letters of China

is admirable. No superstitions, no absurd legends, none of those dogmas which insult reason and nature and to which the bonzes give a thousand different meanings, because they don't have any. The simplest cult has seemed to them the best for more than forty centuries. They are what we think Seth, Enoch, and Noah were; they are content to worship a God with all the sages of the world, while in Europe we are divided between Thomas and Bonaventure, between Calvin and Luther, between Jansenius and Molina.

CHRISTIANISME · CHRISTIANITY
Historical Research into Christianity

A number of scholars have indicated their surprise that there isn't a trace of Jesus Christ in the writings of the historian Josephus; for all true scholars agree today that the short passage in *The Jewish War* dealing with him is an interpolation.* The father of Flavius Josephus must have been one of the witnesses of all of Jesus' miracles. Josephus was of a priestly tribe, related to queen Mariamne, Herod's wife; he goes into the greatest detail about all the actions of that prince; still, he says

---

* The Christians, by one of those frauds called pious, grossly falsified a passage in Josephus. They palm off on that Jew, so obstinate in his religion, four ridiculously interpolated lines, and at the end of this passage they add: "He was the Christ." But if Josephus had heard people talk about so many events that astonish nature, would Josephus have given them only four lines in the history of his country? Would this obstinate Jew have said: "Jesus was the Christ"? Why, if he had believed in Christ, he would then have been a Christian. How absurd to make Josephus talk like a Christian! How can there still be theologians imbecile enough or insolent enough to try to justify that forgery of the first Christians, well known to have been fabricators of impostures a hundred times worse than this!

not one word about either the life or the death of Jesus;
and the historian who disguises none of Herod's cruelties does not mention the massacre of the infants that
Herod ordered after he heard the news that a king of the
Jews had been born. The Greek almanac reckons fourteen thousand children massacred on that occasion.

Of all the actions of all the tyrants, this is the most
horrible. There is no parallel to it in the history of the
whole world. Still, the best writer the Jews ever had,
the only one esteemed by the Romans and the Greeks,
makes no mention of this strange and terrible event. He
says nothing about the new star which had appeared in
the East after the birth of the Savior, a brilliant phenomenon which should not have escaped the attention of a
historian as enlightened as Josephus. He is even silent
about the darkness that covered the whole earth at high
noon, for three hours, on the death of the Savior, the
great number of tombs that opened at that moment, and
the crowd of just men who came back to life.

Scholars never cease to show their surprise that no
Roman historian speaks of these marvels, which occurred in the reign of Tiberius, before the eyes of a Roman governor and a Roman garrison who were duty-
bound to send the emperor and the senate a detailed
report on the most miraculous event men had ever heard
of. Rome itself must have been plunged into profound
darkness for three hours; this marvel should have been
noted in the annals of Rome and in those of all nations.
God did not want these divine things to be recorded by
profane hands.

The same scholars also find some difficulties in the
history of the Gospels. They observe that in St. Matthew, Jesus Christ tells the scribes and Pharisees that all
the innocent blood that has been shed upon earth will
be upon their heads, from the blood of Abel, the just,

down to Zechariah, son of Barachiah, whom they killed
between the sanctuary and the altar. Yet, in the history
of the Hebrews, they say, there is no Zechariah killed in
the temple before the coming of the Messiah, nor in his
time; though they do find in Josephus' history of the
siege of Jerusalem a Zechariah, son of Barachiah, killed
right in the temple by the faction of the zealots. That is
in chapter 19 of book 4. They suspect, on the basis of
this, that the Gospel according to St. Matthew was written after Jerusalem was taken by Titus.

But all doubts and objections of this kind vanish when
we consider the infinite difference there must be between books divinely inspired and the books of men.
God wanted to envelop his birth, his life, and his death in
a dark and respectable cloud. His ways are in everything
different from ours.

Scholars have also much tortured themselves with the
difference between the two genealogies of Jesus Christ.
St. Matthew makes Jacob Joseph's father; Matthan, Jacob's; Eleazar, Matthan's. On the other hand, St. Luke
says that Joseph was the son of Heli; Heli, of Matthat;
Matthat, of Levi; Levi, of Melchi, etc. Nor do they find
it easy to reconcile the fifty-six ancestors that Luke
places between Jesus and Abraham with the forty-two
different ancestors that Matthew mentions. And they are
staggered to see Matthew, who speaks of forty-two generations, nevertheless reporting only forty-one.

They have still more difficulties with Jesus' not being
the son of Joseph but of Mary. They also raise some
doubts about the miracles of our Savior, in citing St.
Augustine, St. Hilary, and others who have given the
accounts of these miracles a mystical sense, an allegorical
sense: such miracles as the fig-tree cursed and withered
for not bearing figs (when it was not the season for
figs); the demons sent into the bodies of swine (in a

country where people did not eat pork); the waters changed into wine at the end of a meal (when the table companions were already overheated).

But the law confounds all these scholars' criticisms—they only make it purer still. The aim of this article is solely to follow the historical thread, and to give a precise idea of facts which are not in dispute. First, Jesus was born under the Mosaic law, he was circumcised in accordance with that law, he fulfilled all its precepts, he celebrated all its feasts, and he preached ethics alone: he did not reveal the mystery of his incarnation; he never told the Jews that he was born of a virgin; he received John's blessing in the waters of the Jordan, a ceremony to which some Jews submitted, but he never baptized anybody; he did not mention the seven sacraments, he did not institute an ecclesiastical hierarchy in his lifetime. He concealed from his contemporaries that he was the son of God, begotten from eternity, consubstantial with God, and that the Holy Spirit proceeded from the Father and the Son. He did not say that his person was composed of two natures and two wills; he wanted these great mysteries to be announced to men in the course of time, by those who would be enlightened by the light of the Holy Spirit. As long as he lived, he did not deviate from the law of his fathers in anything; he revealed to men nothing but a just man pleasing to God, persecuted by men who envied him and had him condemned to death by prejudiced magistrates. Presumably he wanted his holy Church, established by him, to do all the rest.

In chapter xii of his history, Josephus mentions a sect of rigid Jews, newly established by one Judas the Galilean. "They despise," he writes, "the evils of this world; they triumph over torments by their constancy; they prefer death to life, when its cause is honorable. They have suffered iron and fire and have seen their bones broken, rather than say the slightest word against their legislator or eat forbidden meats."

It seems that this portrait describes the Judaites, and not the Essenes. For here are the words of Josephus: "Judas was the creator of a new sect, entirely different from the other three, that is, the Sadducees, the Pharisees, and the Essenes." He continues, and writes: "They are Jews by nationality; they live united among themselves and regard voluptuousness as a vice." The plain sense of this passage makes it clear that the author is speaking of the Judaites. And these Judaites were known before the disciples of Christ began to amount to something in the world.

The Therapeutes were a society different from the Essenes and the Judaites; they resembled the Gymnosophists of India and the Brahmins. "They have," writes Philo, "an emotion of celestial love which throws them into the enthusiasm of bacchants and corybants and puts them into the state of contemplation to which they aspire." That sect was born in Alexandria, which was filled with Jews, and spread widely throughout Egypt.

The disciples of John the Baptist also spread a little into Egypt, but chiefly in Syria and Arabia; there were also some in Asia Minor. It is written in the Acts of the Apostles (chapter 19) that Paul encountered several at Ephesus; he asked them: "Did you receive the Holy Spirit?" They replied: "We have never even heard that there is a Holy Spirit." He asked them: "Into what then were you baptized?" They replied: "Into John's baptism."

Thus, in the first years following the death of Jesus there were seven different societies or sects among the Jews: the Pharisees, the Sadducees, the Essenes, the Judaites, the Therapeutes, the disciples of John, and the disciples of Christ—this last a little troop which God guided in ways unknown to human wisdom.

The man who contributed most to strengthening this newborn congregation was the very Paul who had persecuted it with the greatest cruelty. He was born in Tarsus in Cilicia and was raised by the famous Pharisaic doctor Gamaliel, disciple of Hillel. The Jews claim that he broke with Gamaliel, who refused Paul his daughter in marriage. We find some traces of that anecdote in the sequel to the *Acts of St. Thecla*. These acts report that he had a high forehead, a bald head, joined eyebrows, aquiline nose, a short, thick waist, and crooked legs. In his dialogue *Philopatris*, Lucian draws quite a similar portrait. There are serious doubts whether he was a Roman citizen, for at that time this title was not granted to Jews; they had been chased out of Rome by Tiberius, and Tarsus became a Roman colony only about a hundred years later, under Caracalla, as Cellarius observes in his *Geography*, book 3, and Grotius in his *Commentaries on the Acts*.

The faithful had the name of Christians in Antioch, around the year 60 of our common era; but as we shall see they were known in the Roman Empire under other names. Earlier they distinguished themselves only by the titles of brothers, saints, or the faithful. God, who had descended to earth to set it an example of humility and poverty, thus gave his church the feeblest of beginnings, and established it in the same lowly condition in which he had wished to be born. All the early faithful were obscure men: they all worked with their hands. The apostle Paul testifies that he made his living as a tent maker. St. Peter resurrected Forcas, the seamstress, who made the brothers' robes. The faithful were assembled at Joppa, in the house of a currier named Simon, as we see from chapter 9 of the Acts of the Apostles.

The faithful secretly spread to Greece, and some of them went from there to Rome, living among the Jews, whom the Romans allowed to have a synagogue. At first they didn't separate themselves from the Jews; they retained circumcision, and, as I have already observed elsewhere, the first fifteen bishops of Jerusalem were all circumcised.

When the apostle Paul took along Timothy, who was the son of a gentile father, he himself circumcised him in the little town of Lystra. But Titus, his other disciple, didn't want to undergo circumcision. The brethren who were disciples of Jesus were united with the Jews up to the time Paul suffered persecution in Jerusalem for bringing foreigners into the temple. He was accused by the Jews of wanting to destroy the Mosaic law through Jesus Christ. It was that this accusation might be refuted that the apostle James suggested to the apostle Paul that he should have his head shaved and have himself purified in the temple with four Jews who had taken a vow to shave themselves: "Take these men," James told him (chapter 21, Acts of the Apostles), "and purify yourself along with them; thus all will know that there is nothing in what they have been told about you, but that you yourself live in observance of the law."

So Paul, who at first had been the bloodthirsty perse-cutor of the society established by Jesus, Paul, who afterwards wished to govern that newborn society, Paul, turned Christian, Judaizes "that the world may know that it slanders him when it calls him a Christian"; Paul commits what is considered an abominable crime today, a crime which is punished by fire in Spain, Portugal, and Italy; and he commits it at the urging of the apostle James; and he commits it after receiving the Holy Spirit, that is, after being instructed by God himself that he must renounce all those Jewish rites previously insti-tuted by God himself.

None the less Paul was accused by the Jews of impiety and heresy, and his criminal prosecution lasted a long time; but it is obvious, even from the accusations brought against him, that he had come to Jerusalem to observe the Jewish rites. He tells Festus in these very words (chapter 25 of Acts): "Neither against the law of the Jews, nor against the temple, have I offended."

The apostles proclaimed Jesus Christ a Jew, observer of Jewish law, sent by God to have it observed. "Circumcision is of value," says the apostle Paul (chapter 2, Epistle to the Romans), "if you obey the law; but if you break the law, your circumcision becomes uncircumcision. So if a man who is uncircumcised keeps the precepts of the law, will not his uncircumcision be regarded as circumcision? He is a Jew who is one inwardly."

When this apostle speaks of Jesus Christ in his Epistles, he does not reveal the ineffable mystery of his consubtantiality with God. "We shall be saved by him," he says (chapter 5, Epistle to the Romans), "from the wrath of God. God's free gift has spread over us in the grace of that one man Jesus Christ. . . . As sin reigned in death through one man's trespass, grace also might reign through righteousness to eternal life through one man, Jesus Christ."

And in chapter 8: "We, heirs of God and fellow heirs with Christ." And in chapter 16: "To the only wise God be glory forevermore through Jesus Christ!" ". . . You are Christ's, and Christ is God's." (First Corinthians, chapter 3.)

And (First Corinthians, chapter 15, verse 27): "All things are put into subjection under him, but he is excepted who put all things under him."

There has been some difficulty in explicating the passage from the Epistle to the Philippians: "Do nothing from selfishness or conceit, but in humility count others better than yourselves; let this mind be in you, which was also in Jesus Christ, who, being in the form of God, thought it not grasping to be equal with God." This passage seems to have been thoroughly investigated and fully explained in a letter from the churches of Vienne and Lyon, written in the year 117, a precious relic of antiquity. In this letter the modesty of several faithful is praised: "They did not seek the great title of martyr" (for some tribulations), says the letter, "following the example of Jesus Christ, who, bearing the impress of God, did not think equality with God within his grasp." Origen says in his *Commentary on John:* "The grandeur of Jesus shone more brightly when he humbled himself *than if he had considered equality with God within his grasp.*" In fact, the opposite explanation is obvious nonsense. What does it mean to say: "Count others better than yourself; imitate Jesus who didn't believe that it was grasping and a usurpation to count himself equal with God"? That would be an obvious self-contradiction; it would offer an example of grandeur as one of modesty; it would sin against common sense.

Thus the wisdom of the apostles laid the foundations for the newly born Church. That wisdom was not changed by the dispute which took place between the apostles Peter, James, and John on one side, and Paul on the other. The argument took place in Antioch. The apostle Peter, formerly Cephas, or Simon Barjona, ate with converted gentiles, and did not observe with them either the ceremonies of the law or the distinction of meats; he, Barnabas, and other disciples indiscriminately ate pork, stuffed meat, the flesh of animals with cloven hoofs who did not ruminate; but after several Christian Jews arrived, St. Peter abstained once again from forbidden meats and observed with them the ceremonies of the Mosaic law.

This action seemed highly prudent; he did not want to shock his companions, the Christian Jews, but St. Paul broke out against him with some harshness. "I opposed him to his face, because he stood condemned." (Letter to the Galatians, chapter 2).

This quarrel seems all the more extraordinary, as St. Paul had started out as a persecutor and should have been more moderate; he himself had sacrificed in the temple of Jerusalem, had circumcised his disciple Timothy, and celebrated the Jewish rites with which he now reproached Cephas. St. Jerome claims that the quarrel between Paul and Cephas was feigned. He says in his first *Homily*, volume 3, that they acted like two attorneys who get excited and strut before the bar in order to gain greater authority with their clients; he writes that since Peter Cephas was meant to preach to the Jews, and Paul to the gentiles, they pretended to quarrel, Paul to win over the gentiles, and Peter to win over the Jews. But St. Augustine isn't of this opinion at all: "I am incensed," he writes in his Epistle to Jerome, "that a man as great as that should make himself the patron of a lie,"—*patronum mendacii.*

Moreover, if Peter was meant to go to the Judaizing Jews, and Paul to the foreigners, it is highly probable that Peter never came to Rome. The Acts of the Apostles make no mention of Peter's trip to Italy.

Be that as it may, it was around the year 60 of our era that the Christians began to separate themselves from the Jewish community, and this involved them in quarrels with all the synagogues in Rome, Greece, Egypt, and Asia, and drew down every persecution on their heads. They were accused of impiety, of atheism, by their Jewish brothers, who excommunicated them in their synagogues three times on the sabbath day. But God continued to sustain them in the midst of persecutions.

Little by little, several churches were formed, and before the end of the first century the separation between the Jews and the Christians was complete. The Roman government was unaware of that separation. Neither the senate of Rome nor the emperors took part in the quarrels of a little sect which God had governed in obscurity up to then, and whom he was raising up by imperceptible degrees.

Let us look at the state of religion in the Roman Empire. Mysteries and atonements were authorized virtually throughout the whole world. To be sure, the emperors, the magnates, and the philosophers had no faith in these mysteries; but the people, who give the law to the magnates in religious matters, required them to conform outwardly to their cult. To put chains on the popular religion, the rulers must appear to be wearing the same chains. Cicero himself was initiated into the Eleusinian mysteries. Knowledge of one God was the principal dogma preached in these mysterious and magnificent festivals. We must admit that the prayers and hymns from these mysteries which have survived are the most pious and admirable things in paganism.

This made it easier for the Christians, who also worshiped but one God, to convert some of the gentiles. Several philosophers of the Platonic sect became Christians. And this is why the Church Fathers of the first three centuries were all Platonists.

The thoughtless zeal of some of them did not damage the fundamental truths. St. Justin, one of the first Fathers, has been reproached for saying in his *Commentary on Isaiah* that the saints would be able to enjoy all the sensual pleasures in the millennium of Christ's reign on earth. He has been praised for saying in his *Apology for Christianity* that once God had made the earth, he left it to the care of angels, who fell in love with women and gave them children, which are the devils.

Lactantius and other Fathers have been condemned for inventing Sybilline oracles. Lactantius claimed that the Erythraean sybil composed four Greek verses, which literally translated are as follows:

> *With five loaves and two fish*
> *He will feed five thousand men in the desert;*
> *And, gathering up the pieces that remain,*
> *He will fill twelve hampers with them.*

The first Christians have also been reproached with inventing acrostic verses that they imputed to an ancient sybil, each line of which began with a letter in the name of Jesus Christ, in order. They are reproached with forging letters from Jesus Christ to the king of Edessa, when there was no king of Edessa; with forging letters from Mary, letters from Seneca to Paul, letters and acts of Pilate, false gospels, false miracles, and a thousand other impostures.

We also have the history—that is, the gospel—of the nativity and the marriage of the virgin Mary, where it is said that she was led to the temple when she was three years old and climbed the steps all by herself. It is reported in this gospel that a dove descended from heaven to announce that it was Joseph who was to marry Mary.

We have the proto-gospel of James, Jesus' brother by Joseph's first marriage. It is said that when Mary was pregnant in the absence of her husband, and her husband complained about it, the priests made both of them drink the water of jealousy, and both were declared innocent.

We have the gospel of the infancy, attributed to St. Thomas. According to that gospel, Jesus at the age of five amused himself in the company of children of his age by kneading clay and making little birds; when he was scolded, he breathed life into the birds and they flew away. Another time, when a small boy beat him, he made him die on the spot. We have still another gospel of his childhood in Arabic; this is more serious.

We have a gospel of Nicodemus. It seems to deserve greater attention, because in it we find the names of the men who accused Jesus to Pilate; they were the principals of the synagogue, Annas, Caiaphas, Somne, Dothaim, Gamaliel, Judas, Nephtalim. There are things in that story which can be reconciled with the accepted Gospels, and others which can't be found elsewhere. We read that the woman cured of dysentery was called Veronica. We find in it everything that Jesus did when he descended into hell.

Then, we have the two letters Pilate is supposed to have written to Tiberius concerning the torture of Jesus; but the bad Latin in which they are written easily exposes them as forgeries.

People pushed false zeal so far as to circulate several letters by Jesus Christ. The letter which he is supposed to have written to Abgar, king of Edessa, has been preserved; but at that time Edessa no longer had kings.

They fabricated fifty gospels, which later were declared to be apocryphal. St. Luke himself tells us that many persons made them up. It has been thought that there was one called the Eternal Gospel, about which it is said in the Apocalypse, chapter 14: "I have seen an angel flying in the midst of heaven, carrying the eternal Gospel." In the thirteenth century, the Franciscans twisted these words by making up an Eternal Gospel in which the reign of the Holy Spirit was to be substituted for that of Jesus Christ; but in the first centuries of the Church no book of that title came to light.

Letters of the Virgin were also invented, written to St. Ignatius the martyr, the inhabitants of Messina, and to others.

Abdias, the immediate successor of the apostles, wrote

their history, in which he introduced fables so absurd that these histories were completely discredited with the passage of time; but at first they had wide circulation. It is Abdias who reports the contest of St. Peter with Simon the magician. In fact, there was in Rome a very skillful mechanic, named Simon, who not only arranged for actors to fly on the stage, as is done today, but who himself revived the marvel attributed to Dedalus. He made himself wings, he flew, and like Icarus he fell; this is what Pliny and Suetonius report.

Abdias, who was in Asia, and who wrote in Hebrew, claims that Peter and Simon met in Rome at the time of Nero. A young man, closely related to the emperor, died; the whole court begged Simon to bring him back to life. St. Peter for his part presented himself as competent to perform that operation. Simon employed all the rules of his art; he seemed to be succeeding; the dead man raised his head. "That's not enough," exclaimed St. Peter, "the dead must speak; let Simon leave the bedside, and we'll see if the young man is alive." Simon withdrew, the dead man no longer moved, and Peter returned him to life with a single word.

Simon went to complain to the emperor that a miserable Galilean had taken it into his head to perform greater miracles than he. Peter appeared with Simon, to demonstrate who knew his art better. "Tell me what I'm thinking about," exclaimed Simon to Peter." "Let the emperor," replied Peter, "give me a barley bread, and you'll see if I know what you have in your mind." They gave him a loaf. Immediately Simon had two big mastiffs appear who wanted to devour it. Peter threw them the bread, and while they were eating it, he said: "Well, but didn't I know what you were thinking about? You wanted to have me devoured by your dogs."

After this first session it was suggested that Simon and Peter should engage in combat by flight, to see which of them could ascend higher. Simon went first, St. Peter made the sign of the cross, and Simon broke his legs. This story was copied from a story in the *Sepher toldos Jeschut*, where it is said that Jesus himself flew, and Judas, who wanted to do the same, fell to the ground.

Nero, irritated with Peter for breaking the legs of Simon, his favorite, had Peter crucified head down; and from all this arose the notion of Peter's stay in Rome, his execution, and his sepulchre.

It is this same Abdias who also started the belief that St. Thomas went to preach Christianity in India, to King Gondophares, and that he went there in his capacity as an architect.

The quantity of books of this kind written in the first centuries of Christianity is prodigious. St. Jerome and even St. Augustine claimed that the letters of Seneca and St. Paul were absolutely authentic. In the first letter, Seneca expresses the hope that his brother Paul is well: *Bene te valere, frater, cupio.* Paul doesn't speak Latin nearly so well as Seneca. "I have received your letters yesterday," he writes, "with joy: *Litteras tuas hilaris accepi;* and I should have answered immediately if I had had the attendance of the young man whom I would have sent to you: *si praesentiam juvenis habuissem.*" Besides, these letters, which one would hope to be instructive, are nothing but compliments.

All these lies forged by Christians, uninformed and filled with false zeal, in no way prejudiced the truth of Christianity, nor did they hinder its establishment; on the contrary, they gave evidence that Christian society was growing day by day, and that each member wanted to help with its development.

The Acts of the Apostles don't say that the apostles agreed on a Creed. Actually, if they had drawn up the Creed, the *Credo* that we now have, St. Luke would not have omitted this essential foundation of the Christian religion from his history; the substance of the Credo is scattered through the Gospels, but its articles were not brought together until long afterward.

In a word, our Creed is undeniably the belief of the apostles, but it is not anything they wrote. Rufinus, priest of Aquileia, is the first to mention it; and a homily attributed to St. Augustine is the first document which conjectures how this *Credo* was written. Peter said in assembly: *I believe in God the father almighty;* Andrew said: *and in Jesus Christ;* James added: *who was conceived by the Holy Spirit;* and so on, to the end.

This formula was called *symbolos* in Greek, *collatio* in Latin. I may only observe that the Greek says: *I believe in God the father almighty, maker of heaven and earth: Pisteo eis theon patera pantokratora poieten ouranou Kaiges;* the Latin translates *maker, former,* by *creatorem.* But later, translating the creed of the first council of Nicaea, they put *factorem.*

Christianity at first established itself in Greece. There the Christians had to battle a new sect of Jews who had turned philosophers by dint of frequenting the Greeks: this was the sect of the gnose or Gnostics whom some new Christians mixed with. At that time all these sects enjoyed complete freedom to dogmatize, to meet together, and to write; but under Domitian the Christian religion began to give offense to the government.

The zeal of some of these early Christians, which was not very scientific, didn't prevent the Church from making the progress God intended for it. At first the Christians celebrated their mysteries in secluded houses, in caves, at night; from this comes the title of *lucifugaces* (according to Minutius Felix). Philo calls them **Ges-seans**. Among the gentiles, their most common names in the first four centuries were Galileans and Nazarenes; but Christian has prevailed over all the others.

Neither hierarchy nor practices were established all at once; the apostolic ages were different from the ages that followed them. St. Paul tells us in First Corinthians that when the brethren, circumcised or uncircumcised, were assembled and several prophets wanted to speak, only two or at most three were allowed to speak, and if someone had a revelation right then, the prophet who had the word had to hold his tongue.

It is on this practice of the primitive church that several Christian communities still base themselves today; they hold assemblies without hierarchies. At that time everybody was permitted to speak in church, except the women. Paul forbids them to speak in First Corinthians; but he also seems to authorize them to preach and prophesy in the same epistle, in chapter 11, verse 5: "Any woman who prays or prophesies with her head unveiled dishonors her head"; it is as though she were shaved. Thus women believed that they were allowed to speak provided they wore a veil.

What is Holy Mass today, which is celebrated in the morning, was then Supper, which was held in the evening; these practices changed as the Church grew stronger. An expanded society required more regulations, and the pastors prudently accommodated themselves to time and place.

Saints Jerome and Eusebius report that when the Churches took shape, five different orders were gradually distinguished in them: the inspectors, *episcopoï*, from whom developed bishops; the elders of the society, *presbyteroï*, the priests; the *diaconoï*, the servants or deacons; the *pistoï*, believers, initiates, that is, baptized ones who took part in the love-feast suppers; and the *catechumens* and *energumens*, who attended baptism.

In these five orders no one wore any dress differing from the others; no one was constrained to celibacy— witness the book of Tertullian dedicated to his wife, witness the example of the apostles. No representation, whether in painting or sculpture, was allowed in their assemblies during the first three centuries. The Christians carefully hid their books from the gentiles; they confided them only to the initiates; the catechumens weren't even permitted to recite the Lord's Prayer.

What distinguished the Christians most, and what has lasted down to our time, was the power of expelling devils with the sign of the cross. Origen admits in his *Treatise against Celsus*, at number 133, that Antinoüs, deified by the emperor Hadrian, performed miracles in Egypt by means of spells and magic; but he says that the devils left the bodies of the possessed when the mere name of Jesus was pronounced.

Tertullian goes further, and he writes in his *Apologetics*, chapter 23, from the heart of Africa where he was: "If in the presence of a true Christian your gods don't confess that they are devils, we want you to shed the blood of that Christian." Could there be a clearer demonstration?

In fact, Jesus Christ himself sent his apostles to cast out demons. In his time the Jews also had the gift of casting them out, for, when Jesus had delivered the possessed, sending the devils into the bodies of a herd of two thousand swine, and when he had performed other cures like it, the Pharisees said: "It is only by Beelzebul that this man casts out demons."— "And if I cast out demons by Beelzebul," replied Jesus, "by whom do your sons cast them out?" It is undeniable that the Jews boasted of that power; they had exorcists and exorcisms.

They invoked the name of the God of Jacob and Abraham. They put consecrated herbs in the nose of demoniacs. (Josephus reports part of these ceremonies). This power over devils, which the Jews have lost, was transmitted to the Christians, who also seem to have lost it some time ago.

In the power of casting out demons was included the power of nullifying the workings of magic; for magic was still in force among all the nations. All the Fathers of the Church testified to the force of magic. In his *Apology*, book III, St. Justin admits that the souls of the dead are called up frequently, and draws from this an argument in favor of the immortality of the soul. Lactantius, in book 7 of his *Divine Institutions*, says that "if you dare deny the existence of souls after death, the magician will soon convince you otherwise and make them appear." Irenaeus, Clement of Alexandria, Tertullian, bishop Cyprian, all assert the same thing. True, today everything has changed and there are no more magicians than there are demoniacs; but there'll be some when it pleases God.

When the Christian societies became somewhat larger, and when some of them protested against the cult of the Roman Empire, the magistrates took rigorous measures against them, and the common people above all persecuted them. The Jews, who had special privileges, and who shut themselves up in their synagogues, were not persecuted; they were allowed to practice their religion, as they are today in Rome; all the different cults scattered through the empire were tolerated by the senate. But the Christians, proclaiming themselves the enemies of all these cults, above all of the cult of the empire, were exposed to cruel trials more than once.

One of the first and most famous martyrs was Ignatius, bishop of Antioch, who was sent to Rome on the orders of the emperor Trajan himself (who was then in Asia) and condemned to be thrown to wild beasts, at a time when other Christians in Rome were not being put to death. We don't know what he was charged with before that emperor, who in other respects was famous for his clemency; St. Ignatius must have had some rather violent enemies. Be that as it may, the history of his martyrdom reports that the name of Jesus Christ was found engraved on his heart, in characters of gold; and this is why the Christians in several places took the name of *theophores*, which Ignatius had given to himself.

One of his letters has been preserved to us; in it he entreats the bishops and the Christians not to offer opposition to his martyrdom, indicating that at that time the Christians were powerful enough to set him free, or that there were some of them who had enough influence to obtain his pardon. What is also quite remarkable is that the Christians of Rome were allowed to come to him when he was brought in to the capital, which clearly proves that he was punished in his person, and not for his sect.

The persecutions were not continued. Origen says in his book 3, against Celsus: "It would be easy to count the Christians who have died for their religion, because few of them have died in this way, and only from time to time, and at intervals."

God took such good care of his Church that, despite its enemies, it managed to hold five councils in the first century, sixteen in the second, and thirty in the third— these were tolerated assemblies. Sometimes, when the misguided prudence of the magistrates feared they might become tumultuous, these assemblies were prohibited. Little remains to us of the official reports of the proconsuls and the praetors who condemned Christians to death. These are the only documents from which it would be possible to verify the accusations against them, as well as their tortures.

We have a fragment by Denis of Alexandria, in which he reports an extract from the registry of a proconsul of Egypt, under the emperor Valerian; here it is:

"Denis, Faustus, Maximus, Marcel, and Cheremon were given an audience by prefect Emilianus, who told them: 'From the conversations I had with you and from everything I wrote you about it, you must have known how much indulgence our princes have shown in your behalf; I'd like to tell it to you again: they entrust your preservation and salvation to yourselves; your destiny is in your own hands. They ask only one thing of you, which may be asked of every reasonable person: to worship the two protectors of the empire, and to abandon this other religion, which is so contrary to nature and good sense.'

"Denis replied: 'Everyone doesn't have the same gods, and everyone worships those he truly believes to exist.'

"The prefect Emilianus resumed: 'Clearly, you are ingrates who abuse the indulgence the emperors have shown you. Very well, you may not stay in this town, and I am sending you to Cephro, in the heart of Libya; that will be your place of banishment, according to the order I have received from our emperors; moreover, don't think of holding your assemblies there, or of saying your prayers in those places you call cemeteries; that I absolutely forbid you, and I won't permit it to anyone.' "

Nothing bears the stamp of truth more than this official report. It shows us that there were times when assemblies were prohibited. In just the same way we have forbidden Calvinists to assemble in Languedoc; several times we have even had ministers, or preachers, hanged or broken on the wheel for holding assemblies in defiance of the laws. In just the same way Roman

Catholics are forbidden to hold assemblies in England and Ireland, and there have been occasions when the offenders were condemned to death.

Despite the prohibitions imposed by the Roman laws, God inspired several emperors with indulgence for the Christians. Diocletian himself, whom the ignorant consider a persecutor, Diocletian, whose first year on the throne was still in the era of martyrs, was the declared protector of Christianity for more than eighteen years, so much so that several Christians held high office near his person. He even tolerated the building of a superb church opposite his palace in Nicomedia. Finally, he married a Christian.

The caesar Galerius, who was, unfortunately, prejudiced against the Christians, thinking he had some complaints against them, urged Diocletian to have the cathedral of Nicomedia destroyed. A Christian who was more zealous than wise tore the emperor's edict to pieces, and that set off the famous persecution throughout the length and breadth of the Roman Empire; more than two hundred persons were condemned to death, not counting those whom the enraged common people, aways fanatical and barbarous, may have put to death without judicial formalities.

There have been several periods in which we have had a large number of martyrs, so we must take care not to water the truth of the history of the true confessors of our holy religion with a dangerous mixture of fables and false martyrs.

For example, dom Ruinart, the Benedictine, in other respects a man as well informed as he is estimable and zealous, should have chosen his *Actes sincères* with more discretion. For a document to be authentic it is not enough that the manuscript be taken from the abbey of Saint-Benoît-sur-Loire, or from a convent of nuns in Paris, based on a manuscript of the monks of St. Ber-

nard: the document must be ancient, written by con-
temporaries, and it must also bear all the marks of truth.
He might have dispensed with reporting the adventure
of young Romanus, which occurred in 303. This young
Romanus had obtained his pardon from Diocletian in
Antioch. Nevertheless dom Ruinart says that the judge
Asclepiades condemned him to be burned at the stake.
Jews present at the spectacle made fun of young St.
Romanus, and taunted the Christians that their God
let them burn, the same God who had delivered Shad-
rach, Meshach, and Abednego from the furnace. Immediately a rainstorm came up, in the calmest weather,
which extinguished the flames; whereupon the judge
ordered young Romanus' tongue cut out. The emperor's
chief physician, being present, obligingly performed the
hangman's function and cut his tongue out by the roots;
immediately the young man, who had been a stutterer,
spoke freely. The emperor was astonished to hear him
speak so well without a tongue; the physician, repeating
the experiment, immediately cut out the tongue of a
passer-by, who died on the spot.

Eusebius, from whom the Benedictine Ruinart has
taken this tale, should have shown enough respect for
the true miracles worked in the Old and New Testaments (which nobody will ever doubt) not to associate
them with stories as suspect as this, which might trouble
the weak in faith.

This last persecution did not extend throughout the
empire. At that time there was a trace of Christianity
in England, which soon vanished, reappearing later under the Saxon kings. Southern Gaul and Spain were
filled with Christians. The caesar Constantius Chlorus
gave them strong protection in all these provinces. He
had a concubine who was a Christian: she was the
mother of Constantine and was known by the name of
St. Helena: there was never an authenticated marriage

between her and Constantius, and he even sent her away in the year 292, when he married the daughter of Maximian Herculius; but she retained a great influence over him, and inspired him with a great affection for our holy religion.

By ways that seemed human, divine Providence prepared the triumph of its Church. Constantius Chlorus died in 306, at York, in England, at a time when the young children he had had with a caesar's daughter were still young, and could not claim their empire. Constantine was self-assured enough to have himself elected emperor at York by five or six thousand soldiers, mostly Germans, Gauls, and English. It seemed unlikely that this election, held without the consent of Rome, the senate, and the armies, could stand; but God gave him the victory over Maxentius, elected in Rome, and finally delivered him from all his colleagues. It must be admitted that at first he made himself unworthy of the favors of Heaven by murdering all his relatives, his wife, and his son.

We may be skeptical of what Zosimus reports about this matter. He says that Constantine, troubled by remorse after so many crimes, asked the pontiffs of the empire if there was any expiation for him, and that they told him they knew of none. It is certainly true that there would have been none for Nero, and that he wouldn't have dared participate in the sacred mysteries of Greece. Yet it was still the custom to sacrifice bulls, and I find it hard to believe that an all-powerful emperor couldn't have found a priest willing to perform the expiatory sacrifices for him. It is perhaps even less credible that a Constantine busy with war, his own ambitions, and his projects, and surrounded by flatterers, would have had time for remorse. Zosimus adds that an Egyptian priest, coming from Spain, who had access to the emperor's door, promised him expiation of all his crimes in the Christian religion. It has been thought that this priest was Hosius, bishop of Cordoba.

Be that as it may, Constantine took communion with the Christians, even though he had never been anything but a catechumen, and deferred his baptism until the moment of his death. He had his city of Constantinople built, which became the center of the empire and the Christian religion. It was then that the Church took an august form.

It is worth noting that from the year 314 on, before Constantine lived in his new city, the Christians punished for their cruelties those who had persecuted them. They threw Maximian's wife into the Orontes; they butchered all his relatives; in Egypt and Palestine they massacred the magistrates who had spoken most openly against Christianity. Diocletian's widow and daughter, hiding in Thessalonica, were recognized and their bodies thrown into the sea. It might have been hoped that the Christians would pay less heed to the spirit of vengeance; but God, who punishes justly, wished the hands of the Christians tinted with the blood of their persecutors, as soon as they had freedom of action.

Constantine convoked, assembled, at Nicaea, opposite Constantinople, the first ecumenical council, over which Hosius presided. There they decided the great question agitating the Church—the divinity of Jesus Christ. Some availed themselves of the opinion of Origen, who says in chapter 6 against Celsus: "We present our prayers to God through Jesus, who stands midway between created natures and uncreated nature, who brings us the grace of his father, and presents our prayers to the great God in his capacity as our pontiff." They also relied on some passages from St. Paul, of which several have been handed down. Above all, they based themselves on these words of Jesus Christ: *My father is greater than I;* and they regarded Jesus as the first-born of creation, as the purest emanation of the supreme Being, but not precisely as God.

The others, who were orthodox, cited passages more consistent with the eternal divinity of Jesus, such as this one: *My father and I are one*, words which their adversaries interpreted to mean: *My father and I have the same plan, the same will; I have no desires other than those of my father.* Alexander, bishop of Alexandria, and after him, Athanasius, stood at the head of the orthodox; and Eusebius, bishop of Nicomedia, with seventeen other bishops, the priest Arius, and several other priests, were in the opposition. From the first the quarrel was bitter, since St. Alexander called his adversaries anti-Christs. Finally, after many arguments, the Holy Spirit decided in the council as follows, through the mouth of 299 bishops against eighteen: "Jesus is the only son of God, begotten of the Father, that is, of the substance of the Father, God of God, light of light, true God of the true God, consubstantial with the Father; we also believe in the Holy Spirit, etc." This was the creed of the council. This shows that the bishops had carried the day against the common priests, for two thousand persons of the second order agreed with Arius, according to the two Alexandrian patriarchs who wrote the history of Alexandria in Arabic. Arius was exiled by Constantine; but so was Athanasius soon afterward, whereupon Arius was recalled to Constantinople; but St. Macarius prayed so fervently for Arius to die before the priest could enter the cathedral that God granted his prayer. Arius died on his way to church, in 330. Emperor Constantine's life came to an end in 337. He put his testament into the hand of an Arian priest, and died in the arms of Eusebius, leader of the Arians, bishop of Nicomedia; he had himself baptized only on his death bed, leaving the Church triumphant but divided.

The partisans of Athanasius and Eusebius carried on a

cruel war against each other; and what is called Arianism was established in all the provinces of the empire for a long time to come.

Julian the philosopher, surnamed the *Apostate,* wished to stifle these divisions, and could not manage it.

The second general council was held in Constantinople, in 381. There the doctrine that the Council of Nicaea had not judged it appropriate to utter about the Holy Spirit was set forth and it was added to the Nicaean creed that "the Holy Spirit is the life-giving lord who proceeds from the Father, and that he is worshipped and glorified with the Father and the Son."

Not until about the ninth century did the Latin Church go about decreeing, step by step, that the Holy Spirit proceeds from the Father and the Son.

In 431, the third general council, held at Ephesus, decided that Mary was truly the mother of God, and that Jesus possessed two natures and one person. Nestorius, bishop of Constantinople, who wanted the Holy Virgin to be called the mother of Christ, was pronounced Judas by the council; the two natures were further confirmed by the council of Chalcedonia.

I shall skip lightly over the succeeding centuries, which are familiar enough. Unfortunately, all these disputes led to wars, and the Church was ever compelled to take up arms. To try the patience of the faithful, in the ninth century God also permitted the Greeks and Latins to break with each other forever; he also permitted twenty-nine bloody schisms to rend the West over the see of Rome.

Meanwhile, almost the entire Greek Church, and the entire African Church, became slaves under the Arabs, and then under the Turks, who raised the Mahometan religion on the ruins of the Christian. The Roman Church survived, but continually sullied with the blood of more than six hundred years of discord between the Holy Roman Empire in the West and its priesthood. These very quarrels made it powerful. In Germany, the bishops and the abbots all made themselves into princes, and the popes little by little acquired absolute dominion over Rome and 250 miles of the countryside. Thus God tried his Church through humiliations, through troubles, through crimes, and through splendor.

In the sixteenth century the Latin Church lost half of Germany, Denmark, Sweden, England, Scotland, Ireland, the better part of Switzerland, and Holland; with the Spanish conquests it won more territory in America than it had lost in Europe; but the greater territory has far fewer subjects.

Divine Providence seemed to reserve Japan, Siam, India, and China for obedience to the pope, to repay him for Asia Minor, Syria, Greece, Egypt, Africa, Russia, and all the other lost states I have spoken of. St. Francis Xavier, who carried the Holy Gospel to the East Indies and Japan when the Portuguese went there looking for wares, performed a great number of miracles, all attested to by the Reverend Fathers, the Jesuits; some say that he brought nine dead men back to life; in his *Flowers of the Saints*, the R. F. Ribadeneira limits himself to saying that he revived four: but that's quite enough. Providence willed it that in less than a hundred years there should be thousands of Roman Catholics in the isles of Japan; but the Devil sowed his tares amid the good grain. The Christians started a conspiracy, followed by a civil war, in which they were all exterminated in 1638. Then that nation closed its ports to all foreigners except the Dutch, who were regarded as merchants, not as Christians, and were first made to tread on the cross, in the prison where they were shut up when they landed at Nagasaki, in order to obtain permission to sell their goods.

The Catholic, apostolic, and Roman religion was in recent times proscribed in China, but in a less cruel manner. It is true that the Reverend Fathers, the Jesuits, had not brought the dead back to life at the court of Peking; they had contented themselves with teaching astronomy, casting guns, and being mandarins. But their unhappy disputes with the Dominicans and others shocked the great emperor Yong-tching so much that this prince, who was justice and goodness itself, fell into the blindness of prohibiting the teaching of our holy religion, about which our missionaries didn't agree. He expelled them, but with paternal kindness, furnishing them with food and carriages to the borders of his empire.

All Asia and Africa, half of Europe, all the possessions of the English and the Dutch in America, all the untamed American hordes, all the Australian lands, which are a fifth of the globe, have remained a prey to the Devil, to confirm this holy saying: *Many are called, but few are chosen.* If there are about sixteen hundred million people on the earth, as some scholars claim, the Holy Roman Catholic Universal Church possesses scarcely sixty million of them: which is a little more than the twenty-sixth part of the inhabitants of the known world.

LE CIEL DES ANCIENS
THE HEAVEN OF THE ANCIENTS

If a silkworm were to call the little fluff that surrounds its cocoon *heaven*, it would be arguing as soundly as all the ancients, who gave the name of *heaven* to the atmosphere, which, as M. de Fontenelle has well said in his *Mondes*, is the fluff of our cocoon.

The vapors which rise from our ocean and our earth, and which form the clouds, the meteors, and the thunder, were at first mistaken for the home of the gods. In Homer the gods always descend in clouds of gold; hence painters today still paint them sitting on a cloud; but, since it was fitting that the master of the gods should be more comfortable than the others, they gave him an eagle to carry him, because the eagle flies higher than the other birds.

The ancient Greeks, seeing the rulers of towns living in citadels at the top of a mountain, decided that the gods should have a citadel too, and placed it in Thessaly, on Mount Olympus, whose peak is sometimes hidden in the clouds; so the gods' palace was on the same floor as their heaven.

The stars and planets, which seemed fixed to the blue vault of our atmosphere, later became the dwellings of gods; seven of them had their own planet, the others lived where they could. The general council of the gods was held in a great hall which one reached by the Milky Way; for the gods had to have a hall in the air, since men had town halls on the ground.

When the Titans, a species of animal between gods and men, declared a just war on these gods to reclaim a part of their heritage on their father's side (being sons of Heaven and Earth), they piled only two or three mountains on one another, assuming that this would be quite enough to make them masters of heaven and of the castle of Olympus.

> *Neve foret terris securior arduus aether,*
> *Affectasse ferunt regnum caeleste gigantes,*
> *Altaque congestos struxisse ad sidera montes.*

[*Nor was high heaven safer than the earth.*
The giants attacked the heavenly kingdom,
And piled up mountains to the very stars.
                    Ovid, *Metamorphoses*, I, 151-153]

This natural philosophy of children and old women is tremendously old; however, it is quite certain that the Chaldeans had ideas about what is called Heaven that were as sensible as ours are. They placed the sun in the center of our planetary world, at about the distance from our globe that we have calculated; they had the earth and all the planets revolve around that star: this is what Aristarchus of Samos teaches us. This is the true system of the world which Copernicus has since revived; but the philosophers kept the secret to themselves, in order to be more highly respected by kings and people—or rather, not to be persecuted.

The language of error is so familiar to men that we still give the name of Heaven to our vapors and the space between the earth and moon; we say ascend to Heaven as we say that the sun turns, although we know perfectly well that it does not turn; we are probably heaven for the inhabitants of the moon, every planet placing its heaven in the neighboring planet.

If someone had asked Homer to what heaven Sarpedon's soul had gone, and where was the soul of Hercules, Homer would have been more than a little puzzled: he would have replied with harmonious verses.

What guarantee was there that the ethereal soul of Hercules would have been more comfortable on Venus or on Saturn than on our globe? Could it have been comfortable in the sun? That furnace doesn't seem a very habitable place. Anyway, what did the ancients understand by heaven? They knew nothing about it; they were always exclaiming, "heaven and earth"; that's as though we exclaimed, "infinity and an atom." Properly speaking, there is no heaven; there is a prodigious number of globes revolving in empty space, and our globe revolves like the others.

The ancients believed that to go to the heavens was to ascend; but one does not ascend from one globe to another; the heavenly globes are sometimes above our horizon, sometimes below. Thus let us suppose that Venus, having come to Paphos, returned to her planet when that planet had set; then the goddess would not have ascended in relation to our horizon: she would have descended, and one would have to say in that case, *descend to heaven*. But the ancients weren't as subtle as all this; they had vague, uncertain, contradictory notions about everything connected with natural science. People have written immense volumes to find out what they thought about all sorts of questions of this kind. Four words would have been enough: *they did not think*.

We must always except a small number of sages, but they came late; few of them explained their thoughts, and when they did so the charlatans of this world sent them to heaven by the shortest route.

A writer, called Pluche, I think, has tried to make a great scientist of Moses; another had previously reconciled Moses with Descartes and published the *Cartesius Mosaïzans;* according to him, Moses was the first to invent vortices and subtle matter; but we know perfectly well that God, who made Moses a great legislator and a great prophet, had no intention of making him a professor of science; he instructed the Jews in their duties; he didn't teach them a word of philosophy. Calmet, who compiled much and never thought, speaks of the system of the Hebrews; but that coarse people were far from having a system; they didn't even have a school of geometry; its very name was unknown to them; their only science was that of brokerage and usury.

In their books we find ideas about the structure of heaven that are dubious, incoherent, and in everything worthy of a barbaric people. Their first heaven was the air; the second, the firmament, to which the stars were attached; this firmament was solid, of ice, and supported the superior waters which at the time of the deluge escaped from their reservoir through gates, sluices, cataracts. Above the firmament, or these superior waters, was the third heaven, or empyrean, to which St. Paul was carried. The firmament was a kind of half-vault that embraced the earth. The sun didn't go round the globe, which they didn't know about. When it had arrived in the west, it returned to the east by an unknown path; and if you didn't see it, that was because, as baron de Foeneste put it, it returned at night.

Besides, the Hebrews had taken these fantasies from other peoples. Most nations, except the school of the Chaldeans, regarded heaven as solid; the earth, fixed and immobile, was longer by a third from east to west than from south to north; hence the expressions of longitude and latitude which we have adopted. Obviously, according to this view, there could be no antipodes. Indeed, St. Augustine calls the notion of antipodes an "absurdity," and Lactantius says expressly: "Are there people crazy enough to believe that there are men whose head is lower than their feet?" etc.

Lactantius also writes in book III of his *Institutions:* "I can prove to you with many arguments that it is impossible for heaven to surround the earth."

The author of *Spectacle de la nature* may tell M. le chevalier as often as he likes that Lactantius and St. Chrysostom were great philosophers; we will answer him that they were great saints, and that it is by no means necessary to be a good astronomer in order to be a saint. We will believe that they are in heaven, but we

will admit that we don't know exactly in what part of
heaven.

CIRCONCISION · CIRCUMCISION

When Herodotus relates what he was told by the
barbarians among whom he traveled, he relates nonsense; but most of our travelers do the same. Of course
he doesn't ask us to believe him when he talks about the
adventure of Gyges and Candaules; about Arion, borne
on a dolphin; and about the oracle which, when consulted on what Croesus was doing, replied that he was
cooking a tortoise in a covered cauldron; and about Da-
rius' horse, which proclaimed its master king by being
the first to whinny; and about a hundred other fables fit
to amuse children and to be compiled by rhetoricians;
but when he talks about what he has seen, the customs
of the nations he has surveyed, the antiquities he has consulted, then he speaks to men.

"It seems," he says in his book *Euterpe*, "that the inhabitants of Colchis were of Egyptian origin; I think so,
not because of hearsay, but because I found that in Colchis people remembered the ancient Egyptians much
better than people in Egypt remembered the ancient customs of Colchis.

"These inhabitants of the shores of the Black Sea
claimed to be a colony founded by Sesostris; as for me,
I conjectured this not merely because they are swarthy
and have curly hair, but because the nations of Colchis,
Egypt, and Ethiopia are the only ones in the world who
have always practised circumcision: for the Phoenicians
and Palestinians admit that they borrowed circumcision
from the Egyptians. The Syrians, who inhabit the banks

of Thermodon and Parthenius, and their neighbors the Macronians, admit that they adopted this Egyptian custom only recently; it is chiefly through this that they have been recognized as having an Egyptian origin.

"As for Ethiopia and Egypt, since this ceremony is very ancient in these two nations, I am unable to say which of them taught circumcision to the other; nevertheless it is likely that the Ethiopians took it from the Egyptians; whereas the Phoenicians, on the other hand, abolished the custom of circumcising newborn infants when they began to have more dealings with the Greeks."

It is obvious from this passage in Herodotus that several nations had taken circumcision from Egypt; but no nation has ever claimed to have taken circumcision from the Jews. To whom then can we attribute the origin of this custom—to the nation from which five or six others confess having taken it, or to another nation, much less powerful, less engaged in trade, less warlike, hidden in a corner of Arabia Petraea, which never passed on the least of its practices to any people?

The Jews say that of old they were admitted to Egypt out of charity; isn't it highly probable that the small nation imitated a practice of the great nation, and that the Jews borrowed several customs from their masters?

Clement of Alexandria reports that Pythagoras, traveling among the Egyptians, was obliged to have himself circumcised to be admitted to their mysteries; in other words, it was absolutely necessary to be circumcised to be one of the priests in Egypt. These priests existed at the time when Joseph arrived there; the government was very ancient, and the antique ceremonies of Egypt were observed with the most scrupulous exactitude.

The Jews admit that they stayed in Egypt for two

hundred and five years; they say they didn't practice circumcision during that time; thus it is clear that during these two hundred and five years the Egyptians did not adopt circumcision from the Jews. Would they have taken it from them after the Jews, according to their own testimony, had stolen all the vessels they had borrowed and fled into the desert with their booty? Would a master adopt the principal badge of his thieving and fugitive slave? That's not in human nature.

In the Book of Joshua it is said that the Jews were circumcised in the desert: "I have rolled away the reproach of Egypt from you." Now what could this reproach be for a people who found themselves between the nations of Phoenicia, the Arabs, and the Egyptians, if it was not something that made them contemptible to these three nations? How was this reproach removed? By removing a bit of their foreskin. Isn't that the natural meaning of this passage?

Genesis says that Abraham had been circumcised earlier; but Abraham traveled in Egypt, which had been a flourishing kingdom for a long time, governed by a powerful king. It seems likely that in a kingdom as ancient as Egypt, circumcision was in use long before the Jewish nation came into being. Moreover, the circumcision of Abraham was not followed up; his descendants were not circumcised until the time of Joshua.

Now, before Joshua, the Israelites took many customs from the Egyptians, by their own admission; they imitated them in several sacrifices and in several ceremonies, as in the fasts observed on the eve of the feasts of Isis; in ablutions; in the custom of shaving the head of priests; incense, candelabra; the sacrifice of the red heifer; purification with hyssop, abstinence from pork, abhorrence of the cooking utensils of foreigners—all attest that the little Hebrew people, despite its aversion for the

great Egyptian nation, had retained an infinite number
of practices of its former masters. The goat Azazel,
which was sent into the desert laden with the sins of the
people, was an obvious imitation of an Egyptian practice; the rabbis even admit that that the word *Azazel*
is not Hebrew. It seems likely, therefore, that the Hebrews imitated the Egyptians in circumcision, as did the
Arabs, their neighbors.

It is not extraordinary that God, who sanctified baptism, so ancient a practice among the Asiatics, also sanctified circumcision, no less ancient among the Africans.
I have already observed that he is at liberty to attach his
grace to any sign he deigns to choose.

Still, ever since the Jewish people was circumcised
under Joshua, it has retained this practice right down to
our day; the Arabs too have always remained faithful
to it; but the Egyptians, who circumcised boys and girls
in the earliest times, ceased after a while to perform the
operation on females, and finally restricted it to priests,
astrologers, and prophets. This is what Clement of
Alexandria and Origen teach us. In fact, it is not apparent
that the Ptolemies ever were circumcised.

The Latin authors who treat the Jews with such profound contempt that they call them *curtus Apella* in
derision, *credat Judaeus Apella, curti Judaei,* don't apply these epithets to the Egyptians. The whole Egyptian
people is circumcised today, but for another reason: because Mahometism adopted Arabia's ancient custom of
circumcision. It is this Arabian circumcision which spread
to the Ethiopians, where boys and girls are circumcised
still.

We must admit that the ceremony of circumcision
seems very strange at first; but we must note that from
the beginning the priests of the Orient consecrated
themselves to their divinities by special signs. An ivy leaf

was engraved with a needle on the priests of Bacchus. Lucian tells us that the votaries of the goddess Isis printed letters on their wrist and neck. The priests of Cybele turned themselves into eunuchs.

It seems very probable that the Egyptians, who revered the instrument of generation, and who carried its image in pomp in their processions, thought of offering to Isis and Osiris, by whom everything on earth was begotten, a small part of the member with which these gods wished mankind to perpetuate itself. Ancient oriental manners are so very different from ours that nothing should seem extraordinary to anyone who has done a little reading. A Parisian is greatly astonished when he is told that the Hottentots cut one testicle off their male children; the Hottentots are perhaps astonished that the Parisians should keep both of them.

CONCILES · COUNCILS

All councils are infallible, no doubt; for they are composed of men. It is impossible that these assemblies should ever be dominated by passions, intrigues, a wrangling spirit, hatred, jealousy, prejudice, ignorance.

But why, you will ask, have so many councils opposed each other? To try our faith; they were all of them right, each in its time.

Today Roman Catholics believe only in councils approved by the Vatican; and the Greek Catholics believe only in those approved by Constantinople. The Protestants make fun of the former and the latter; and so everybody should be satisfied.

We shall speak here only of the great councils; the small ones aren't worth the trouble.

The first one was that of Nicaea. It was assembled in 325 of our common era, after Constantine had written and sent with Hosius that noble letter to the somewhat muddle-headed clergy of Alexandria: "You are quarreling over a rather trivial subject. These subtleties are unworthy of reasonable people." The question was whether Jesus was created or uncreated. This in no way affects ethics, which is the essential thing. Whether Jesus was in time or before time, we must be decent men just the same. After many altercations, it was finally decided that the Son was as old as the Father, and *consubstantial* with the Father. This decision is hardly comprehensible, but that makes it all the more sublime. Seventeen bishops protested against the decree, and an ancient chronicle of Alexandria, preserved at Oxford, says that two thousand priests protested too; but the prelates made light of these ordinary priests, who were generally poor. Be that as it may, there was no mention of the Trinity in this first council. The Creed runs: "We believe Jesus consubstantial with the Father, God of God, light of light, begotten and not made; we also believe in the Holy Spirit." It must be acknowledged that the Holy Spirit was treated pretty cavalierly.

It is reported in the supplement to the Council of Nicaea that the Fathers, much perplexed over which were the authentic and which were the apocryphal books of the Old and New Testament, put them all together in a heap on the altar; and the books to be rejected fell to the ground. It's a pity this pretty prescription should be lost to our time.

After the first Council of Nicaea, composed of three hundred and seventeen infallible bishops, another one was held at Rimini; and this time the number of infallibles was four hundred, without counting a big detachment at Seleucia of about two hundred. After four months of quarreling, these six hundred bishops unanimously deprived Jesus of his *consubstantiality*. It has since been restored to him, except by the Socinians; so all goes well.

One of the great councils was that of Ephesus, in 431; Nestorius, bishop of Constantinople, great persecutor of heretics, was himself condemned as a heretic for maintaining that while Jesus was indeed God, his mother was not absolutely the mother of God, but the mother of Jesus. It was St. Cyril who had Nestorius condemned; but the partisans of Nestorius also had St. Cyril deposed in the same council: which embarrassed the Holy Spirit greatly.

Here observe very carefully, dear reader, that the Gospel never said a word either about the consubstantiality of the Word, or about the honor Mary had of being mother of God, or anything about the other disputes for which infallible councils have assembled.

Eutyches was a monk who had shouted a great deal against Nestorius, whose heresy went so far as to suppose two persons in Jesus: which is appalling. The better to contradict his adversary, the monk argued that Jesus had only one nature. One Flavian, bishop of Constantinople, argued against him that it was absolutely necessary that there should be two natures in Jesus. A numerous council was assembled at Ephesus in 449; this one was conducted in the form of hand-to-hand combat, like the minor Council of Cirta in 355 and a certain conference in Carthage. Flavian's nature was bruised by blows, and two natures were assigned to Jesus. At the Council of Chalcedon, in 451, Jesus was reduced to one nature.

I skip councils held for minutiae, and come to the sixth general council of Constantinople, assembled to find out precisely whether Jesus, having only one nature, had two wills. You understand how important all this was to please God.

This council was convoked by Constantine the Bearded, just as all the others had been by preceding emperors: the legates of the bishop of Rome were on the left, the patriarchs of Constantinople and Antioch on the right. I don't know if the train-bearers at Rome claim that the left is the place of honor. Be that as it may, Jesus obtained two wills from that affair.

The Mosaic law had prohibited images. Painters and sculptors had never made a hit with the Jews. It is not apparent that Jesus ever had any pictures, except perhaps that of Mary, painted by Luke. But in any event Jesus nowhere recommends that men worship images. The Christians nevertheless worshiped them around the end of the fourth century, when they had become familiar with the fine arts. The abuse was carried so far in the eighth century that Constantine Copronymus assembled a council of three hundred and twenty bishops in Constantinople, which anathematized the cult of images and called it idolatry.

The empress Irene, the same who later had her son's eyes torn out, convoked the second Council of Nicaea in 787: there the worship of images was restored. Today people justify this council by saying that such worship was a cult of *dulie* and not of *latrie*.

But, be it *dulie*, be it *latrie*, in 794 Charlemagne held another council at Frankfurt which branded the second Council of Nicaea idolatrous. Pope Adrian I sent two legates to it, but he did not convoke it.

The first great council convoked by a pope was the first Lateran Council of 1139; about a thousand bishops were there; but they did almost nothing except to anathematize those who said that the Church was too rich.

Another Lateran Council, in 1179, was held by pope

Alexander III, where the cardinals for the first time took precedence over the bishops; the only matters considered had to do with discipline.

Another great Lateran Council, in 1215. There pope Innocent III stripped the count of Toulouse of all his possessions, by virtue of his excommunication. This is the first council to speak of *Transubstantiation*.

In 1245, the general Council of Lyon, then an imperial city. Here, pope Innocent IV excommunicated emperor Frederick II, and accordingly deposed him, forbidding him fire and water: it was in this council that cardinals were given a red hat, to remind them that they must bathe in the blood of the emperor's partisans. This council caused the destruction of the house of Suabia, and thirty years of anarchy in Italy and Germany.

General Council at Vienne, in Dauphiny, in 1311, where they abolished the Order of Templars, whose principal members had been condemned to the most horrible tortures on the flimsiest of charges.

In 1414, the great Council of Constance, where they were satisfied with deposing pope John XXIII, convicted of a thousand crimes, and where they burned John Hus and Jerome of Prague for being obstinate, since obstinacy is a far greater crime than murder, rape, simony, and sodomy.

In 1430, the great Council of Basel, not recognized in Rome because it deposed pope Eugenius IV, who would not let himself be deposed.

The Romans count as a general council the fifth Lateran Council in 1512, convoked against Louis XII, king of France, by pope Julius II; but with the death of that warrior-pope, the council went up in smoke.

Finally, we have the great Council of Trent, which is not accepted in France in matters of discipline; but its dogma is incontestable, since the Holy Spirit came from

Rome to Trent every week in the courier's bag, as fra Paolo Sarpi says; but fra Paolo Sarpi smells a little of heresy.

(*By M. Abausit the younger*)

CONFESSION

It remains a problem whether confession, considering only its political effects, has done more harm than good.

There was confession in the mysteries of Isis, Orpheus, and Ceres, before the hierophant and the initiated; for, since these mysteries were rites of expiation, it was necessary to acknowledge that one had crimes to expiate.

The Christians adopted confession in the first centuries of the Church, just as they adopted pretty nearly all the rites of antiquity, like temples, altars, incense, candles, processions, lustral water, priestly habits, formulas of the mysteries: the *Sursum corda*, the *Ite missa est*, and so many others. The scandal of the public confession of a woman, which happened in Constantinople in the fourth century, led to the abolition of confession.

The secret confession one man makes to another was not admitted in our West until about the seventh century. The abbots began by demanding that their monks come twice a year to acknowledge all their faults. It was these abbots who invented the formula: *I absolve you as much as I can and as much as you need*. It might have been more respectful to the supreme Being, and more proper, to say, "May he pardon your faults and mine!"

Confession has done some good, in that it has sometimes obtained restitution from petty thieves. The trouble is that during political unrest, it has sometimes forced men to be rebellious and sanguinary in good conscience. The Guelf priests refused absolution to the Ghibellines, and the Ghibelline priests took good care not to absolve the Guelfs. The assassins of the Sforzas, the Medicis, the princes of Orange, and the kings of France prepared themselves for parricide by the sacrament of confession.

Louis XI and la Brinvilliers went to confession after they had committed a great crime; they confessed often, as gourmands take medicine to improve their appetites.

If we may be astonished at anything, it is at a bull of pope Gregory XV, emanating from His Holiness on 30 August 1622, in which he decrees that confessions should be revealed in certain cases.

The Jesuit Coton's reply to Henry IV will last longer than the Jesuit order: "Would you reveal the confession of a man determined to assassinate me?" *No; but I would put myself between you and him.*

CONVULSIONS

Around the year 1724 there was dancing at the cemetery of St. Médard; many miracles were performed there; and here is one, reported in a song by Madame, duchess du Maine:

> *Un décrotteur à la royale,*
> *Du talon gauche estropié,*
> *Obtint pour grâce spéciale*
> *D'être boiteux de l'autre pied.*

> [*A shoe-shine boy from Port Royale*
> *This special grace he claimed:*
> *His left leg dragged behind at first,*
> *And now both legs are maimed.*]

It is well known that the miraculous convulsions continued until a guard was posted in the cemetery.

> *De par le roi, défense à Dieu*
> *De plus fréquenter en ce lieu.*
>
> [*To God an order from the throne:*
> *The Lord must leave this place alone.*]

As is also well known, the Jesuits tried to counterbalance the vogue of the Jansenists. But as they could no longer perform such miracles, for their Xavier had exhausted the company's supply of grace by resurrecting a total of nine dead men, they decided to engrave a print of Jesus Christ dressed as a Jesuit. A wit in the Jansenist party, as is also well known, put at the bottom of the print:

> *Admirez l'artifice extrême*
> *De ces moines ingénieux:*
> *Ils vous ont habillé comme eux,*
> *Mon Dieu, de peur qu'on ne vous aime.*
>
> [*Admire the clever stratagem*
> *Of these monks: O Lord,*
> *They've dressed you up to look like them—*
> *For fear you'll be adored.*]

The Jansenists, the better to prove that Jesus Christ could never have worn the habit of a Jesuit, filled Paris with convulsions and attracted everybody to their monastery. Carré de Montgeron, councilor to *parlement*, went to the king and presented him with a collection of these miracles in quarto, attested to by a thousand witnesses. Reasonably enough, he was put in a *château* where they tried to restore his brains by diet; but truth always prevails over persecutions: the miracles continued for thirty years in a row, without letup. Sister Rose, sister Illuminée, sister Promise, sister Confite, were sent for: they had themselves scourged without any of it showing the next day; they were hit with faggots on their armored, well-padded stomachs, without suffering any harm; they were put before a big fire, their faces rubbed with pomade, and were not scorched; finally, as all arts achieve perfection in due course, they finished them off by sticking swords into their flesh and crucifying them. A famous theologian also had the good fortune to be put on the cross: all this to convince everybody that a certain bull was ridiculous, which they could have proved at less expense. However, Jesuits and Jansenists all united against *l'Esprit des lois,* and against . . . and against . . . and against. . . . And after that we dare to make fun of Laplanders, Samoyedes, and Negroes!

CORPS · BODY

Just as we don't know what a spirit is, so we are ignorant of what a body is: we see some of its properties; but what is the subject in which these properties reside? "There are only bodies," said Democritus and Epicurus; "There are no bodies," said the disciples of Zeno of Elea.

Bishop Berkeley of Cloyne is the last who claims, with a hundred sophisms, to have proved that bodies don't exist. They have, he says, neither color, nor odor, nor heat; these modalities are in your own sensations and not in the objects. He could have saved himself the trouble of proving this truth; it was known well enough. But from there he moves on to extension and solidity, which are the essence of a body; he thinks he can prove that there is no extension in a piece of green cloth, because the cloth is not really green; the sensation of green is in you alone, hence the sensation of extension also is in you alone. And, after he has thus destroyed extension, he concludes that solidity, which is attached to it, falls of its own weight—and thus there's nothing in the world but our ideas. So that, according to this scholar, ten thousand men killed by ten thousand cannon shots are fundamentally nothing but ten thousand apprehensions of our soul.

My lord, the bishop of Cloyne, had only himself to blame if he went to such ridiculous lengths. He believes he can show that there is no extension because a body seemed to him four times larger through his glasses than it was through his eyes, and four times smaller with the aid of another glass. From this he concludes that since a body cannot be at the same time four feet, sixteen feet, and a single foot in length, extension doesn't exist: hence there's nothing. All he needed to do was take a measure, and say: "Of whatever extension a body may appear to me, it is extended so many of these measures."

It would have been quite easy for him to see that extension and solidity are not like sounds, colors, tastes, odors, etc. Clearly, these are feelings excited in us by the configuration of parts; but extension is not a feeling. When this burning wood is extinguished, I am no longer warm; when the air no longer vibrates, I no longer hear anything; when this rose withers, I no longer smell it; but this wood, this air, and this rose have extension without any participation on my part. Berkeley's paradox isn't worth refuting.

It is useful to know how he was drawn into this paradox. A long time ago I had some conversations with him; he told me that he came to this opinion when he observed how men were unable to conceive what it is that receives extension. And in fact he triumphs in his book when he asks Hylas what that *substratum*, that substance, is. "It is the extended body," replies Hylas. Then the bishop (under the name of Philonous) laughs at him; and poor Hylas, seeing he has said that extension is subject to extension, and has therefore talked nonsense, is crestfallen, and admits that he doesn't understand it, that there is no body, the material world doesn't exist, there is nothing but a world of mind.

Hylas should merely have told Philonous: "We know nothing about the heart of this subject, this primal substance, extended, solid, divisible, mobile, shaped, etc.; I know it no better than I know the thinking, feeling, and willing subject; but still, that subject none the less exists, since it has essential properties of which it cannot be deprived."

We are all like most of the ladies of Paris: they live extremely well without knowing what goes into the stew; in the same way we enjoy bodies without knowing what they are composed of. What is the body made of? Of parts, and these parts resolve themselves into other parts. What are these last parts? Always bodies; you can go on dividing endlessly and never get any further.

Finally, a subtle philosopher, observing that a picture is made of elements none of which is a picture, and a house of materials none of which is a house, fancied (in a little different fashion) that bodies are built from an infinity of little things which are not bodies; and these are called *monads*. This system nevertheless has its good side, and, were it a part of revealed religion, I would think it quite plausible; all these little beings would be mathematical points, a species of souls who only wait for clothes to get into; it would be a perpetual metempsychosis; a monad would sometimes go into a whale, sometimes into a tree, sometimes into a juggler. This system is as good as any other; I like it quite as well as the declination of atoms, substantial forms, versatile grace, and the vampires of dom Calmet.

CREDO · CREED

I recite my Lord's Prayer and my Creed every morning; I'm not like Broussin, of whom Reminiac said:

> *Broussin, dès l'âge le plus tendre,*
> *Posséda la sauce-Robert,*
> *Sans que son précepteur lui pût jamais apprendre*
> *Ni son Credo ni son Pater.*

> [*Broussin, from the tend'rest age*
> *Knew the sauce Robert,*
> *But his teacher could never teach the young sage*
> *His Creed or his Lord's Prayer.*]

Symbol, collation, or *creed*, comes from the word *symbolein*, which the Latin Church adopted, as it has taken everything, from the Greek Church. Theologians who know something know that the so-called Apostles' Creed is not by the apostles at all.

The Greeks called *symbol*, or *creed*, the words, the signs by which those initiated into the mysteries of Ceres, Cybele, and Mythra recognized one another;* as time went by, the Christians had their own creed. If it had existed in the time of the apostles, it is to be presumed that St. Luke would have mentioned it.

A history of the creed is attributed to St. Augustine in his sermon 115; there he is made to say that Peter had begun the creed by saying: *I believe in God the Father Almighty;* John added: *Creator of heaven and earth;* James added: *I believe in Jesus Christ his only son, our Lord;* and so on to the end. This fable was suppressed in

---

* *Arnobius*, book 5, *Symbola quae rogata sacrorum*, etc. See also Clement of Alexandria, in his protreptic sermon, or *Cohortatio ad gentes.*

the last edition of Augustine. I leave it to the reverend Benedictine fathers to know precisely whether this curious little piece should have been suppressed or not.

The fact is that nobody ever heard anything about this creed for more than four hundred years. The common people say that Paris wasn't built in a day; the common people are often right in their proverbs. The apostles had our creed in their hearts, but they didn't put it in writing. One, which does not resemble the one we recite, was made up in the time of St. Irenaeus. Our creed, as it is today, derives from the fifth century. It is subsequent to that of Nicaea. The article which says that Jesus descended into hell, the one mentioning the communion of saints, can't be found in any of the creeds that precede ours. And in fact neither the Gospels nor the Acts of the Apostles say that Jesus descended into hell. But it was an accepted view from the third century on that Jesus had descended into Hades, into Tartarus, words that we translated as hell. In that sense, hell is not the Hebrew word *Scheol*, which means underground, pit. And that is why St. Athanasius has since informed us how our Savior descended into hell. "His humanity," he says, "was neither wholly in the tomb, nor wholly in hell. It was in the tomb according to the flesh, and in hell according to the soul."

St. Thomas claims that the saints who came back to life at the death of Jesus Christ died again to revive once more with him; that is the most widely accepted view. All these opinions have nothing to do with ethics; we must be decent men whether the saints revived twice, or whether God revived them only once. Our creed was written late, I admit it; but virtue is from all eternity.

If I may cite moderns in a matter as grave as this, let me quote the *Credo* of the abbé de Saint-Pierre, as it is written in his own hand in his book (it has not been printed) on the purity of religion and which I have copied faithfully:

"I believe in the one only God, and I love him. I believe that he illuminates every soul that comes into the world, as St. John says. Every soul, I mean, that seeks him faithfully.

"I believe in the one only God, because there can be but a single soul of the great whole, a single vivifying being, a unique creator.

"I believe in God the Father Almighty, because he is the common father of nature and of men, who are equally his children. I believe that he who made all to be born after the same fashion, who arranges the springs of our life in the same manner, who has given the same moral principles to all, which we can grasp as soon as we are able to reflect, has established no difference between his children except as they do good or ill.

"I believe that the just and beneficent Chinese is more precious in his eyes than a hairsplitting, arrogant scholar from Europe.

"I believe that as God is our common father, we are obligated to regard all men as our brothers.

"I believe that the persecutor is abominable, and that he walks close behind the poisoner and the parricide.

"I believe that theological disputes are at once the most ridiculous farce and the most terrible scourge of the word, immediately after war, pestilence, famine, and syphilis.

"I believe that ecclesiastics should be paid, and well paid, as servants of the public, teachers of morals, keepers of the registers of birth and death; but that they should not be given either the wealth of a farmer general or the rank of a prince, because one or the other corrupts the soul, and because nothing is more revolting than to see men so rich and so proud make people with only a hundred *écus* in wages sing the praises of humility and love of poverty.

"I believe that all parish priests should be married, not only so as to have a good wife who will take care of their household, but so as to be better citizens, provide good subjects to the state, and have many well-brought-up children.

"I believe that monks absolutely must be extirpated; this would render a very great service to the country and to themselves; they are men whom Circe has changed into pigs; the sage Ulysses should restore them to their human shape."

Paradise for charitable men!

CRITIQUE · CRITICISM

I don't intend to say anything about the kind of scholastic criticism that in the restoration ruins a phrase by an ancient author which had been understood perfectly well before. Nor shall I touch on that true criticism which disentangles whatever it can of ancient history and philosophy. I have in mind the criticism whose real aim is satire.

One day a patron of letters read Tasso with me; he came upon this stanza:

> *Chiama gli abitator dell' ombre eterne*
> *Il rauco suon della tartarea tromba.*
> *Treman le spaziose atre caverne;*
> *E l'aer cieco a quel rumor rimbomba:*
> *Nè si stridendo mai dalle superne*
> *Regioni del cielo il folgor piomba;*
> *Nè si scossa giammai trema la terra,*
> *Quando i vapori in sen gravida serra.*

[*The spirits gathered in eternal shade*
Are now convened with raucous trumpet sounds,
The open spacious caverns tremble,
The air reverberates as noise resounds.
Just so do distant regions quake
When thunderous roaring fills the skies
Just so does laboring earth travail
When pent-up vapor for release applies.
                    Gerusalemme liberata, IV, 3]

After this he read at random several more stanzas of such force and harmony that he exclaimed: "Ah! so that's what your Boileau calls tinsel? So that's how he wants to belittle a great man who lived a hundred years before him, and who himself had done justice to Tasso!" —"Console yourself," I told him; "let's look at Quinault's librettos."

So we did, and right off we found something to make us incensed against criticism; where that admirable poem *Armide* appears, we found these words:

SIDONIE
La haine est affreuse et barbare,
L'amour contraint les coeurs dont il s'empare
A souffrir des maux rigoureux.
Si votre sort est en votre puissance,
Faites choix de l'indifférence:
Elle assure un repos heureux.

ARMIDE
Non, non, il ne m'est pas possible
De passer de mon trouble en un état paisible,
Mon coeur ne se peut plus calmer;
Renaud m'offense trop, il n'est que trop aimable;
C'est pour moi désormais un choix indispensable
De le haïr ou de l'aimer.

[SIDONE
Hatred is a barbarous scourge,
Love can master hearts and urge
*   Patience under grievous wrong.*
If your fate is in your hands,
*   Choose indifference: it sends*
*   Sweet repose for which you long.*

ARMIDE
No, no, I really cannot be
Pacified; and the perplexity
*   Of my heart cannot be moved.*
Renaud offends me—for he's lovable,
Choice is therefore inescapable:
*   He must be hated or be loved.*

Armide, Act III, scene 2]

We read all of *Armide,* in which Tasso's genius gains still greater charms at Quinault's hands. "Well!" I told my friend, "nevertheless, this is the Quinault whom Boileau is perpetually straining to get people to think is the worst possible writer; he even persuaded Louis XIV that this graceful, moving, touching, and elegant poet had no merit but what he had borrowed from the musician Lulli." —"I can easily understand that," my friend replied; "Boileau was not jealous of the musician, he was jealous of the poet. How can we rely on the judgment of a man who, just to find a rhyme for a verse ending in *aut,* sometimes denigrated Boursault, sometimes Hénault, sometimes Quinault, depending on whether he was on good or bad terms with these gentlemen?

"But, lest your zeal against injustice cool, only put your head out the window, look at the Louvre's beautiful façade, with which Perrault achieved immortality: this clever man was the brother of a very learned Academician whom Boileau had had some dispute with; and that was enough to get Perrault branded as an ignorant architect."

After musing for a minute, my friend resumed with a sigh: "Human nature is like that. In his *Mémoires*, the duke de Sully found that cardinal d'Ossat and secretary of state Villeroi were poor ministers; Louvois did everything possible to have a poor opinion of the great Colbert." —"They published nothing against one another during their lifetime," I replied; "that kind of foolishness is usually reserved to literature, legal chicanery, and theology."

"We once had a man of merit, Lamotte it was, who wrote beautiful stanzas:

> *Quelquefois au feu qui la charme*
> *Résiste une jeune beauté,*
> *Et contre elle-même elle s'arme*
> *D'une pénible fermeté.*
> *Hélas! cette contrainte extrême*
> *La prive du vice qu'elle aime*
> *Pour fuir la honte qu'elle hait.*
> *Sa sévérité n'est que faste,*
> *Et l'honneur de passer pour chaste*
> *La résout à l'être en effet.*
>
> *En vain de sévère stoïque*
> *Sous mille défauts abattu*
> *Se vante d'une âme héroïque*
> *Toute vouée à la vertu:*
> *Ce n'est point la vertu qu'il aime;*
> *Mais son coeur, ivre de lui-même,*
> *Voudrait usurper les autels,*
> *Et par sa sagesse frivole*
> *Il ne veut que parer l'idole*
> *Qu'il offre au culte des mortels.*
>
> *Les champs de Pharsale et d'Arbelle*
> *Ont vu triompher deux vainqueurs,*

L'un et l'autre digne modèle
Que se proposent les grands coeurs.
Mais le succès a fait leur gloire;
Et, si le sceau de la victoire
N'eût consacré ces demi-dieux
Alexandre, aux yeux du vulgaire,
N'aurait été qu'un téméraire,
Et César qu'un séditieux.

[*Sometimes a young beauty resists*
The dangers of passion's charms;
With firmness she enters the lists:
Against herself she arms.
Alas! this restraint removes
The vice she dearly loves—
All to flee hateful shame.
Her jeweled honor is paste,
And the pleasure of being called chaste
Makes her chaste in more than name.

In vain this serious Stoic,
By a thousand defects bowed,
Boasts of her soul heroic
All to virtue vowed.
But Virtue! This boast isn't true,
She's drunk with herself, not with you.
She sets up a cult of herself
While true religion she scorns;
Her idol she adorns
While God is put on the shelf.
            L'amour propre, ode à l'évêque
            de Soissons, stanzas 5, 9]

[*Two victors in heavy fighting*
(*At Pharsal and Arbela in war*)—
These models look inviting;
No noble heart asks for more.
But their glory was made by success.
The victors became only less

Than the gods. But the herd
(Without such success) would have called Alexander
Reckless, foolhardy, absurd,
And Caesar, a mutinous ranter.

> *La sagesse du roi supérieure à*
> *tous les événements*, stanza 4]

"This author," he said, "was a sage who more than once lent the charm of verse to philosophy. If he had always written stanzas like these, he would have been the greatest lyric poet; still, when he presented these fine things to his contemporaries, one of them called him:

Certain oison, gibier de basse-cour.

[*A certain gosling, bird of the poultry-yard.*]

Elsewhere, the same critic says of Lamotte:

De ses discours l'ennuyeuse beauté.

[*The boring beauty of his speech.*]

And elsewhere:

. . . Je n'y vois qu'un défaut:
C'est que l'auteur les devait faire en prose.
Ces odes-là sentent bien le Quinault.

[*There is but one fault I see—*
He should have written them in prose.
These odes smell of Quinault to me.
>   Jean-Baptiste Rousseau, *Epître aux Muses*]

He pursues Lamotte everywhere, reproaching him with harshness and lack of harmony. Would you like to see the odes that this same censor, who considered Lamotte his master and disparaged him as his enemy, wrote a few years later? Read:

Cette influence souveraine
N'est pour lui qu'une illustre chaîne
Qui l'attache au bonheur d'autrui;
Tous les brillans qui l'embellissent;
Tous les talens qui l'ennoblissent,
Sont en lui, mais non pas à lui.

Il n'est rien que le temps n'absorbe, ne dévore,
Et les faits qu'on ignore
Sont bien peu différens des faits non avenus.

La bonté qui brille en elle
De ses charmes les plus doux
Est une image de celle
Qu'elle voit briller en vous.
Et, par vous seule enrichie,
Sa politesse, affranchie
Des moindres obscurités,
Est la lueur réfléchie
De vos sublimes clartés.

Ils ont vu par ta bonne foi
De leurs peuples troublés d'effroi
La crainte heureusement déçue,
Et déracinée à jamais
La haine si souvent reçue
En survivance de la paix.

Dévoile à ma vue empressée
Ces déités d'adoption,
Synonymes de la pensée,
Symboles de l'abstraction.
N'est-ce pas une fortune,
Quand d'une charge commune
Deux moitiés portent le faix,
Que la moindre le réclame,
Et que du bonheur de l'âme
Le corps seul fasse les frais?

[*This influence, so sovereign,*
Is for him but an illustrious chain
Which him to others binds.
All the jewels that make it shine,
All the talents that make it fine,
He in him, but not of him, finds.

Time all absorbs, time eats up all,
And facts that we don't know at all
Are almost like facts that never were.

The goodness which shines in her,
Which is her sweetest delight,
Is nothing but a picture
Of your shining light.
Her manners which now seem
Freed from the slightest obscurities,
Are but a reflected beam
Of your sublimest clarities.

Their people troubled and frightened,
Your faith their burden has lightened:
They were quite happy to err.
And now forever will cease
The hate we so often transfer
Into conditions of peace.

To my earnest view are brought
Adopted deities—they're mine:
Truly synonyms of thought,
Of abstraction they're the sign.
Aren't we truly fortunate
(When a joint burden is our fate)
When both halves fill their role?
When the lesser half asks
To let the body shoulder the tasks
Of making the bliss of the soul?]

"One shouldn't," my judicious patron of letters then remarked, "doubtless one shouldn't offer such dreadful works as models to the man one has criticized with such bitterness; it would have been better to let one's adversary enjoy his own merits in peace, and to preserve what merits one had oneself. But what do you expect? The *genus irritabile vatum* is sick with the same bile that tormented him in earlier days. The public forgives this wretched behavior toward men of talent, for it thinks only of its own amusement. In an allegory entitled *Pluton*, it sees judges condemned to be flayed and to sit in hell on seats covered with their own skin instead of *fleur-de-lis;* the reader doesn't care whether these judges deserve it or not, whether the plaintiff who brings them before Pluto is right or wrong. He reads these verses solely for his pleasure; if he gets that, he doesn't ask for more; if they displease him, he lets the allegory go, and won't do a single thing to have the sentence confirmed or set aside.

"Racine's inimitable tragedies have all been criticized, and inadequately; that's because they were criticized by rivals. True, artists are competent judges of art, but these competent judges are nearly always corrupt.

"An artist with a great deal of knowledge and taste, no prejudices, and no envy—that would be an excellent critic. He's hard to find."

DAVID

When a young peasant finds a kingdom while he is looking for asses—that's not a common occurrence; when another peasant cures his king of an attack of madness by playing the harp, that case is still quite rare; but when that little harp player becomes a king himself because he meets a village priest in some out of the way place who empties a bottle of olive oil on his head, the thing is even more marvelous.

When were these marvels written down and by whom? I have no idea; but I'm quite sure that it was neither by a Polybius nor a Tacitus. I greatly revere the worthy Jew, whoever he was, who wrote the true history of the mighty kingdom of the Hebrews for the instruction of the universe, under the dictation and inspiration of the God of all the worlds; but I am displeased to see my friend David start by assembling a band of thieves numbering four hundred, and come to an understanding, at the head of this troop of honest men, with Abimelech, the high priest, who arms him with the sword of Goliath and gives him consecrated loaves (I Kings, chapter 21, verse 13).

I'm a little shocked that David, the anointed of the Lord, the man after God's own heart, should rebel against Saul, another anointed of the Lord, should depart with four hundred brigands to lay the country under contribution, rob good old Nabal, and immediately after Nabal is dead, marry his widow without delay (chapter 25, verses 10, 11).

I have some reservations about his behavior toward the great king Achish, owner of five or six villages in the canton of Gath, if I'm not mistaken. David, then at

the head of six hundred brigands, made the rounds of the
allies of Achish, his benefactor; he pillaged everywhere,
he killed everybody, old men, women, infants at the
breast. And why did he cut the throats of infants at the
breast? "For fear," writes the divine Jewish author,
"that these children might carry the news to king Achish" (chapter 27, verses 8, 9, 11).

The brigands got angry with him and wanted to stone
him. What does this Jewish Mandrin do? He consults the
Lord, who replies that he must attack the Amalekites,
where these brigands shall collect good spoils and enrich
themselves (chapter 30).

Meanwhile, Saul, the anointed of the Lord, loses a
battle against the Philistines and is killed. A Jew brings
the news to David. David, who apparently had nothing
on him to give the courier for the *buona nuncia*, has him
killed by way of reward (II Kings, chapter 1, verse 10).

Ishbosheth succeeds his father Saul; David is strong
enough to make war on him: finally Ishbosheth is assassinated.

David seizes the whole kingdom; he surprises the little
town or village of Rabbah, and he puts all the inhabitants to death, by means of quite extraordinary tortures;
they are sawed in two, they are torn to pieces with iron
harrows, they are burned in brick kilns; quite a noble
and generous manner of making war (II Kings, chapter 12).

After these fine expeditions, there was a famine of
three years in the land. I can well believe it, for given
the way in which good David made war, the soil must
have been poorly sown indeed.

The Lord is consulted and asked why there should be
a famine. The reason was self-evident: surely when you
have peasants cooked in brick kilns or sawed in two, in a
country which barely produces any wheat, very few

men remain to cultivate the earth; but the Lord replied that it was because Saul had formerly killed Gibeonites.

What does the good David do then? He assembles the Gibeonites; he tells them that Saul had done a great wrong to make war on them; that unlike him, Saul was not after God's own heart, that it was right to punish his race; and he gave them seven of Saul's grandsons to hang—and they were hanged, because there had been a famine (II Kings, chapter 21).

It is a pleasure to see how that imbecile, dom Calmet, justifies and canonizes all these actions which would make us shudder with horror if they were not incredible.

I won't mention here the abominable assassination of Uriah, and the adultery of Bathsheba: it is familiar enough, and the ways of God are so different from the ways of men that he permitted Jesus Christ to be descended from this infamous Bathsheba, the whole line being purified by this holy mystery.

I won't ask now how Jurieu had the insolence to persecute the virtuous Bayle for not approving all the actions of good king David; but I do ask how they tolerated a man like Jurieu molesting a man like Bayle.

DES DÉLITS LOCAUX
OF LOCAL OFFENSES

Survey the whole world, you will find that theft, murder, adultery, calumny, are regarded as offenses which society condemns and curbs; but should something approved in England and condemned in Italy be punished as if it were an outrage against all mankind? This is what I call a local offense. Doesn't something

that is criminal only within the precincts of a few mountains or between two rivers require more indulgence of
the judges than the outrages which are abhorred in
all countries? Shouldn't the judge say to himself: "I
wouldn't dare to punish at Ragusa what I'm punishing at
Loretto"? Shouldn't this reflection soften the harshness
of heart he all too easily contracts in the long practice of
his profession?

We all know the carnivals of Flanders: in the last century they were carried to a degree of indecency that
could revolt eyes unaccustomed to these spectacles.

This is how the feast of Christmas used to be celebrated in some towns. At first a young man appeared,
half naked, with wings on his back; he recited the *Ave
Maria* to a young girl who replied with *fiat*, and the
angel kissed her on the mouth; later a child shut in a big
cardboard cock cried out in imitation of a cock's crow:
puer natus est nobis. A stout ox, lowing, said *ubi*, which
he pronounced *oobi*; a ewe bleated, crying out *Bethle-
hem*. A donkey cried out *hihanus*, to signify *eamus;* a
long procession, led by four fools with rattles, caps and
bell, concluded the parade. Today some traces of these
popular devotions, which better educated people would
take for profanations, still remain. A Swiss, in a bad
mood and perhaps more drunk than those who acted
the role of the ox and the donkey, had some words with
them in Louvain; blows were exchanged; they wanted to
hang the Swiss, who barely escaped.

The same man had a violent quarrel at the Hague in
Holland for loudly taking the side of Barneveldt against
an extreme Gomarist. He was put in prison in Amsterdam for saying that priests are the scourge of humanity
and the cause of all our miseries. "So," he said, "if you
think good works can help to save one, you are thrown
in prison; if you make fun of a cock and a donkey, you

risk the rope." This adventure, comical as it is, makes it clear enough that one may be guilty in one or two places in our hemisphere, and absolutely innocent in the rest of the world.

DESTIN · FATE

Of all the books that have come down to us, the oldest is Homer; there we find the ways of profane antiquity, coarse heroes, coarse gods made in the image of man; but there, too, we find the seeds of philosophy, and above all the idea of fate, which is the master of the gods, as the gods are the masters of the world.

In vain does Jupiter wish to save Hector; he consults the fates; he weighs in a scale the fates of Hector and Achilles; he finds that the Trojan must absolutely be killed by the Greek; he can't do anything against it; and from that moment on Apollo, the guardian spirit of Hector, is obliged to give him up (*Iliad*, book 22). To be sure, in his poem Homer often throws out quite contrary ideas, following the privilege of antiquity; but still he is the first in whom the notion of fate is to be found. So, it must have been quite fashionable in his time.

Among the little Jewish people, the Pharisees adopted the idea of fate only several centuries later; for the Pharisees, who were the first Jews to be scholars, were new men themselves. In Alexandria they mixed a part of Stoic dogma with ancient Jewish ideas. St. Jerome even claims that their sect does not antedate our common era by very much.

The philosophers never needed either Homer or the Pharisees to convince themselves that everything happens according to immutable laws, that everything is arranged, that everything is a necessary effect.

Either the world subsists by its own nature, by its own physical laws, or a supreme Being has created it in accordance with his supreme law: in either case, these laws are immutable; in either case, everything is necessary; heavy bodies tend toward the center of the earth, and cannot tend to rest in the air. Pear trees can never bear pineapples. The instinct of a spaniel cannot be the instinct of an ostrich. Everything is regulated, correlated, and circumscribed.

Man can only have a certain number of teeth, hairs, and ideas; there comes a time when he must lose his teeth, his hair, and his ideas.

It is a contradiction to say that what existed yesterday didn't exist, that what exists today does not exist; it is equally a contradiction to say that what has to exist doesn't have to exist.

If you could unsettle the destiny of one fly, there would be no reason on earth why you couldn't fashion the fate of all the other flies, all the animals, mankind, and nature; finally you would find yourself more powerful than God.

Imbeciles say: "My doctor pulled my aunt through a mortal illness; he has made my aunt live ten years longer than she should have." Others, who know better, say: "The prudent man makes his own fate."

> *Nullum numen abest, si sit prudentia, sed te*
> *Nos facimus, fortuna, deam, caeloque locamus.*
>
> [*Had we but wisdom we would see that Fortune*
> *Is not divine: we make her so, place her in heaven.*
> Juvenal, *Satires*, X, 365-366.]

But often the prudent man, far from making his own destiny, succumbs to it; prudent men are created by fate.

Profound statesmen argue that if Cromwell, Ludlow, Ireton, and a dozen other parliamentary leaders had been assassinated a week before they cut off Charles I's head, this king could have gone on living and died in his bed: they are right; they might add that if all England had been engulfed in the sea, this monarch wouldn't have died on the scaffold at *Witehall*, or white hall; but things were arranged in such a way that Charles had to have his throat cut.

Cardinal d'Ossat was doubtless more prudent than a lunatic in a madhouse; but isn't it obvious that the organs of the sage d'Ossat were fashioned differently from the organs of a harebrain, just as the fox's organs are different from a crane's or lark's?

Your doctor saved your aunt; but he certainly didn't negate the order of nature to do so: he followed it. It is clear that your aunt couldn't prevent herself from being born in a certain town, that she couldn't prevent herself from having a certain illness at a certain time, that the doctor could not be anywhere but in the town where he was, that your aunt had to call him, that he had to prescribe the drugs that cured her.

A peasant believes that hail fell on his field by chance; but the philosopher knows there is no chance, and that, given the way this world is constituted, it couldn't possibly not have hailed on that day and in that place.

There are people who, afraid of this truth, grant only half of it, like debtors who offer their creditors half and demand remission for the rest. There are necessary events, they say, and others which are not necessary. It would be amusing indeed if one part of this world were ordered, and the other not; if part of what happens has to happen, and another part of what happens does not have to happen. If we examine this closely, we see that the anti-fatalistic doctrine is absurd; but there are many people fated to think badly, others not to think at all, and others to persecute those who think.

There are people who tell you: "Don't believe in fatalism; for then everything will seem inevitable to you,

you won't work at anything, you will stagnate in indifference, you will love neither riches, honors, nor
praises; you won't want to acquire anything, you will
think of yourself as without capacities and without
power; you will cultivate no talent; everything will perish in apathy."

Gentlemen, fear not, we shall always have passions
and prejudices, since it is our destiny to be subjected to
prejudices and passions; we know perfectly well that
having great capacities and great talents no more depends
on us than having beautiful hair or well-shaped hands;
we are convinced that we ought not to be vain about
anything, and yet we are always vain.

I necessarily have the passion to write this; and you—
you have the passion to condemn me; both of us are
equally foolish, equally the plaything of destiny. Your
nature is to do evil, mine is to love the truth and to publish it in spite of you.

The owl which feeds on mice in his ruin, said to the
nightingale: "Stop singing in your beautiful shade, come
into my hole so I can eat you"; and the nightingale replied: "I was born to sing here and to laugh at you."

You ask me what will become of liberty. I don't understand you. I don't know what this liberty is that you
speak of; you have been arguing about its nature for so
long that it is certain you know nothing about it. If you
would like to know, or rather if you could peacefully
examine with me what it is, then turn to the letter L.

DIEU · GOD

In the reign of Arcadius, Logomachos, a theologian of
Constantinople, went to Scythia and stopped at the foot
of the Caucasus, in the fertile plains of Zephirim, at the

frontier of Colchis. Dondindac, a kind old man, was in
his great lower hall, between his large sheepfold and his
spacious barn; he was on his knees with his wife, five
sons and five daughters, relations and servants, and all
were singing the praises of God after a light meal.
"What are you doing there, idolator?" Logomachos
asked him. —"I'm not an idolator," said Dondindac.
—"You must be an idolator," said Logomachos, "because you are a Scythian and not a Greek. Come, tell
me, what were you singing in your barbarous Scythian
jargon?" —"All languages count equally in the ears
of God," replied the Scythian. "We were singing his
praises." —"Now that's quite extraordinary," rejoined
the theologian; "a Scythian family that prays to God
without having been instructed by us!" And he started a
conversation with Dondindac, the Scythian; for the
theologian knew a little Scythian, and the other a little
Greek. This conversation has been rediscovered in a
manuscript preserved in the library at Constantinople.

LOGOMACHOS. Let's see if you know your catechism.
Why do you pray to God?

DONDINDAC. Because it is right to worship the supreme
Being, from whom we have everything.

LOGOMACHOS. Not bad for a barbarian! And what do
you ask of him?

DONDINDAC. I thank him for the blessings I enjoy, and
even for the evils with which he tries me; but I take care
not to ask anything of him: he knows what we need
better than we do; and besides, I would be afraid to ask
for good weather when my neighbor is asking for rain.

LOGOMACHOS. Ah! I thought he'd say something foolish. Let's begin farther back. Barbarian, who told you
that there is a God?

DONDINDAC. All nature.

LOGOMACHOS. That's not enough. What is your idea of
God?

DONDINDAC. The idea of my creator, of my master, who will reward me if I do good, and who will punish me if I do evil.

LOGOMACHOS. All these are bagatelles, platitudes! Let's come to the essential. Is God infinite *secundum quid*, or according to his essence?

DONDINDAC. I don't understand you.

LOGOMACHOS. Brute beast! Is God in one place or outside every place, or in every place?

DONDINDAC. I have no idea . . . just as you like.

LOGOMACHOS. Ignoramus! Can he cause things that existed, never to have existed? Or a stick not to have two ends? Does he see the future as future or as present? What does he do to draw being from non-being, and to annihilate being?

DONDINDAC. I've never examined these matters.

LOGOMACHOS. What a lout! All right, I must lower my level, adapt myself. Tell me, my friend, do you believe that matter can be eternal?

DONDINDAC. What do I care whether it exists from all eternity or not? I myself don't exist from all eternity. God is always my master; he has given me the notion of justice; I must follow it; I don't want to be a philosopher, I want to be a man.

LOGOMACHOS. One has a lot of trouble with these fatheads. Let's go step by step: what is God?

DONDINDAC. My sovereign, my judge, my father.

LOGOMACHOS. That's not what I asked. What is his nature?

DONDINDAC. To be powerful and good.

LOGOMACHOS. But is he corporeal or spiritual?

DONDINDAC. How should I know that?

LOGOMACHOS. What? You don't know what a spirit is?

DONDINDAC. Not in the slightest: what good would it do me? Would I be more just then? Would I be a better husband, better father, better employer, better citizen?

LOGOMACHOS. It's absolutely necessary to teach you what a spirit is; listen: it's, it's, it's. . . . I'll tell you some other time.

DONDINDAC. I'm afraid you will tell me less what it is than what it is not. Permit me to ask you a question in my turn. Once I saw one of your temples: why do you paint God with a long beard?

LOGOMACHOS. That's a very difficult question, and demands preliminary instruction.

DONDINDAC. Before I receive your instruction, I must tell you what happened to me one day. I had just had a toilet built at the end of my garden, when I heard a mole arguing with a June bug: "Here's a fine building," said the mole. "It must have been a pretty powerful mole who did this work." —"You're joking," said the June bug; "it's a mighty talented June bug who is the architect of this building." From that time on I resolved never to argue.

DIVINITÉ DE JÉSUS
DIVINITY OF JESUS

The Socinians, who are considered blasphemers, don't recognize the divinity of Jesus Christ. They dare to maintain, with the philosophers of antiquity, with the Jews, the Mohammedans, and so many other nations, that the idea of a God-man is monstrous, that the distance between a God and man is infinite, and that it is impossible for the infinite, immense, eternal Being to have been contained in a perishable body.

They have the effrontery to cite Eusebius, bishop of Caesarea, in support of their view. In his *Ecclesiastical History*, book I, chapter 11, he declares that it is absurd that the unbegotten, immutable nature of almighty God should take the form of a man. They cite the Church Fathers Justin and Tertullian, who said the same thing: Justin in his Dialogue with Tryphon, and Tertullian in his Discourse against Praxeas.

They cite St. Paul, who never calls Jesus Christ God, and who very often calls him man. They push audacity to the point of maintaining that the Christians spent three entire centuries inventing the apotheosis of Jesus, bit by bit, and that they raised this astonishing edifice only in imitation of the pagans, who had deified mortals. According to them, Jesus was at first regarded merely as a man inspired by God; later, as a creature more perfect than others. Some time later, as St. Paul says, he was given a place above the angels. He became an emanation of God manifested in time. This was not enough; they had him born before time itself. Finally, he was made God, consubstantial with God.

Crellius, Voquelsius, Alexander Natalis, Hornebeck, have supported all these blasphemies with arguments that astound the wise and pervert the feeble. It was Faustus Socinus above all who spread the seeds of this doctrine through Europe; and at the end of the sixteenth century it almost established a new Christian sect of which there were already more than three hundred brands.

DOGMES · DOGMAS

On the 18th of February of the year 1763 of the common era, with the sun entering the sign of Pisces, I was conveyed to heaven, as all my friends know. Borac, Mahomet's mare, was not my mount; Elijah's fiery chariot was not my car; I was carried neither on the elephant of Sammonocodom the Siamese, nor on the horse of St. George, patron saint of England, nor on St. Anthony's pig: I confess without guile that I took my trip I don't know how.

You can imagine how dazzled I was; but what you won't believe is that I saw the judging of all the dead. And who were the judges? They were, if you please, all those who had done well by mankind. Confucius, Solon, Socrates, Titus, the Antonines, Epictetus, all the great men who, having taught and practiced the virtues God demands, alone seemed to have the right to pronounce his judgments.

I won't say what thrones they were sitting on, nor how many million celestial beings were prostrated before the creator of all globes, nor what a crowd of inhabitants from these innumerable globes appeared before the judges. Here I shall only give an account of a few small, quite interesting details that struck me.

I observed that every dead man who pleaded his case and paraded his fine sentiments was instantly surrounded by all the witnesses of his true actions. For example, when the cardinal of Lorraine boasted that he had got the Council of Trent to adopt some of his views, and demanded eternal life as a reward for his orthodoxy, immediately courtesans (or ladies of the court) appeared, each bearing on her forehead the number of her rendezvous with the cardinal. I saw those who had laid the foundations of the League with him; all the accomplices of his perverse plans surrounded him.

Opposite the cardinal of Lorraine was C . . . . . , who boasted in his crude dialect that he had kicked the papal idol with his feet after others had thrown it down. "I wrote against painting and sculpture," he said; "I made it clear that good works count for nothing at all, and I proved that it is diabolical to dance the minuet: drive the cardinal of Lorraine away quickly, and put me at the side of St. Paul."

As he was speaking, I saw a burning stake near him; a frightful specter, wearing a half-burned Spanish frill around his neck, rose from the flames with dreadful cries. "Monster," he shouted, "execrable monster, tremble! recognize S . . . . , whom you put to death by the cruelest of tortures, because he had argued with you about the manner in which three persons can make a single substance." Then all the judges ordered the cardinal of Lorraine thrown into the abyss, but C . . . . . to be punished even more severely.

I saw an immense crowd of dead who said: "I believed, I believed"; but on their foreheads it was written, "I acted" and they were condemned.

The Jesuit Le Tellier proudly appeared, the bull *Unigenitus* in his hand. But at his side a pile of two thousand *lettres de cachet* suddenly heaped itself up. A Jansenist set fire to them: Le Tellier was burned to a cinder; and the Jansenist, who had plotted no less than the Jesuit, received his share of burning too.

I saw troops of fakirs arriving right and left, Buddhist priests, white, black, and grey monks, who all imagined that in order to pay their court to the supreme Being, they must either chant, or scourge themselves, or walk stark naked. I heard a terrible voice ask them: "What good did you do mankind?" This question was succeeded by a gloomy silence; no one dared to answer; presently they were all led off to the madhouse of the universe: that's one of the biggest buildings you could imagine.

One shouted: "We must believe in the metamorphoses of Xaca"; another: "In those of Sammonocodom." — "Bacchus stopped the sun and the moon," said this one. "The gods resurrected Pelops," said that one. "Here is the bull *In Coena Domini*," said a newcomer; and the judges' usher shouted: "To the madhouse, to the mad-house!"

When all these cases were completed, I heard this judgment promulgated:

"By order of the eternal Creator, Conserver, Rewarder, Avenger, Forgiver, etc., etc., be it known to all the inhabitants of the hundred thousand millions of billions of worlds it has pleased us to create, that we will never judge any of the said inhabitants on their chimerical ideas, but solely on their actions; for such is our justice."

I confess that this was the first time I heard such an edict: all the ones I have read on the little grain of sand where I was born end with these words: *For such is our pleasure.*

ÉGALITÉ · EQUALITY

What does a dog owe to a dog, and a horse to a horse? Nothing. No animal depends on his kind; but since man has received the gleam of divinity called *reason*, what is the result? He becomes a slave almost everywhere in the world.

If this world were what it seems it should be, that is, if man found easy and assured subsistence everywhere, and a climate congenial to his nature, it is clear that one man couldn't possibly have enslaved another. If this globe were covered with wholesome fruits; if the air which should contribute to our life gave us neither diseases nor death; if man needed no other lodging and no other bed than do deer and roe: then the Genghis Khans and Tamerlanes would have no valets but their children, who would be people good enough to help them in their old age.

In this natural condition, which all the quadrupeds, birds, and reptiles enjoy, man would be as happy as they, and domination would then be a chimera, an absurdity no one would think of; for why seek servants when you need no service?

If some individual with a tyrannical head and muscular arm got the idea of enslaving his weaker neighbor, the business would be impossible; the oppressed would be two hundred miles away before the oppressor had made his preparations.

Thus all men would necessarily be equal, if they were without needs. It is the misery attached to our species that subordinates one man to another; it is not inequality which is the real evil, it is dependence. It matters very little if some man is called His Highness, and another, His

Holiness; but it is hard to have to serve one or the other.

A numerous family cultivates good soil; two small neighboring families till sterile and obstinate fields: the two poor families must either serve the opulent family or cut its collective throat; there's no problem about that. One of the two poor families offers its services to the rich one so it may have bread; the other attacks the rich family and is beaten. In the serving family we see the origin of domestics and laborers; in the beaten family, the origin of slaves.

On our miserable globe it is impossible for men living in society not to be divided into two classes, one the rich who command, the other the poor who serve; and these two subdivide themselves into a thousand, and these thousand have still several further divisions.

All the poor are not absolutely miserable. Most of them are born in that condition, and continual labor prevents them from feeling their situation too keenly; but when they do feel it, then you see wars, like that of the popular party against the senatorial party in Rome, or the peasant wars in Germany, England, and France. Sooner or later all these wars end with the enslavement of the people, because the powerful have money, and within a state money is the master of all: I say within a state, because the same is not true between nation and nation. The nation that puts the sword to the best use will always subjugate the one that has more gold and less courage.

Every man is born with a powerful urge toward domination, wealth, and pleasures, and with a strong taste for laziness; consequently every man would like the money and the women or the girls of others, to be their master, to subject them to all his caprices, and to do nothing, or at least to do only the very agreeable things. Obviously, with such benign dispositions it is just as impossible for men to be equal as it is impossible for two preachers or two professors of theology not to be jealous of one another.

Mankind, such as it is, cannot go on existing unless there is an infinite number of useful men who possess nothing at all; for surely a man who is well off will not leave his land to labor on yours; and if you need a pair of shoes, it won't be a *maître des requêtes* who'll make them for you. Thus, equality is at once the most natural and at the same time the most chimerical of things.

Since men go to excess in everything whenever they can, they have exaggerated this inequality; in some countries they maintain that a citizen is not permitted to leave the country in which he was born by chance; obviously the meaning of this law is: *This country is so bad, and so badly governed, that we forbid every individual to leave it, lest everybody leave it.* Do better: create in all your subjects the desire to remain at home, and in foreigners, the desire to come there.

In his heart of hearts every man has the right to think himself entirely equal to other men; it doesn't follow from this that a cardinal's cook should order his master to cook him a dinner; but the cook can say: "I am a man like my master, like him I was born crying; like me, he will die in anguish, with the same ceremonies. Both of us perform the same animal functions. If the Turks took Rome and I became a cardinal and my master a cook, I should take him into my service." This whole speech is reasonable and right; but while he waits for the Grand Turk to take Rome, the cook must do his duty, or human society is perverted.

As for the man who is neither a cardinal's cook nor clothed with any other public office; as for the private person who has no connections, but who is offended at being received everywhere with an air of patronage or contempt, who clearly sees that several *monsignori* have neither more knowledge, nor more wit, nor more vir-

tue than he, and who is bored when he is in their ante-
rooms on occasion, what should he do? He should leave.

ENFER · HELL

As soon as men started to live in society, they must
have noticed that some guilty persons were able to escape the severity of the laws. Public crimes were punished: it was necessary to establish a check on secret
crimes; religion alone could be that check. The Persians,
the Chaldeans, the Egyptians, the Greeks, invented
punishments after life; and, of all the ancient nations we
know, the Jews were the only ones who accepted none
but temporal punishment. It is ridiculous to believe, or to
pretend to believe, on the basis of some highly obscure
passages, that hell had a place in the ancient laws of the
Jews, in their Leviticus, in their Decalogue, when
the author of these laws says not a single word that
could have the slightest reference to punishment in an
after-life. We should have the right to tell the editor of
the Pentateuch: "You are an inconsistent man, without
probity or reason, and quite unworthy of the name of
legislator which you arrogate to yourself. What! You
know a doctrine with as restraining an influence, as
necessary to the people, as the doctrine of hell, and you
don't expressly proclaim it? And, while it is accepted in
all the nations around you, you are content to let this
dogma be inferred by several commentators who come
four thousand years after you and torture some of your
words to find in them what you didn't say? Either you
are an ignoramus, who doesn't know that this belief
was universal in Egypt, Chaldea, and Persia; or you
used bad judgment if, knowing this dogma, you didn't
make it the basis of your religion."

At best the authors of the Jewish laws might reply: "We concede that we are exceedingly ignorant; that we learned to write only very late; we concede that our people was a savage and barbaric horde that wandered through impassable deserts for nearly half a century; that it finally usurped possession of a small country by means of the most terrible pillage and the most detestable cruelties ever recorded in history. We had no traffic with civilized nations: how can you expect us (us, the most terrestrial of men) to invent a wholly spiritual system?

"We employed the word corresponding to *soul* only to signify *life;* we knew our God and his ministers, his angels, only as corporeal beings; the distinction between soul and body, the idea of a life after death, can only be the fruit of long meditation and highly refined philosophizing. Ask the Hottentots and the Negroes, who inhabit a country a hundred times more extensive than ours, whether they are acquainted with the life to come. We thought we had done enough when we persuaded our people that God punishes malefactors to the fourth generation, whether with leprosy, sudden death, or with the loss of whatever little property they may possess."

One might reply to this apology: "You have invented a system whose absurdity is obvious; for the malefactor who is in good health and whose family flourishes will certainly laugh at you."

Then the apologist for the Jewish law might answer: "You are wrong; for every criminal who thinks clearly there are a hundred who don't think at all. The man who had committed a crime and felt himself punished neither in himself nor in his son, would fear for his grandson. More, if he didn't at the time have some stinking sore (which used to be very common among us), he would surely get one in the course of a few years: there are always calamities to afflict a family, and one could easily awaken the belief that these calamities had been sent by a divine hand, the avenger of secret offenses."

It would be easy to reply to this reply, and say: "Your excuse is worthless, for it happens every day that honest men lose their health and wealth; and, since there is no family to which calamities do not happen, if these calamities are God's punishments, all your families must have been families of rascals."

The Jewish priest might then reply further; he would say that there are calamities attached to human nature, and others sent expressly by God. But we could show this logician how ridiculous it is to think that fever and hail are sometimes a divine punishment, sometimes a natural event.

In a word, the Pharisees and the Essenes among the Jews accepted a belief in hell after their own fashion; this dogma had already spread from the Greeks to the Romans, and was adopted by the Christians.

Several Church Fathers did not believe in eternal punishments: it seemed absurd to them that some poor man should burn through eternity for stealing a goat. Vergil may very well say in the sixth book of the *Aeneid:*

> *Sedet aeternumque sedebit*
> *Infelix Theseus*
>
> [*So sits and will forever sit*
> *Unhappy Theseus.*
>   *Aeneid*, VI, 617-618]

But he claims in vain that Theseus sits forever in a chair, and that this is his punishment. Others believed that Theseus was a hero with a seat, not in hell, but in the Elysian fields.

Not long ago a good and honest Huguenot minister preached and wrote that the damned would one day be pardoned, that sin and suffering must be commensurate, and that the slip of a moment cannot deserve an infinite punishment. His colleagues, the preachers, dismissed this indulgent judge; one of them told him: "My friend, I no more believe in eternal hell than you do; but it is a good thing for your servant, your tailor, and even your lawyer to believe in it."

ENTHOUSIASME · ENTHUSIASM

This Greek word signifies a convulsion of the entrails, internal agitation. Did the Greeks invent the word to express the jolts experienced by the nerves, the dilation and tightening of the intestines, the violent contraction of the heart, the sudden flow of those fiery spirits which mount from the entrails to the brain whenever we are passionately moved?

Or was the word enthusiasm, trouble in the entrails, first applied to the contortions of the Pythia who, on the tripod at Delphi, received the spirit of Apollo in a place that seems made to receive bodies only?

What do we understand by enthusiasm? What nuances there are in our feelings! Approval, sensibility, emotion, distress, possession, passion, frenzy, madness, fury, rage: these are all the states this poor human soul can pass through.

A geometer attends a moving tragedy; he notices only that it is well directed. A young man beside him is moved and notices nothing; a woman cries; another young man is so carried away that, unhappily for him, he decides to write a tragedy too: he has caught the disease of enthusiasm.

The centurion or military tribune who thought war merely a profession in which he might make a small fortune went as calmly to battle as a roofer climbs a roof. Caesar wept when he saw the statue of Alexander.

Ovid speaks of love only wittily. Sappho expressed the enthusiasm of that passion and if it is true that it cost her her life, then in her case enthusiasm became madness.

Partisan spirit is a marvelous spur to enthusiasm; there is no faction that doesn't have its fanatics.

Enthusiasm is above all the characteristic of misdirected piety. The young fakir who sees the end of his nose when he says his prayers gradually warms up until he believes that if he loads himself with chains weighing fifty pounds, the supreme Being will be deeply obligated to him. He goes to sleep with his imagination filled with Brahma, whom he then naturally sees in a dream. In that state, when he is neither asleep nor awake, sparks sometimes come from his eyes; he sees Brahma refulgent with light, he falls into ecstacies, and often the malady becomes incurable.

It is extremely rare to see reason joined with enthusiasm; reason consists in always seeing things as they are. The man who experiences double vision in his drunkenness is deprived of his reason at that moment.

Enthusiasm is exactly like wine; it can excite so much tumult in the blood vessels, and violent vibrations in the nerves, that reason is completely overthrown by it. It may cause only slight jolts that merely stimulate a little more activity in the brain; this is what happens in great outbursts of eloquence, and above all in sublime poetry. Reasonable enthusiasm is the characteristic of great poets.

This reasonable enthusiasm is the perfection of their art; at one time it was responsible for the belief that they were inspired by the gods, which has never been said of other artists.

How can rationality govern enthusiasm? When a poet begins by sketching in the design of his painting then reason holds the pencil. But when he wishes to animate his characters and mark them with the passions, his imagination kindles and enthusiasm is at work; it is a race horse speeding along its course; but the course has been correctly laid out.

ESPRIT FAUX · UNSOUND MIND

We have blind men, one-eyed men, squint-eyed men, far-sighted and near-sighted men, clear-sighted and con-fused men, weak-eyed and indefatigable men. All this is a pretty faithful image of our understanding; but there is very little sight that is wholly erroneous. There are hardly any men who always mistake a cock for a horse, or a chamber pot for a house. Why then do we often meet minds, in other respects tolerably sound, that are absolutely unsound in important matters? Why does the same Siamese who will never allow himself to be de-ceived when it is a question of paying him three rupees, believe firmly in the metamorphoses of Sammonoco-dom? Through what strange caprice do sensible men resemble Don Quixote, who thought he saw giants where others saw only windmills? Still, Don Quixote had more excuse than the Siamese who believes that Sammonocodom came to this earth several times, and the Turk who is persuaded that Mahomet put half the moon in his sleeve; for Don Quixote, smitten with the notion that he must combat giants, might have imagined that a giant must have a body as big as a windmill, and arms as long as the mill's sails; but on what supposition can a sensible man persuade himself that half the moon en-tered into a sleeve, or a Sammonocodom descended from heaven to fly kites in Siam, cut down a forest, and do all kinds of hocus-pocus?

The greatest geniuses may be unsound about a principle they have accepted without examination. Newton was thoroughly unsound when he commented on the Apocalypse.

All that certain tyrants over souls wish for the men they teach is that they should have unsound minds. A fakir trains an extremely promising child; he employs five or six years to drive it into his head that the god Fo appeared to men in the shape of a white elephant, and he persuades the child that he shall be whipped for five hundred thousand years after his death if he doesn't believe in such metamorphoses. He adds that at the end of the world, the enemy of the god Fo will appear to do battle with this divinity.

The child studies and becomes a prodigy; he bases arguments on the lessons of his master; he finds that Fo could have changed himself into a white elephant only because that is the most beautiful of animals. "The kings of Siam and of Pegu," he says, "made war on each other over a white elephant; surely, if Fo had not been hidden in that elephant, these kings would not have been so mad as to fight for the possession of a mere animal. The enemy of Fo will appear to defy him at the end of the world; surely that enemy must be a rhinoceros, for the rhinoceros wars with the elephant."

This is how the fakir's learned pupil argues at a mature age, and he becomes one of the lights of India; the subtler his mind, the more unsound; and later he will shape minds as unsound as his own.

Show all these fanatics a little geometry, and they learn it easily enough; but, strange to say, their understanding is not thus corrected; they perceive the truths of geometry, but it doesn't teach them to weigh probabilities; they have decided on their course; all their life their thinking will be askew, and I am sorry for them.

ÉTATS, GOUVERNEMENTS
STATES, GOVERNMENTS
Which Is the Best?

Up to this very day I haven't met anybody who didn't govern some state. I'm not speaking of messieurs the ministers, who actually govern, some for two or three years, others for six months, others for six weeks; I'm speaking of all those other men who parade their systems of government at dinner or in their study, who reform armies, the Church, the judiciary, and the finances.

The abbé de Bourzeis set about to govern France around the year 1645; under the name of cardinal de Richelieu, he composed that *Testament politique* in which he would enlist the nobility in the cavalry for three years, have the property tax paid to the Courts of Finance and the *parlements*, deprive the king of the yield of the salt-tax; above all he asserts that to begin a war with fifty thousand men, one should raise a hundred thousand for the sake of economy. He claims that Provence alone has many more seaports than Spain and Italy put together.

The abbé de Bourzeis never traveled. Besides, his work teems with anachronisms and errors; he makes the cardinal de Richelieu sign his name in a way he never did, just as he makes him speak as he never spoke. Moreover, he devotes an entire chapter to telling us how *reason should rule a state*, and to try to prove the validity of his new idea. This compendium of obscurities, this bastard of the abbé de Bourzeis, has long been considered the legitimate son of the cardinal de Richelieu; and all the Academicians, in their acceptance speeches, make a point of praising it extravagantly as a masterpiece of politics.

Sieur Gratien de Courtilz, seeing the success of Richelieu's *Testament politique*, had the *Testament de Colbert* printed at The Hague, with a fine letter from M. Colbert to the king. It is clear that if this minister had made such a testament, it must have been suppressed; yet this book has been cited by several authors.

Next, another scoundrel, whose name we don't know, came up with the *Testament de Louvois*, if possible still worse than that of Colbert; an abbé de Chevremont also made Charles, duke of Lorraine, write a testament. We have had the *Testaments politiques* of cardinal Alberoni, of Marshal de Belle-Isle, and finally of Mandrin.

M. de Bois-Guillebert, author of the *Détail de la France*, printed in 1695, proposed the impracticable project of a royal tithe in the name of marshal de Vauban.

In 1720, a madman named La Jonchère, who had nothing to eat, wrote a financial project in four volumes; and several fools have cited this production as a work of La Jonchère, the chief of the treasury, fancying that a treasurer couldn't write a bad book on finance.

But it must also be admitted that quite intelligent men, perhaps quite worthy of governing, have written on the administration of states, France, or Spain, or England. Their books have done a great deal of good: not that they reformed the ministers who were in office when these books appeared, for a minister does not and cannot reform himself; he has attained his growth; he doesn't have time to listen to instruction and advice; the current of business sweeps him along; but these good books educate young men destined for office; they educate princes, and the next generation is well trained.

In recent times the strength and weakness of all the different kinds of governments has been closely examined. Tell me then, you who have traveled, who have read and observed, in what state, under what form of government would you like to have been born? I imagine that a great landowner in France would not object to being born in Germany; he would be a sovereign instead of being a subject. A peer of France would be highly pleased with the privileges of the English peerage; he would be a legislator. The judge and the financier would be better off in France than elsewhere.

But what country would a wise and free man choose, a man of middle station and without prejudices?

A very learned member of the council of Pondichery returned to Europe by land with a Brahmin, who was better educated than Brahmins commonly are. "What do you think of the government of the Grand Mogul?" asked the councilor. "It's abominable," replied the Brahmin. "How do you expect a state to be well governed by Tartars? Our rajahs, our omras, our nabobs, are very well satisfied, but the citizens really aren't, and millions of citizens amount to something."

The councilor and the Brahmin traversed all upper Asia, discussing government. "I have been thinking," said the Brahmin; "there isn't a republic in all this vast part of the world." —"There used to be one at Tyre," said the councilor, "but it didn't last long. There was another one near Arabia Petraea, in a little corner called Palestine, if one can honor with the name of republic a horde of thieves and usurers, sometimes governed by judges, sometimes by a kind of king, sometimes by grand pontiffs. These people were enslaved seven or eight times, and were finally driven from the country they had usurped."

"I imagine," said the Brahmin, "that we should find only very few republics on this earth. Men rarely deserve to govern themselves. This happiness should belong only to small nations hiding themselves on islands, or between mountains, like rabbits who steal away from

carnivorous beasts; but in the long run they are discovered and devoured."

When the two travelers had arrived in Asia Minor,
the councilor said to the Brahmin: "Can you believe it,
there was once a republic established in a corner of Italy
that lasted more than five hundred years and possessed
the Asia Minor we are in now, Asia, Africa, Greece,
Gaul, Spain, and all of Italy?" —"Then it quickly
changed into a monarchy?" suggested the Brahmin.
—"You've guessed it," said the other, "but that monarchy has fallen, and every day we write fine disserta-
tions to discover the causes of its decline and fall."
—"You're wasting your time," said the Indian; "that
empire fell because it existed. All must fall; I hope that
the same thing will happen to the empire of the Grand
Mogul." —"By the way," said the European, "do you
think that a despotic state requires more honor, and a
republic more virtue?" When it had been explained to
the Indian what was meant by honor, he replied that
honor was more necessary to a republic, and that a mon-
archical state needed a good deal more virtue. "For,"
he said, "a man who claims election by the people won't
receive it if he has dishonored himself; whereas at court
he might easily obtain some sort of office, according to
the maxim of a great prince that to succeed, a courtier
must have neither honor nor temper. As for virtue, one
must have a prodigious lot of it to dare to speak the
truth at court. The virtuous man has it much easier in a
republic; he has nobody to flatter."

"Do you think," asked the man from Europe, "that
laws and religions are made for climates, just as furs are
needed in Moscow and gauzy stuff in Delhi?" —"Yes,
certainly," said the Brahmin; "all the laws dealing with
physical matters are calculated for the meridian we inhabit; a German needs only one woman, a Persian needs
three or four. The same is true of religious rites. If I were

a Christian, how would you expect me to say mass in my province, where there is neither bread nor wine? As for dogmas, that's another matter; climate has nothing to do with them. Didn't your religion begin in Asia, whence it was driven out? Doesn't it now exist near the Baltic Sea, where it was unknown?"

"In what state, under what kind of rule, would you like to live best?" asked the councilor. "Anywhere else but at home," said his companion, "and I've found many Siamese, Tonkinese, Persians, and Turks who say the same." —"But, once again," asked the European, "which state would you choose?" The Brahmin replied: "The one in which men obeyed the laws alone." —"That's an old answer," said the councilor. "That doesn't make it any worse," said the Brahmin. "Where is that country?" asked the councilor. The Brahmin said: "We must look for it." (*See* the article GENÈVE.)

ÉVANGILE · GOSPEL

Which are the first gospels?—That is an important question to solve. Whatever Abbadie says about it, it is an established truth that none of the first Church Fathers, up to and including Irenaeus, cites a single passage of the four Gospels we know. On the contrary, the Alogi, the Theodotians, steadily rejected the Gospel of St. John, and always spoke of it with contempt, as St. Epiphanius asserts in his 34th homily. Our enemies further observe that the first Church Fathers not only do not ever cite our Gospels but quote several passages which are found only in the apocryphal gospels refused a place in the canon.

For example, St. Clement reports that our Lord, asked about the time his kingdom would come, replied: "That shall come to pass when two make only one, when what is outside shall resemble what is inside, and when there shall be no more male or female." Now it must be admitted that this passage cannot be found in any of our Gospels. There are a hundred examples to prove this truth; they can be found in the *Examen critique* by M. Fréret, permanent secretary of the Académie des Belles Lettres in Paris.

The learned Fabricius took the trouble of assembling all the ancient gospels which time has preserved; that of James seems to be the first. It is certain that it still has much authority in some churches of the East. It is called *first Gospel*. The Passion and the Resurrection, supposedly written by Nicodemus, remain to us. The Gospel of Nicodemus is quoted by St. Justin and Tertullian; there we find the names of the accusers of our Savior, Annas, Caiaphas, Somne, Dothaim, Gamaliel, Judas, Levi, Nephtalim: the care with which these names are reported gives the work an appearance of authenticity. Our adversaries have concluded that since there are so many false gospels which were at first accepted as true, those which are the basis of our belief today might also have been forged. They dwell at length on the faith of the first heretics who died for these apocryphal gospels. Therefore, they say, there were dupes, and also forgers and seducers, who died for error: that martyrs should have died for the truth of our religion is no proof of it.

They add further that the martyrs were never asked: "Do you believe in the Gospel of John or the Gospel of James?" The pagans could not base interrogations on books they didn't know: the magistrates punished some Christians as disturbers of the public peace, but they never interrogated them about our four Gospels. It was only under Trajan that these books became at all known to the Romans, and they were not to be found in the hands of the public until the last years of the reign of Diocletian. For these reasons the rigid Socinians regard our four Gospels as clandestine works only, fabricated about a century after Jesus Christ and carefully hidden from the gentiles for another century; works, they say, written crudely by crude men, who addressed themselves only to the mob for a long time. We don't wish to repeat their other blasphemies here. This sect, although rather widespread, is today as hidden as the first gospels were. It is all the more difficult to convert them since they believe in their reason alone. The other Christians battle against them only in the holy way of Scripture: thus it is impossible that the one and the other, having always been enemies, should ever agree.

(*By the abbé de Tilladet*)

D'ÉZÉCHIEL · OF EZEKIEL

About Some Peculiar Passages in This Prophet, and about Some Ancient Practices

We all know today that we shouldn't judge ancient practices by modern ones: the man who would reform the court of Alcinous in the *Odyssey* on the model of the Grand Turk's or Louis XIV's would not be well received by scholars; the man who would criticize Vergil for representing king Evander covered with a bear skin and accompanied by two dogs, in order to receive ambassadors, would be a poor critic.

The morals of the ancient Egyptians and Jews were even more different from ours than those of king Alcinous, his daughter Nausicaa, and good old Evander.

Ezekiel, a slave among the Chaldeans, had a vision near the little river of Chebar which flows into the Euphrates. We must not be surprised that he saw ani-

mals with four heads and four wings or with calves'
feet; or wheels revolving by themselves, having the
spirit of life; these images even please the imagination.
But several critics have been repelled by the Lord's command to him to eat bread made of barley, wheat, and
millet, smeared with human excrement, for three hundred and ninety days.

The prophet exclaimed: "Phew! phew! phew! Up to
now my soul hasn't been polluted," and the Lord replied: "Very well, instead of human excrement I'll allow you cow dung; you shall knead your bread with
cow dung."

Since it isn't customary to eat such jam on one's
bread, most men have found these orders unworthy of
the divine majesty. Still, it must be admitted that cow
dung and all the diamonds of the Grand Mogul are perfectly equal, not only in the eyes of a divine being, but
in those of a true philosopher; and as for the reasons
God might have to command the prophet to eat such a
lunch, it is not for us to inquire into them.

It is enough to see that these commands, which seem
strange to us, did not appear so to the Jews.

True, in the time of St. Jerome the Synagogue did
not permit the reading of Ezekiel before the age of
thirty; but that was because in chapter 18 he says that
the son shall no longer be visited with the sins of his
father, and that it shall no longer be said: "The fathers
have eaten sour grapes, and the children's teeth are set
on edge."

This was in express contradiction to Moses, who declares in chapter 28 of Numbers that the sins of the
fathers are visited on the children unto the third and
fourth generation.

In chapter 20, Ezekiel further makes the Lord say that
he has given the Jews *statutes which are not good.* This
is why the Synagogue prohibited young men reading

that which might make them doubt the indisputability of the laws of Moses.

The censors of our time are still more astonished by chapter 16 of Ezekiel: here is how the prophet sets about publishing the crimes of Jerusalem. He introduces the Lord as speaking to a girl, and the Lord says to her: "On the day you were born, your navel string was not cut, nor were you rubbed with salt; you were naked, I took pity on you; you grew up, your breasts were formed, and your hair had grown; I passed by you and looked upon you, behold, you were at the age for love; I covered your nakedness, I spread my skirt over you; you became mine; I washed you, anointed you, clothed you, and shod you with leather; I decked you with ornaments, bracelets, and a chain on your neck; I put a ring on your nose, and earrings in your ears, and a crown on your head, etc.

"But you trusted in your beauty, and lavished your harlotries on any passer-by. . . . And you built yourself a house of prostitution . . . , and you played the harlot even in public places, and you opened your legs to all passers-by . . . , and you played the harlot with Egyptians . . . , and finally you paid your lovers, you gave your gifts to all your lovers that they might sleep with you . . . ; and you gave hire, while no hire was given to you, so you were different from other women. . . . The proverb is, *like mother, like daughter;* this is what they will say of you, etc."

They object still more to chapter 23. A mother had two daughters who had lost their virginity early: the elder was called Ohola, and the younger Oholibah . . . : "Ohola doted on warriors, governors, commanders; she had lain with Egyptians from her earliest youth. . . . Oholibah, her sister, committed far more fornications with officers, governors, and desirable horsemen; she uncovered her nakedness; she multiplied her fornications; she doted upon the embraces of those whose members were like those of asses, and whose issue was like that of horses. . . ."

Still, these descriptions, which shock so many weak spirits, merely signify the iniquities of Jerusalem and Samaria; the expressions that appear bold to us were not so then. The same naiveté shows itself fearlessly in more than one scriptural passage. There is frequent talk of opening the vulva. The terms Scripture uses to describe the coupling of Boaz with Ruth, or Judah with his daughter-in-law, are not indecent in Hebrew, but would be so in our language.

People unashamed of their nakedness do not cover themselves with a veil; why should people have blushed in those days over naming the genitals, since they touched the genitals of those to whom some promise was being made? It was a mark of respect, a symbol of fidelity, as formerly in our country manorial lords put their hands into those of their feudal overlords.

We have translated the genitals as "thigh." Eliezer puts his hand over Abraham's thigh; Joseph puts his hand under Jacob's thigh. This custom was extremely ancient in Egypt. The Egyptians were so far from attaching any ignominy to what we neither dare uncover nor name, that they carried in procession a large image of the virile member, called *phallum*, to thank the gods for making this member serve for the propagation of mankind.

All this proves that our decorum is not the decorum of other nations. When was there more politeness among the Romans than in the century of Augustus? Nevertheless, Horace has no difficulty in saying, in a moral piece,

Nec vereor ne dum futuo vir rure recurrat

[*Nor do I, while fucking, fear her husband's return from the country.*

Horace, *Satires*, I, ii, 127]

Augustus employs the same expression in an epigram against Fulvia. With us, a man who would use the word that corresponds to *futuo* would be regarded as a drunken porter; this word, and several others employed by Horace and other authors, seems to us even more indecent than the expressions of Ezekiel. Let us get rid of all our prejudices when we read ancient authors or travel among far-away nations. Nature is the same everywhere, and practices are everywhere different.

One day I met a rabbi in Amsterdam, full of this subject. "Ah! my friend," he said, "how deeply we are obliged to you! You have revealed all the sublimities of Mosaic law, Ezekiel's lunch, his fine attitudes concerning the left side; Ohola and Oholibah are admirable things; those are models, brother, models forecasting that some day the Jewish people shall be the master of the whole world; but why have you omitted so many others which have nearly the same force? Why didn't you show the Lord telling the sage Hosea, in the second verse of the first chapter: 'Hosea, go take to yourself a wife of harlotry and have children of harlotry.' These are his very words. Hosea takes the young lady and has a son by her, and then a daughter, and later another son; and that too was a model, and the model lasted for three years. 'That is not all,' says the Lord in the third chapter, 'love a woman who is beloved of a paramour and is an adulteress.' Hosea obeyed; but it cost him fifteen écus and eighteen bushels of barley; for you know that there is very little grain in the promised land. But do you know what all this means?" —"No," I told him. "Neither do I," said the rabbi. A grave scholar approached and told us that these were ingenious fictions, all full of charm. "Ah, monsieur," a well-educated young man told him, "if you want fictions, believe me, take those of Homer, Vergil, and Ovid. Whoever likes the prophecies of Ezekiel deserves to have lunch with him."

FABLES

Aren't the most ancient fables obviously allegorical? Isn't the first fable we know, after our method of reckoning time, the one recorded in the ninth chapter of the Book of Judges? A king was to be chosen among the trees; the olive tree didn't wish to give up the care of its oil, nor the fig tree of its figs, nor the vine of its wine, nor the other trees of their fruits; the thistle, which wasn't good for anything, was made king, because it had thorns and could do mischief.

Isn't the ancient fable of Venus, as recorded in Hesiod, an allegory of nature as a whole? The means of generation had fallen from the ether onto the shore of the sea; Venus sprang from this precious foam; her first name was "lover of generation": could there be a more evident image? Venus is the goddess of beauty; beauty ceases to be lovable if it walks without the graces; beauty gives birth to love; love has features that pierce every heart; love wears a bandage that hides the faults of the beloved.

Wisdom, under the name of Minerva, is conceived in the brain of the master of the gods; the soul of man is a divine fire which Minerva shows to Prometheus, who employs this divine fire to give life to man.

It is impossible not to recognize in these fables a vivid picture of all nature. Most other fables are either corrupted ancient stories or the caprice of imagination. These ancient fables are like our modern tales: there are moral ones which are charming; there are also insipid ones.

The fables of the clever nations of antiquity were crudely imitated by the cruder nations; witness those of Bacchus, Hercules, Prometheus, Pandora, and so many others; they were the amusement of the ancient world. The barbarians who vaguely heard them talked about, accepted them into their savage mythology; and then they dared to say: "We were the ones who invented them." Alas! Poor unknown and unknowing nations who knew neither useful nor agreeable arts, who never even heard the name of geometry, can you say that you invented anything? You knew neither how to discover truths nor how to lie skillfully.

FANATISME · FANATICISM

Fanaticism is to superstition what delirium is to fever and rage to anger. The man visited by ecstasies and visions, who takes dreams for realities and his fancies for prophecies, is an enthusiast; the man who supports his madness with murder is a fanatic. Jean Diaz, in retreat at Nuremberg, was firmly convinced that the pope was the Antichrist of the Apocalypse, and that he bore the sign of the beast; he was merely an enthusiast; his brother, Bartholomew Diaz, who came from Rome to assassinate his brother out of piety, and who did in fact kill him for the love of God, was one of the most abominable fanatics ever raised up by superstition.

Polyeucte, who goes to the temple on a solemn holiday to knock over and smash the statues and ornaments, is a less dreadful but no less ridiculous fanatic than Diaz. The assassins of the duke François de Guise, of William, prince of Orange, of king Henri III, of king Henri IV, and of so many others, were fanatics sick with the same mania as Diaz'.

The most detestable example of fanaticism was that of the burghers of Paris who on St. Bartholomew's Night went about assassinating and butchering all their fellow citizens who did not go to mass, throwing them out of windows, cutting them in pieces.

There are cold-blooded fanatics: such as judges who condemn to death those who have committed no other crime than failing to think like them; and these judges are all the more guilty, all the more deserving of the execration of mankind, since, unlike Clément, Châtel, Ravaillac, Damiens, they were not suffering from an attack of insanity; surely they should have been able to listen to reason.

Once fanaticism has corrupted a mind, the malady is almost incurable. I have seen convulsionaries who, speaking of the miracles of St. Pâris, gradually grew impassioned despite themselves: their eyes got inflamed, their limbs trembled, madness disfigured their faces, and they would have killed anyone who contradicted them.

The only remedy for this epidemic malady is the philosophical spirit which, spread gradually, at last tames men's habits and prevents the disease from starting; for, once the disease has made any progress, one must flee and wait for the air to clear itself. Laws and religion are not strong enough against the spiritual pest; religion, far from being healthy food for infected brains, turns to poison in them. These miserable men have forever in their minds the example of Ehud, who assassinated king Eglon; of Judith, who cut off Holofernes' head while she was sleeping with him; of Samuel, who chopped king Agag in pieces. They cannot see that these examples which were respectable in antiquity are abominable in the present; they borrow their frenzies from the very religion that condemns them.

Even the law is impotent against these attacks of rage; it is like reading a court decree to a raving maniac. These fellows are certain that the holy spirit with which they are filled is above the law, that their enthusiasm is the only law they must obey.

What can we say to a man who tells you that he would rather obey God than men, and that therefore he is sure to go to heaven for butchering you?

Ordinarily fanatics are guided by rascals, who put the dagger into their hands; these latter resemble that Old Man of the Mountain who is supposed to have made imbeciles taste the joys of paradise and who promised them an eternity of the pleasures of which he had given them a foretaste, on condition that they assassinated all those he would name to them. There is only one religion in the world that has never been sullied by fanaticism, that of the Chinese men of letters. The schools of philosophers were not only free from this pest, they were its remedy; for the effect of philosophy is to make the soul tranquil, and fanaticism is incompatible with tranquility. If our holy religion has so often been corrupted by this infernal delirium, it is the madness of men which is at fault.

> *Ainsi du plumage qu'il eut*
> *Icare pervertit l'usage;*
> *Il le reçut pour son salut,*
> *Il s'en servit pour son dommage.*

> [*Thus Icarus abused*
> *His newly-acquired plumage:*
> *He got it for his flight,*
> *He used it to his damage.*
> Bertaut, Bishop of Séez]

FAUSSETÉ DES VERTUS HUMAINES
FALSENESS OF HUMAN VIRTUES

After the duke de La Rochefoucauld had set down his thoughts on egotism, and had laid bare this human motive, one monsieur Esprit, of the Oratory, wrote a captious book entitled: *De la fausseté des vertus humaines*. This Esprit said that there is no virtue, but was gracious enough to end each chapter by referring to Christian charity. Thus, according to sieur Esprit, neither Cato, nor Aristides, nor Marcus Aurelius, nor Epictetus were good men; for such can be found only among Christians. Among the Christians, there is virtue only among Catholics; among the Catholics, we must still exclude the Jesuits, the Oratorians' enemies; hence, virtue is to be found among the Jesuits' enemies alone.

This M. Esprit begins by saying that prudence is not a virtue, and his reason is that it is often deceived. That is like saying that Caesar was not really a great general because he was beaten at Dyrrhachium.

If M. Esprit had been a philosopher, he would not have examined prudence as a virtue but as a talent, as a useful, pleasing quality; for a scoundrel can be extremely prudent, and I have known some like that. Oh, what madness to claim that,

Nul n'aura de vertu *que nous et nos amis!*

[*No one has* virtue *but we and our friends!*]

What is virtue, my friend? It is to do good: let us do it, and that's enough. But we won't look into your motives. What! According to you there is no difference between the *président* de Thou and Ravaillac, between Cicero and that Popilius whose life he had saved and who still cut off Cicero's head for money? And you pronounce Epictetus and Porphyry rascals because they didn't follow our dogmas? Such insolence is revolting. I'll say no more about it, lest I grow furious.

FIN, CAUSES FINALES
END, FINAL CAUSES

A man, it seems, must be mad to deny that stomachs were made to digest, eyes to see, ears to hear.

On the other hand, a man must have a strange love of final causes to assert that rocks were created to build houses, and that silkworms are born in China so that we might have satin in Europe.

But, you say, if God evidently did one thing by design, then he did all things by design. It is ridiculous to admit Providence in one case and deny it in others. Everything that was done was foreseen, was arranged. No arrangement without object, no effect without cause; hence everything is equally the result, the product, of a final cause; hence it is as true to say that noses were made to wear glasses, and fingers to be decorated with diamonds, as it is to say that ears were shaped to hear sounds and eyes to receive light.

I think this difficulty can be cleared up easily. When the effects are invariably the same at all times and in all places, when these uniform effects are independent of the beings to which they belong, then there is evidently a final cause.

All animals have eyes, and they see; all have ears, and they hear; all a mouth, with which they eat; a stomach, or something approximately like it, with which they digest; all an opening through which they void excrement, all an instrument of generation: and these gifts of nature work in them without human skill taking a hand. Here are final causes clearly established, and it is to pervert our thinking faculty to deny so universal a truth.

But rocks do not make buildings at all times and in all places; all noses do not wear glasses; all fingers do not have a ring; all legs are not covered with silk stockings. Hence a silkworm is not made to cover my legs as your mouth is made to eat and your behind to sit on the toilet. Hence there are effects produced by final causes, and a very large number of effects which cannot be so named.

But the former and the latter take part equally in the plan of general Providence: surely nothing happens despite it, nor even without it. All that belongs to nature is uniform, immutable, the immediate work of the Master; it is he who created the laws by which the moon is three-quarters responsible for the ebb and flow of the ocean, and the sun one-quarter; it is he who gave a rotating movement to the sun, by which this star sends light rays into the eyes of men, crocodiles, and cats, in five and a half minutes.

But if after many centuries we hit on the idea of inventing shears and spits, to clip the wool of sheep with the first, and to roast them with the second in order to eat them, what may we infer from this but that God made us so that some day we might necessarily become skillful and carnivorous?

To be sure, sheep were not made expressly to be roasted and eaten, since several nations abstain from this enormity; men were not essentially created to massacre one another, for the Brahmins and the Quakers kill no one; yet the clay from which we are kneaded often produces massacres, as it produces slanders, futilities, persecutions, and impertinences. It is not that the creation of man is the final cause of our madness and our idiocies: for a final cause is universal and invariable at all times and in all places; yet the horrors and absurdities of the human species are no less in the eternal order of things. When we thresh our wheat, the flail is the final cause of the separation of the grains. But if that flail, threshing my grain, crushes a thousand insects, that doesn't happen by my settled will—nor does it happen by chance: these insects found themselves under my flail at this time, and they had to find themselves there.

It is a consequence of the nature of things that a man should be ambitious, that he should sometimes enlist other men, that he should be victor or vanquished; but we can never say: Man was created by God to be killed in war.

The instruments nature has given us cannot always be final causes in action, with an unfailing effect. Eyes made to see are not always open; every sense has its time of rest. There are even senses which we never use. For example, a miserable imbecile, shut up in a cloister at fourteen, forever shuts the door through which a new generation might emerge; but the final cause exists in her no less: it will operate as soon as she is free.

FOI · FAITH

One day, prince Pico della Mirandola met pope Alexander VI at the house of the courtesan Emilia, while Lucretia, the holy father's daughter, was in labor. There was some uncertainty in Rome whether the child's father was the pope, or the pope's son, the duke of Valentinois, or Lucretia's husband, Alphonse of Aragon, who was thought to be impotent. From the outset the conversation was lively. Cardinal Bembo relates part of it. "Little Pico," said the pope, "who do you think is the father of my grandson?" —"I believe it's your son-in-law," replied Pico. —"Eh! how can you believe such nonsense?" —"I believe it by faith." —"But don't you know perfectly well that an impotent man can't have children?" —"Faith," returned Pico, "consists in believing things because they are impossible; moreover, the honor of your house demands that Lucretia's son should not be considered the fruit of incest. You make me believe in more incomprehensible mysteries than that. Am I not compelled to be convinced that a serpent spoke, that from that time on all men have been damned, that Balaam's ass talked, very eloquently too, and that the walls of Jericho tumbled down at the sound of trumpets?" Without hesitation, Pico threaded together a litany of all the marvelous things he believed. Alexander dropped on a sofa with laughter. "I believe all that just as you do," he said, "for I know that I can be saved by faith alone, and that I won't be saved by my works."

"Ah! Holy father," said Pico, "you need neither works nor faith; that's all right for poor outsiders like me; but you, you are vice-God, you can believe and do whatever you like. You have the keys to heaven; and surely St. Peter won't shut the door in your face. But as for me, I confess that I, being nothing but a poor prince, would need some powerful protection if I had slept with my daughter, and if I had employed the stiletto and Spanish Fly as often as your Holiness." Alexander VI had a sense of humor. "Let's talk seriously," he said to the prince della Mirandola. "Tell me what merit attaches to telling God that one is convinced of things of which, as a matter of fact, it is impossible to be convinced? What pleasure can this give God? Just between us, to say that one believes something that is impossible to believe, is to lie."

Pico della Mirandola made a great sign of the cross. "Eh! Heavenly father," he exclaimed, "may your Holiness forgive me, but you're not a Christian." —"No, upon my faith," said the pope. —"I thought not," said Pico della Mirandola.

(By a descendant of Rabelais)

FOY · FAITH

What is faith? Is it to believe what appears quite evident? No: it is evident to me that there is a Being, necessary, eternal, supreme, intelligent; this is not a matter of faith, but of reason. I deserve no credit for thinking that this eternal, infinite Being, which I perceive as virtue and goodness itself, wishes me to be good and virtuous. Faith consists in believing, not what seems true, but what seems false to our understanding. By faith alone can the Asiatics believe in the journey of Mahomet to the seven planets, the incarnations of the god Fo, of Vishnu, of Xaca, of Brahma, of Sammonocodom, etc., etc., etc. They subordinate their understanding, they fear to investigate, they want neither to be impaled nor burned; they say: "I believe."

We are far from making the slightest allusion to the Catholic faith here. Not only do we venerate it, but it is ours: we are only speaking of the lying faiths of other nations of the world, of the faith that is not faith, and consists only of words.

There is faith in astonishing things, and faith in contradictory and impossible things.

Vishnu incarnated himself five hundred times; that is quite astonishing, but still it is not physically impossible; for if Vishnu had a soul, he could have put his soul into five hundred bodies to enjoy himself. To be sure, the Indian's faith isn't very ardent; he isn't deeply convinced of these metamorphoses, but he will nevertheless say to his bonze: "I have faith; you will have it that Vishnu passed through five hundred incarnations; that's worth five hundred rupees of annuity to you. Very well: you will clamor against me, you will denounce me, you

will ruin my trade, if I don't have faith. All right, I have
faith, and here are ten more rupees for you." The Indian
can swear to this bonze that he believes, without swear-
ing a false oath; for after all it hasn't been demonstrated
to him that Vishnu did not come to India five hundred
times.

But if the bonze requires him to believe a contradictory, impossible thing, that two and two make five, that
the same body can be in a thousand different places,
that being and non-being are precisely the same thing;
then, if the Indian says he has faith, he lies; and if he
swears that he believes, he perjures himself. So he says
to the bonze: "Reverend Father, I can't guarantee to
you that I believe these absurdities, even if they were
worth ten thousand rupees of annuity instead of five
hundred."

"My son," replies the bonze, "give me twenty rupees,
and God will give you grace to believe all that you
don't believe."

"How do you expect God to do in me what he cannot
do in himself?" the Indian asks. "It is impossible for
God to make or believe contradictions. I'd be happy to
tell you that I believe in what is obscure, to give you
pleasure; but I cannot tell you that I believe in the impossible. God wants us to be virtuous; he doesn't want
us to be absurd. I've given you ten rupees, and here are
twenty more; believe at thirty rupees; be an honest man
if you can, and don't worry me any more."

FOLIE · MADNESS

I have no intention of reviving Erasmus' *In Praise of
Folly*, which would seem only insipid and commonplace
today.

We call madness that sickness of the organs of the brain which forcibly keeps a man from thinking and acting like others. Unable to manage his property, he is prohibited from doing so; unable to entertain ideas suitable to society, he is excluded from it; if he is dangerous, he is locked up; if he is violent, he is tied down.

What is important to note is that this man does not lack ideas; he has them like all other men while he is awake, and often when he sleeps. We might ask how his spiritual, immortal soul, which is lodged in his brain and receives all its ideas through clear and distinct senses, yet never makes a sane judgment. It sees objects as the soul of Aristotle and Plato, Locke and Newton, saw them; it hears the same sounds, it has the same sense of touch; how then, receiving the perceptions experienced by the wisest, does it make of them an extravagant collection, and cannot do otherwise?

If this simple and eternal substance has the same means of action as the souls of the wisest brains, it should think like them. What could stop it? If my madman saw red and the sages blue; if, when the sages heard music, my madman heard the braying of an ass; if, when they listened to a sermon, my madman thought he was in the theater; if, when they heard yes, he heard no—then I could understand perfectly well why his soul should think the wrong way. But my madman has the same perceptions as others; there is no apparent reason why his soul, having been provided with all its equipment by the senses, can't make use of it. It is pure, they say; by itself it is subject to no infirmity; here it is, provided with all the necessary aid; whatever may be going on in its body, nothing can change its essence; yet it is taken to the madhouse in a closed vehicle.

These reflections may raise the suspicion that the faculty of thinking, given by God to man, is subject to derangement like the senses. A madman is a sick man whose brain is in distress, as the gouty man is a sick man who suffers in his feet and hands; he thinks with his brain, as he walks with his feet, without any knowledge of his incomprehensible ability to walk, or of his no less incomprehensible ability to think. People have gout in the brain as in the feet. In a word, after a thousand arguments, it may be faith alone that can convince us that a simple and immaterial substance can be sick.

Learned men or medical men will say to the madman: "My friend, even though you have lost your common sense, your soul is as spiritual, as pure, as immortal as ours; but our soul is well housed, and yours is not; the windows of its house are shut up; it lacks air, it is suffocating." In his sane moments, the madman would answer them: "My friends, you take for granted the very thing we are inquiring into, as you generally do. My windows are as wide open as yours, since I see the same objects and hear the same words: it must therefore be that my soul makes bad use of its senses, or that my soul is itself merely a tainted sense, a corrupted faculty. In a word, either my soul is mad by itself, or I have no soul."

One of the doctors might reply: "My brother, God perhaps created mad souls, as he created wise souls." The madman would answer: "If I believed what you tell me, I'd be even madder than I am. Please, you who know so much about it, tell me why I am mad?"

If the doctors had a little sense left, they would answer him: "We have no idea." They don't understand why a brain has incoherent ideas; they don't understand any better why another brain has orderly and consistent ideas. They think themselves wise, and they are as mad as he.

FRAUDE · FRAUD

Should Pious Frauds Be Practiced on the Common People?

One day the fakir Bambabef met one of the disciples of Confutzee, whom we call *Confucius*, and that disciple's name was Ouang. Bambabef maintained that the people needed to be deceived, and Ouang maintained that we should never deceive anyone; and here's the abstract of their debate.

BAMBABEF. We must imitate the supreme Being, who does not show us things as they are; he makes us see the sun as having a diameter of two or three feet, although that star is a million times larger than the earth; he makes us see the moon and the stars as being attached to the same blue ground, while they are at different distances. He wishes us to see a square tower as being round from a distance; he wishes us to feel fire as hot, although it is neither hot nor cold; in short, he surrounds us with errors that suit our nature.

OUANG. What you call error isn't one at all. The real sun, placed millions and millions of lis* from our globe, is not the one we see. We really perceive, and we can only perceive, the sun that is painted on our retina, at a fixed angle. We were not given our eyes to know sizes and distances; other aids and other methods are needed to know them.

Bambabef appeared quite astonished at this remark. Ouang, who was extremely patient, explained the theory of optics to him; and Bambabef, who had a good brain, yielded to the demonstration that Confucius' disciple gave him; then he resumed the debate:

* A li is 124 feet.

BAMBABEF. If God does not deceive us through the agency of our senses, as I had thought, at least admit that doctors always deceive children for their own good: they tell them they are giving them sugar when they are really giving them rhubarb. Hence, as a fakir, I may deceive the common people, who are as ignorant as children.

OUANG. I have two sons, and I have never deceived them; I told them when they were sick: "Here is a very bitter medicine, you must have the courage to take it; it would harm you if it were sweet." I have never allowed their governesses and their tutors to scare them with ghosts, spirits, goblins, witches: in this way I have made courageous and sensible young citizens of them.

BAMBABEF. When the common people are born, they are not as fortunate as your family.

OUANG. All men resemble one another; they are born with the same dispositions. It is the fakirs who corrupt the nature of men.

BAMBABEF. We teach them errors, I confess; but it is for their own good. We make them believe that if they don't buy our blessed nails, if they don't expiate their sins by giving us money, they will turn into post-horses, dogs, or lizards in another life: that intimidates them, and they become decent people.

OUANG. Don't you see that you are perverting these poor people? Far many more of them are rational than you might believe; they laugh at your miracles, at your superstitions; they know perfectly well that they will not be changed into lizards or post-horses. What happens? They have enough good sense to see that you preach an insolent religion to them, but they don't have enough sense to raise themselves to a pure religion, free from superstitions, such as our own. Their passions lead them to believe that there is no religion, since the

only religion they are taught is ridiculous; you make
yourself guilty of all the vices into which they plunge.

BAMBABEF. Not at all, for we teach them only good
morals.

OUANG. You'd be stoned by the people if you taught
them impure morals. Men are so made that, though they
would enjoy doing evil, they don't want it preached to
them. But a wise morality should not be mixed up with
absurd fables, because with your impostures, which you
could dispense with, you weaken the very morality you
are obliged to teach.

BAMBABEF. Really! Do you think that one can teach
the common people the truth without sustaining it with
fables?

OUANG. I believe it firmly. Our men of letters are of
the same stuff as our tailors, our weavers, and our
day laborers. They worship a God who creates, rewards,
and avenges. They sully their cult neither by absurd
systems nor by extravagant ceremonies; and there are
far fewer crimes among the men of letters than among
the common people. Why not deign to instruct our
workers as we instruct our men of letters?

BAMBABEF. You'd be doing something very foolish;
you might as well ask them to have the same politeness,
or to be lawyers: that's neither possible nor desirable.
There must be white bread for the master and brown
bread for his servants.

OUANG. I admit that all men should not have the
same education; but there are things that all men need.
Everyone needs to be just, and the surest method of
instilling justice into all men is to instill them with a
religion free from superstition.

BAMBABEF. That's a fine project, but it's impracticable.
Do you think that it is enough for men to believe in a
God who punishes and rewards? You said to me that it

often happens that the shrewdest among the common people rebel against my fables; they will rebel just as much against your truth. They will say: "Who will guarantee that God punishes and rewards? Where is the proof? What authority do you have? What miracle have you performed that I should believe you?" They will laugh at you much more than at me.

OUANG. That is where you are wrong. You imagine that men will shake off the yoke of an idea that is honest, probable, useful to everybody, an idea about which human reason is in agreement, just because they reject things that are dishonest, absurd, useless, dangerous, which make good sense shudder. The common people are strongly inclined to believe their magistrates: when their magistrates simply suggest to them a reasonable belief, they happily embrace it. They need no prodigies to believe in a just God, who reads the hearts of men; that idea is too natural to be opposed. It is not necessary to say precisely how God will punish and reward; it is enough to believe in his justice. I assure you that I have seen whole towns which had practically no other dogmas, and they were the ones in which I saw the most virtue.

BAMBABEF. Watch out; in those towns you'll find philosophers who will deny both punishments and rewards.

OUANG. You must concede that those philosophers will deny your inventions far more vehemently; so you won't gain anything by that. If there should be philosophers who don't accept my principles, they will be no less virtuous for that; they will cultivate virtue, which should be embraced out of love and not fear. But, further, I maintain that no philosopher will ever be sure that Providence does not reserve punishments for evil men and rewards for good; for if they ask me who told me that God punishes, I shall ask them who told them that God doesn't punish. In a word, I maintain that the philosophers, far from contradicting me, will help me. Would you like to be a philosopher?

BAMBABEF. Gladly; but don't tell the fakirs that.

GENÈSE · GENESIS

We shall not anticipate here what we say about Moses in the article devoted to him; we shall trace several principal features of Genesis, one after the other.

> *In the beginning God created the heavens and the earth.*

That is how they translate it; but the translation is not accurate. No man who has had the slightest schooling doesn't know that the text runs: "In the beginning the gods made the heavens and the earth." Moreover, this reading is consistent with the ancient idea of the Phoenicians, who had supposed that God employed inferior gods to bring order out of the chaos, the *chautereb*. The Phoenicians were a powerful people, with their own theogony, long before the Hebrews seized a few villages adjacent to their country. It is quite natural to suppose that when the Hebrews finally made a small settlement near Phoenicia, they began to learn its language, especially since they were slaves there. Then those who took the trouble to write copied something of the ancient theology of their masters: such is the progress of the human spirit.

In the period into which Moses has been placed, the Phoenician philosophers probably knew enough to consider the earth a point, in comparison with the infinite multitude of globes which God had placed into that immensity of space called the *heavens*. But the idea, so old and so false, that the heavens were made for the earth, has nearly always prevailed among ignorant people. It's almost like saying that God created all the mountains and a grain of sand, and imagining that the mountains were made for the grain of sand. It is hardly likely that the Phoenicians, who were such good navigators, did not have good astronomers; but the old prejudices prevailed, and these old prejudices were the only science the Jews knew.

> *The earth was* tohu-bohu *and void, and darkness was upon the face of the deep; and the Spirit of God was moving over the face of the waters.*

The precise meaning of *tohu-bohu* is chaos, disorder; it is one of those imitative words found in all languages, like hurly-burly, hubbub, tric-trac. The earth was not yet in its final state; matter existed, but the divine power had not yet ordered it. The spirit of God signifies the *breath*, the *wind*, which moved the waters. This idea is expressed in the fragments of Sanchuniathon, the Phoenician author. Like all other nations, the Phoenicians believed matter to be eternal. There is not a single author of antiquity who ever said that something had been drawn from nothing. Even in the whole Bible there is not one passage saying that matter was made out of nothing.

Men have always been divided on the question of the eternity of the world, but never about the eternity of matter.

> ### Gigni
> *De nihilo nihilum nil posse reverti.*

> [*Nothing*
> *Can come from nothing, nothing to nothing return.*
>   Persius, *Satire* III, 83-84]

That was the opinion of all antiquity.

> *God said, "Let there be light"; and there was light. And God saw that the light was good; and God separated the light from the darkness. God called the light*

*Day, and the darkness he called Night. And there was
evening and there was morning, one day. And God said,
"Let there be a firmament in the midst of the waters,
and let it separate the waters from the waters." And
God made the firmament and separated the waters
which were under the firmament from the waters which
were above the firmament. And God called the firmament Heaven. And there was evening and there was
morning, a second day. And God saw that it was good.*

Let us begin by examining whether Huet, bishop of
Avranches, and Leclerc are not clearly right to oppose
those who claim that this is just a burst of sublime
eloquence.

No history written by the Jews affects eloquence. Here
as in the rest of the work, the style is of the greatest
simplicity. If an orator, to reveal the power of God,
simply employed this expression: "He said, 'Let there be
light,' and there was light," that would be sublime. So,
too, is the passage in one of the psalms: *Dixit, et facta
sunt.* This is a touch, standing by itself in that passage,
and put there to create a great image, that moves and
elevates the mind. But here the narrative is at its
simplest. The Jewish author speaks of light as he speaks
of the other objects of creation; he says impartially of
each item: *and God saw that it was good.* Surely everything is sublime in the creation; but the creation of light
is no more so than that of the grass in the fields: the
sublime is what is elevated above the rest, but the same
style pervades this whole chapter.

It was another very ancient opinion that the light did
not come from the sun. It was seen diffused in the air
before the rising and after the setting of that star; people
thought that the sun only served to impel it more strongly.
The author of Genesis also follows this popular error,
and, by an odd reversal of the order of things, has the
sun and moon only created four days after the light. It

is inconceivable that there should be a morning and an evening before there was a sun. There is a confusion here which cannot possibly be explained away. The inspired author followed the vague and crude prejudices of the nation. God did not claim to teach the Jews philosophy. He could have raised their spirit to the truth; but he preferred to descend to them.

The separation of light and darkness is no better as natural science; it seems that night and day were mixed together like different sorts of grains which are separated from one another. It is well known that darkness is nothing but the absence of light, and that there is actually no light until our eyes receive that sensation; but in those days they were far from knowing these truths.

The idea of a firmament is also of the greatest antiquity. People conjectured that the heavens were quite solid, because they always observed the same phenomena in them. The heavens rotated over our heads; they were therefore of a very hard material. How could they calculate that the exhalations of the earth and the seas could furnish water to the clouds? They did not have a Halley who could make this calculation. There were, then, reservoirs of water in the heavens. These reservoirs could rest only on a sound arch; one could see through this arch; it was therefore of crystal. For the higher waters to fall from this arch to the earth, it must have doors, sluices, cataracts, which opened and closed. This was the astronomy of the time; and since the author was writing for Jews, he had to adopt their ideas.

> God made the two great lights, the greater light to rule the day, and the lesser light to rule the night; he made the stars also.

The same ignorance of nature throughout. The Jews did not know that the moon shines only by a reflected

light. The author here speaks of the stars as of a baga-
telle, although they are so many suns each of which has
earths rotating around it. The Holy Spirit accommodated
himself to the spirit of the times.

> God said, "Let us make man in our image, and let
> them have dominion over the fish of the sea, etc."

What did the Jews understand by, *Let us make man in
our image?* That which all antiquity understood by it:

> *Finxit in effigiem moderantum cuncta deorum.*

One makes images only of bodies. No nation imagined
a god without a body, and it is impossible to picture
him in any other way. Of course we might say: "God is
no part of anything we know"; but then we can't have
any idea of what he is. The Jews, like all other nations,
always believed that God was corporeal. All the first
Fathers of the Church also believed God to be corporeal,
until they embraced the ideas of Plato.

> *Male and female he created them.*

If God or the secondary gods created man male and
female in their likeness, it would seem that the Jews
believed God and the gods to be male and female. It
is not known whether the author wants to say that at the
beginning man had both sexes, or if he thinks that God
made Adam and Eve in the same day. The most natural
interpretation is that God created Adam and Eve at the
same time; but this meaning would completely contradict the creation of woman, made from the rib of man
long after the seven days.

> *And on the seventh day he rested.*

The Phoenicians, the Chaldeans, the Indians, said that
God made the world in six periods, which the ancient Zo-

roaster calls the six *gahambârs,* famous among the Persians.

It is undeniable that all these nations had a theology before the Jewish horde inhabited the deserts of Horeb and Sinai, before it could have had scribes. It is therefore extremely probable that the story of the six days is borrowed from that of the six periods.

> *A river flowed out of Eden to water the garden, and there it divided and became four rivers. The first is called Pishon; it is the one which flows around the whole land of Havilah, where there is gold. . . . The name of the second river is Gihon; it is the one which flows around Ethiopia. . . . The name of the third river is Tigris, and the fourth the Euphrates.*

According to this version, the earthly paradise would have contained nearly a third of Asia and Africa. The Euphrates and the Tigris have their sources at more than a hundred and fifty miles from one another, in terrible mountains which hardly resemble a garden. The river which borders Ethiopia, and which can only be the Nile or the Niger, rises more than seventeen hundred miles from the sources of the Tigris and the Euphrates; and if the Pishon is the Phasis, it is rather surprising to find the source of a Scythian river and that of an African river in the same place.

Besides, the Garden of Eden is obviously taken from the gardens of Eden at Saada, in Arabia Felix, famous through all antiquity. The Hebrews, a very recent people, were an Arabian horde. They did themselves the honor of possessing the finest place in the best district of Arabia. They have always taken for their own use the ancient traditions of the great nations in whose midst they were an enclave.

> *The Lord God took the man and put him in the Garden of Eden to cultivate it.*

It is a good thing for a man to *cultivate his garden,*
but it must have been difficult for Adam to cultivate a
garden seventeen or eighteen hundred miles long: apparently he was given some helpers.

> *Of the tree of the knowledge of good and evil you
> shall not eat.*

It is difficult to conceive of a tree that taught good
and evil, as there are pear trees and apricot trees. Besides,
why didn't God want man to know good and evil?
Wouldn't the opposite have been much more worthy of
God, and much more necessary to man? To our poor
reason, it would seem that God should order us to eat
a great deal of that fruit; but we must submit our reason
to his.

> *For in the day that you eat of it you shall die.*

Nevertheless Adam ate of it, and didn't die. On the
contrary, he was allowed to live nine hundred and thirty
years more. Several Fathers have regarded all this as an
allegory. In fact, one could say that the other animals
don't know that they will die, but that man knows it
through his reason. This reason is the tree of knowledge
that makes him foresee his end. This explanation is perhaps the most reasonable one.

> *Then the Lord God said, "It is not good that the man
> should be alone; I will make him a helper fit for him."*

We expect the Lord is about to give him a wife. Not
at all: the Lord brings him all the animals.

> *And whatever Adam called every living creature, that
> was its real name.*

The real name of an animal is understood to be a
name that would designate all the properties of its species,

or at least its principal ones; but it is not that way in any language. Every language has some imitative words, like *coq* in Celtic, which somewhat resembles the crowing of the cock, *lupus* in Latin, etc. But these imitative words are very few in number. Moreover, if Adam had known all the properties of animals so well, either he had already eaten of the fruit of knowledge, or God didn't need to forbid him the fruit.

Note that this is the first time Adam is named in Genesis. Among the ancient Brahmins, who greatly antedate the Jews, the first man was called Adimo, child of the earth, and his wife Procriti, life; this is recorded in the Vedas, which is perhaps the oldest book in the world. "Adam" and "Eve" have the same meanings in the Phoenician language.

> *While Adam slept, the Lord took one of his ribs and closed up its place with flesh; and the rib which the Lord God had taken from Adam he made into a woman and brought her to Adam.*

A chapter before, the Lord had already created male and female; why then take a rib from the man to make him a female who already exists? It has been suggested that the author announces in one place what he explains in another.

> *Now the serpent was more subtle than any other wild creature on the earth, etc.; he said to the woman, etc.*

In this whole article there is no mention of the Devil; everything in it is natural. All the oriental nations considered the serpent not only the subtlest of animals, but even immortal. The Chaldeans had a fable about a quarrel between God and the serpent; that fable has been preserved by Pherecydes, and Origen quotes it in his book VI against Celsus. A serpent was carried in the feasts of Bacchus. The Egyptians attached a kind of divinity to the serpent, as Eusebius reports in his *Evangelical Preparation*, book I, chapter x. In Arabia, in India, and even in China, the serpent was regarded as the symbol of life; that is why the emperors of China always bore the image of a serpent on their chest, long before Moses.

Eve is not surprised that the serpent should speak to her. Animals talked in all the ancient histories; and that is why no one was surprised when Pilpay and Lokman made the animals talk.

This whole adventure is so natural, and so stripped of all allegory, that it even explains why from that time on the serpent has crawled on its belly, why we always try to crush it, and why it always tries to bite us; precisely as the ancient metamorphoses explained why the crow, which was once white, is black today, why the owl leaves its hole only at night, why the wolf loves carnage, etc.

> *I will greatly multiply your pain and your childbearing; in pain you shall bring forth children; you will be under the power of your husband, and he shall rule over you.*

It is hard to see why the multiplication of pregnancies is a punishment. On the contrary, one might say it is a great blessing, and especially among the Jews. The pains of childbirth are considerable only for fragile women; those who are accustomed to labor are delivered very easily, especially in hot climates. Sometimes there are animals that suffer greatly in giving birth; there are even some who die of it. And as for the superiority of man over woman, that is a perfectly natural thing; it is the result of the strength of his body and even of his mind. Men in general have organs more capable of sustained attention than women, and are better fitted for labors of head and hand. But when a woman has a stronger wrist and mind than her husband, she is master in all things: then the husband is subject to the wife.

The Lord made them garments of skin.

This passage proves that the Jews thought of God as corporeal, since they have him exercise the tailor's craft. A rabbi named Eliezer has written that God clothed Adam and Eve in the skin of the very serpent that had tempted them; and Origen claims that this garment of skin was a new flesh, a new body that God made for man.

Then the Lord said, "Behold, the man has become like one of us."

One must renounce common sense not to agree that the Jews worshiped several gods at first. It is harder to know what they meant by the word God, *Elohim.* Several commentators have claimed that this phrase, *one of us,* signifies the Trinity; but surely there is no mention of the Trinity in the Bible. The Trinity is not a composite of several gods, it is one God, triple; and the Jews never heard of a God in three persons. It is very likely that by these words, *like one of us,* the Jews understood the angels, *Elohim,* and that therefore the book was written only after they had come to believe in these subordinate gods.

The Lord sent him forth from the Garden of Eden, to cultivate the ground.

But the Lord had put him into the Garden of Eden *that he might cultivate that garden.* If Adam the gardener turned into a farm hand, it must be admitted that he was not any the worse for that: a good farm hand is easily worth a gardener.

According to overly audacious commentators, this

whole story rests on an idea all men used to have, and still do: that primitive ages were better than recent ones. People have always deplored the present and extolled the past. Men overburdened with labor see happiness in idleness, never thinking that the worst of conditions is that of a man who has nothing to do. Often they see themselves unhappy, and conjure up the idea of a time when everybody had been happy. That is almost like saying: "Once upon a time no tree perished; no animal either fell ill, or became feeble, or was devoured by others." Hence the idea of the golden age, the egg pierced by Arimanes, the serpent that robbed the ass of the recipe of happy and immortal life which man had put into its pack-saddle; hence the combat of Typhon against Osiris, of Ophion against the gods; and that celebrated Pandora's box, and all those old tales, of which some are amusing and none is instructive.

> *And he placed in the Garden of Eden a cherub with a flaming sword which turned every way, to guard the way to the tree of life.*

The word *kerub* signifies *ox*. An ox armed with a flaming sword makes a strange figure at the door. But later the Jews represented the angels in the shape of oxen and hawks, even though they were forbidden to make any images. Obviously they took these oxen and hawks from the Egyptians, whom they imitated in so many things. In the beginning the Egyptians venerated the ox as the symbol of agriculture and the hawk as that of the wind; but they never made an ox into a door-keeper.

> *The gods, Elohim, saw that the daughters of man were fair, and they took to wife such of them as they chose.*

This fancy, too, was common to all nations. China excepted, there is no nation in which some god did not have children by young women. These corporeal gods often descended to earth to visit their domains, they saw our young women and took the prettiest ones for themselves; the children born from the intercourse of these gods and mortals had to be superior to other men; so Genesis too does not neglect to mention that the gods who lay with our young women produced giants.

I will bring a flood of waters upon the earth.

I shall merely observe here that St. Augustine says in his *City of God*, no. 8, *Maximum illud diluvium graeca nec Latina novit historia:* "Neither Greek nor Latin history knew of this great deluge." In fact, the Greeks knew only the floods of Deucalion and Ogyges, which were considered universal in the fables collected by Ovid but were totally unknown in East Asia.

God said to Noah: "I establish my covenant with you and your descendants after you, and with every living creature that is with you."

God make a covenant with animals! What a covenant, exclaim the unbelievers. But if he covenants with man, why not with an animal? It has feeling, and there is something as divine in feeling as in the most metaphysical of thoughts. Moreover, animals feel better than most men think. It is apparently by virtue of this pact that Francis of Assisi, founder of the Seraphic order, said to the grasshoppers and the hares: "Sing, my sister grasshopper; browse, my brother hare." But what were the terms of the treaty? That all the animals should devour one another; that they should feed on our flesh, and we on theirs; that after eating, we should exterminate the rest in rage; all that was missing was that we should eat our fellow men slain by our hand. If there was such a pact, it must have been concluded with the devil.

Probably the whole passage means nothing more than this: God is impartially the absolute master of everything that breathes.

> *I shall set my bow in the cloud, and it shall be a sign of the covenant, etc.*

Observe that the author doesn't say: "I have set my bow in the cloud," he says, "I shall set," which evidently supposes the general opinion that the rainbow had not always existed. It is a phenomenon caused by the rain; and it is here represented as something supernatural, announcing that the earth shall no longer be inundated. It is strange that the sign of rain should be chosen to affirm that men will not be drowned. But one might reply to this that when there is danger of inundation one is reassured by the sign of the rainbow.

> *The two angels came to Sodom in the evening, etc.*

The whole story of the two angels whom the Sodomites tried to rape is perhaps the most extraordinary story invented in antiquity. But we must remember that almost all of Asia believed that there were demons, both incubi and succubi; that, besides, these two angels were creatures more perfect than men, and that they must have been more beautiful, and stimulated the desires of a corrupt people more than ordinary men.

As for Lot, who offered his two daughters to the Sodomites in place of the two angels, and Lot's wife, changed into a pillar of salt, and all the rest of that story—what can we say about it? The ancient Arab fable of Cinyras and Myrrha has some analogy to Lot's incest with his daughters; and the adventure of Philemon and Baucis is not without resemblance to the two angels who appeared

to Lot and his wife. As for the pillar of salt, we don't
know what that resembles: is it the story of Orpheus
and Eurydice?

There are scholars who claim that we should suppress
all these incredible things in the canonical books which
shock the weak; but it has been suggested that these
scholars are corrupt in heart, men to be burned, and
that it is impossible to be an upright man unless one
believes that the Sodomites tried to rape two angels.
This is the argument of a species of monster who seeks
to dominate men's minds.

Several famous Fathers of the Church were prudent
enough to turn all these stories into allegories, following
the Jews and above all Philo. Popes, still more prudent,
wanted to prevent the translation of these books into
the vernacular, lest men be enabled to judge what they
were told to worship.

Surely we must conclude from all this that those who
understand the Book of Genesis perfectly should tolerate those who don't; for if the latter don't understand
it at all, that is not their fault; but those who don't comprehend it at all should also tolerate those who comprehend all of it.

GLOIRE · GLORY

Ben-al-Betif, that worthy chief of the dervishes, said
to them one day: "My brethren, it is a very good thing
that you often employ the sacred formula of our
Koran: *In the name of the most merciful God;* for God
uses mercy, and you will learn to do so by frequently
repeating the words that recommend a virtue without
which few men would be left in the world. But, my

brethren, beware of imitating those reckless men who boast at every opportunity that they are working for the glory of God. If a young imbecile defends a thesis on the categories, a thesis over which an ignoramus in furs presides, he'll be sure to write in large letters at the head of his thesis: *Ek Allah abron doxa: ad majoram Dei gloriam.* When a good Muslim has his drawing room whitewashed, he engraves this nonsense on his door; a saka carries water for the greater glory of God. This is an impious practice, which is piously practiced. What would you think of a little *chiaoux* who exclaims as he empties our sultan's toilet: "To the greater glory of our invincible monarch"? Yet surely there is a greater distance between the sultan and God than between the sultan and the little *chiaoux.*

"Miserable earthworms called men, what do you have in common with the glory of the infinite Being? Can he love glory? Can he receive it from you? Can he appreciate it? Two-legged, featherless animals, how long will you make God in your image? What! Because you are vain, because you love glory, you want God to love it too! If there were several gods, each of them might wish to obtain the approval of his fellow creatures. That would be the glory of a god. If one could compare infinite grandeur with the humblest station, such a god would be like king Alexander or Scanderbeg, who would enter the lists only with kings. But you, you poor fellows, what glory can you give God? Cease to profane his sacred name. An emperor called Octavius Augustus forbade people to praise him in the schools of Rome, for fear his name might be debased. But you can neither debase the supreme Being nor honor him. Prostrate yourselves, worship, and be silent."

Thus spoke Ben-al-Betif; and the dervishes shouted: "Glory to God! Ben-al-Betif has spoken well."

GRÂCE · GRACE

Sacred counsellors of modern Rome, illustrious and infallible theologians, nobody has more respect for your divine decisions than I; but you will admit that if Aemilius Paullus, Scipio, Cato, Cicero, Caesar, Titus, Trajan, and Marcus Aurelius returned to the Rome for whose reputation they once did a little, they would be rather taken aback at your decisions on grace. What would they say if they heard about health-giving grace according to St. Thomas, and medicinal grace according to Cajetan; about exterior and interior, gratuitous, sanctifying, actual, habitual, cooperating grace; about efficacious grace which is sometimes without effect; about sufficient grace which sometimes does not suffice; about versatile and congruent grace? Now, honestly, would they understand it any better than you and I?

What need would these poor fellows have of your sublime instructions? I seem to hear them saying:

"Reverend Fathers, you are terrible demons; we foolishly thought that the eternal Being never acts by particular laws like vile humans, but by his general laws, eternal like himself. Not one of us ever imagined that God was like an insane master who gives a hoard to one slave and refuses nourishment to another; who orders a one-armed man to knead meal, a mute to read to him, a legless cripple to be his courier.

"With God all is grace: he has extended to the globe we inhabit the grace of creating it; to trees the grace of making them grow; to animals the grace of feeding them. But would you say that when a wolf finds a lamb in his path for supper, and another wolf dies of hunger, God gave the first wolf a private grace? Does he

occupy himself, by a preferential grace, with having one
oak grow in preference to another oak which lacks sap?
If all beings in all of nature are subject to general laws,
how can a single species of animal not be subject to
them?

"Why should the absolute master of all be busier
directing the interior of a single man than guiding all of
the rest of nature? By what caprice would he change
something in the heart of a Kurlander or a Biscayan,
while he changes nothing in the laws he has imposed on
all the stars?

"How pathetic to suppose that he continually makes,
unmakes, remakes, feelings within us! And how audacious of us to think that we, of all creatures, should have
been singled out! And what's more, all these changes
have been thought up only for those who go to confession! On Monday, a Savoyard, a Bergamasque, will
have the grace to have a mass said for twelve sous; on
Tuesday, he will go to the tavern and lack grace; on
Wednesday, he will have a cooperating grace which
will lead him to confession, but he won't have the
efficacious grace of perfect contrition; on Thursday,
there will be sufficient grace which will not suffice, as I
have already said. God will be working continually in
the head of this Bergamasque, sometimes powerfully,
sometimes feebly—and the rest of the world will be
nothing to God! He will not deign to meddle with the
insides of Indians and Chinese! Reverend Fathers, if
you have a grain of reason left, don't you find this
system enormously ridiculous?

"Miserable man, look at this oak which raises its head
to the clouds, and this reed groveling at its feet; you
will not say that efficacious grace was given to the oak
and is lacking to the reed. Raise your eyes to heaven,
see the eternal Demiurge creating millions of worlds
which all gravitate toward one another by general and

eternal laws. See the same light reflected from the Sun to Saturn, and from Saturn to you; and, in this harmony of so many stars, hurried along in their rapid course, in this general obedience of all nature, dare to believe, if you can, that God is busy giving a versatile grace to sister Theresa and a concomitant grace to sister Agnes!

"Atom! A foolish atom tells you that the Eternal has private laws for some atoms in your neighborhood; that he gives his grace to this one and refuses it to that one; that somebody who did not have grace yesterday will have it tomorrow; don't repeat this nonsense. God made the universe, and he will not create new winds to move some blades of straw in a corner of this universe. Theologians are like the warriors in Homer, who believed that the gods sometimes took arms against them, sometimes for them. If Homer had not been considered a poet, he would have been considered a blasphemer."

This is Marcus Aurelius speaking, not I: for God, who inspires you, has given me the grace of believing everything you say, everything you have said, and everything you will say.

GUERRE · WAR

Famine, plague, and war are the three most precious ingredients of this vile world.

Under the classification of famine we may include all the unhealthy nourishment we are compelled to resort to in times of scarcity, abridging our life in the hope of sustaining it. In plague we include all the contagious illnesses, which number two or three thousand. These two gifts come to us from Providence.

But war, which unites all these gifts, comes to us from

the imagination of three or four hundred people scattered over the surface of the globe under the name of
princes or ministers; and it is perhaps for this reason that
in dedications to some books they are called the living
images of divinity.

The most determined courtier will easily agree that
war always brings plague and famine in its train, if he
has seen even a little of the hospitals of the German
armies, and passed through some villages in which some
great exploit of war had taken place.

Surely the art that desolates the countryside, destroys
habitations, and, in an average year, leads to the death
of forty thousand out of a hundred thousand men, is a
very fine art. At first it was cultivated by nations who
mobilized for their common good; for instance, the Diet
of the Greeks declared to the Diet of Phrygia and
neighboring nations that it intended to arrive on a
thousand fishing boats in order to exterminate them if
it could. The Roman people in assembly decided that it
was to its interest to fight before harvest time against
the people of Veii, or the Volscians. And some years
later all the Romans, angry at all the Carthaginians,
fought them for a long time on land and on sea. It's not
this way today.

A genealogist proves to a prince that he is the direct
descendant of a count whose parents had made a family
compact, three or four hundred years ago, with a house
that has disappeared even from memory. This house
had farfetched claims to a province whose last proprietor died of apoplexy: the prince and his council conclude without difficulty that the province belongs to him
by divine right. The province, which is several hundred
miles away, protests in vain that it does not know him,
that it has no desire to be governed by him, that one
must at least have a people's consent before one gives it

laws: these speeches don't even reach the ears of the
prince, whose right is incontestable. At once he assembles a large number of men who have nothing to lose; he
dresses them in coarse blue cloth at a hundred and ten
sous the ell, edges their hats with coarse white yarn,
makes them turn right and left, and marches to glory.

The other princes who hear of this escapade take part
in it, each according to his strength, and cover a small
space of land with more mercenary murderers than
Genghis Khan, Tamerlane, or Bajazet ever had in their
train.

Distant nations hear that there is going to be some
fighting, and that they can make five or six sous a day if
they want to join in: right away they divide themselves
into two groups, like reapers, and sell their services to
anyone ready to employ them.

These multitudes become infuriated with each other,
not only without having any business in the proceedings,
but even without knowing what is at stake.

At once there are five or six belligerent powers, sometimes three against three, sometimes two against four,
sometimes one against five, all detesting one another
equally, uniting and fighting with each other in turn; all
in agreement on a single point, to do as much harm as
possible.

The marvelous part of this infernal enterprise is that
every murderer's chief has his flags blessed, and solemnly
invokes the Lord before he goes out to exterminate his
neighbors. If a chief has had the good fortune to butcher
only two or three thousand men, he does not thank God
for it; but when he has had ten thousand exterminated
by fire and sword, and when, his grace abounding, some
town has been destroyed from top to bottom, then they
sing a long song in four parts, composed in a language
unknown to all who did the fighting, and which be-

sides is crammed with solecisms. The same song serves
for marriages and births, as well as for murders: which
is unforgivable, above all in the nation best known for
new songs.

A thousand times natural religion has prevented citizens from committing crimes. A well-disposed soul is
unwilling to commit them; a tender soul is afraid of
them—a just and avenging God appears before it. But
artificial religion encourages all the cruelties which are
committed in company—conspiracies, seditions, pillagings, ambushes, taking towns by surprise, plundering,
murders. Everyone marches gaily off to crime under the
banner of his saint.

Everywhere a certain number of orators are paid to
celebrate these murderous days; some are dressed in a
long black jerkin, encumbered by a cropped cloak;
others have a shirt over a gown; some wear two pend-
ants of motley cloth over their shirt. All talk for a long
time; they point to what was done of old in Palestine,
applying it to a battle in Veteravia.

The rest of the year, these fellows declaim against
vices. They prove in three propositions and by antith-
eses that ladies who spread a little rouge on their bloom-
ing cheeks will be the eternal objects of the eternal
vengeance of the Eternal; that *Polyeucte* and *Athalie* are
works of the Devil; that a man who has two hundred
écus worth of fresh-water fish served at his table during
Lent will infallibly be saved, while a poor man who eats
two and a half sous worth of mutton will forever go to
all the devils.

Of five or six thousand declamations of this kind,
there are at most three or four, composed by a Gaul
named Massillon, which an honest man can read without
disgust; but among all these speeches you will hardly
find two in which the orator dares to stand up against

war, this scourge and crime which includes all other scourges and crimes. These miserable orators ceaselessly speak against love, which is the sole consolation of mankind and the sole means of restoring it; they say nothing about our abominable efforts to destroy mankind.

O Bourdaloue, you have delivered a very poor sermon on impurity! But not one on these murders, so widely varied, on these rapes, these pillagings, this universal mania which desolates the world. All the vices of all ages and all places put together can never equal the evils produced by a single campaign.

Miserable physicians of souls, you shout for an hour and a quarter about some pin pricks, and you say nothing about the malady that tears us in a thousand pieces! Moral philosophers, burn all your books. As long as thousands of our brothers are honestly butchered for the caprice of some men, the part of mankind consecrated to heroism will be the most horrible thing in all nature.

What becomes of humanity, modesty, temperance, gentleness, wisdom, piety; and what do I care about them, while half a pound of lead, shot from six hundred feet away, shatters my body, and while I die at the age of twenty in inexpressible torments in the midst of five or six thousand dying men; while my eyes, opening for the last time, see the town in which I was born destroyed by iron and fire, and while the last sounds in my ears are the cries of women and children expiring under the ruins —all for the alleged interest of a man whom we don't know?

What is worse is that war is an inevitable scourge. If we look at it closely, we see that all men have worshipped the god Mars: Sabaoth, among the Jews, signifies the god of arms; but Minerva, in Homer, calls Mars a savage, insane, infernal god.

HISTOIRE DES ROIS JUIFS
ET PARALIPOMÈNES

HISTORY OF JEWISH KINGS
AND CHRONICLES

All nations have written down their history as soon as they could write. The Jews have also written theirs. Before they had kings, they lived under a theocracy; they were supposedly governed by God himself.

When the Jews desired a king like other neighboring nations, the prophet Samuel, strongly intent on not having a king, announced to them in God's name that they were rejecting God himself: thus, among the Jews theocracy ended when monarchy began.

Therefore we may say without blaspheming that the history of the Jewish kings has been written like that of other nations, and that God himself didn't take the trouble to dictate the history of a people he no longer governed.

We advance this opinion only with the most extreme diffidence. What might confirm it is that the Chronicles very often contradict the Book of Kings in chronology and in facts, just as our profane historians sometimes contradict one another. Moreover, if God had always written the history of the Jews, we would then have to believe that he is still writing it, for the Jews are still his cherished people. One day they will be converted, and then apparently they will have as much right to regard the history of their dispersion as sacred as they have the right to say that God wrote the history of their kings.

We might add a reflection: since God was their only king for a very long time, and then was their historian, we should have the profoundest respect for all Jews. There isn't a single Jewish peddler who isn't infinitely superior to Caesar and Alexander. Why not prostrate ourselves before a peddler who can prove to you that his history was written by Divinity itself, while Greek and Roman history were transmitted to us by mere profane men?

While the style of the Book of Kings and of Chronicles is divine, still, the actions reported in these histories are perhaps not so divine. David assassinates Uriah; Ishbosheth and Mephibosheth are assassinated; Absalom assassinates Amnon; Joab assassinates Absalom; Solomon assassinates Adonijah, his brother; Baasha assassinates Nadab; Zimri assassinates Elah; Omri assassinates Zimri; Ahab assassinates Naboth; Jehu assassinates Ahab and Joram; the inhabitants of Jerusalem assassinate Amaziah, son of Joash; Shallum, son of Jabesh, assassinates Zachariah, son of Jeroboam; Menahem assassinates Shallum, son of Jabesh; Pekah, son of Remaliah, assassinates Pekahiah, son of Menahem; Hoshea, son of Elah, assassinates Pekah, son of Remaliah. I pass over in silence many other minor assassinations. It must be admitted that if the Holy Spirit wrote this history, he didn't choose a very edifying subject.

IDÉE · IDEA

What is an idea?

It is an image painted in my brain.

Are all your thoughts images, then?

Certainly; for the most abstract ideas are nothing but the consequences of all the objects I have perceived. Generally I pronounce the word *being* only because I have known particular beings. I can only say the word *infinite* because I have seen limits, and extend those limits in my understanding as far as I can; I have ideas only because I have images in my head.

And who is the painter who paints this picture?

Not I; my draftsmanship isn't good enough; he who made me, made my ideas.

Do you then agree with Malebranche, who said that we see all in God?

At least I'm quite sure that if we don't see things in God himself, we see them through his almighty action.

And how is that action produced?

I've told you a hundred times in our conversations that I haven't the slightest idea and that God hasn't revealed his secret to anybody. I don't know what makes my heart beat, my blood circulate in my veins; I don't know the principle of all my movements; and you want me to tell you how I feel and how I think! That isn't fair.

But do you at least know if your faculty of having ideas is linked to extension?

I know nothing of the sort. Indeed, it is true that Tatian says in his address to the Greeks that the soul is manifestly made up of a body. Irenaeus says, in his chapter xxv of the second book, that the Lord taught that our souls retain the shape of our body to preserve it in memory. Tertullian maintains in his second book on the soul that it is a body. Arnobius, Lactantius, Hilary, Gregory of Nyssa, Ambrose, held the same opinion. It is said that other Church Fathers maintain that the soul is without any extension, and that here they agree with Plato; but that's highly doubtful. As far as I am concerned, I dare not have any opinion; I see nothing but incomprehensibility in one system or another; and after pondering it my whole life long, I am as far advanced as I was on the first day.

It wasn't worth thinking about, then?

True, the man who enjoys knows more about his pleasure than the man who reflects knows about his thinking—or at least he knows better, he is happier; but what do you expect? It's not up to me to accept or reject all the ideas that have crowded into my head to battle one another and have taken my medullary cells for their battlefield. When they have battled long enough, all I have collected from their remains is uncertainty.

It's rather sad to have so many ideas and not to know the nature of ideas precisely.

I admit it; but it's much sadder, and a great deal more foolish, to think you know what you don't know.

—————————

IDOLE, IDOLÂTRE, IDOLÂTRIE
IDOL, IDOLATOR, IDOLATRY

Idol comes from the Greek εἶδος, form; εἴδωλον, representation of a form; λατρεύειν, to serve, revere, adore. The word *adore* is Latin, and has many different meanings: it signifies putting one's hand to one's mouth in speaking respectfully, to bow down, to kneel, to hail, and finally, in general, to offer supreme worship.

It is useful to observe here that the *Dictionnaire de Trévoux* begins its article on idolatry by saying that all pagans were idolators, and that the Indians are still an idolatrous people. But first of all no one was called *pagan* before Theodosius the Younger. At that time, this name was applied to the inhabitants of the Italian cities, *pagorum incolae, pagani,* who retained their ancient religion. Secondly, Hindustan is Mahommedan, and the Mahommedans are the implacable enemies of images and idolatry. Thirdly, the name idolator shouldn't be applied to many Indian nations who are of the ancient religion of the Parsis, nor to certain castes which have no idols.

EXAMINATION

Whether There Has Ever Been an Idolatrous Government

Apparently there has never been a nation on earth that took the name of *idolator*. The word is an insult, a term of abuse, like the name *gavaches*, cowards, which the Spaniards used to apply to Frenchmen, and the name *maranes*, Marranos, which Frenchmen applied to Spaniards. If you had asked the senate of Rome, the areopagus of Athens, the court of the kings of Persia: "Are you idolators?" they would hardly have understood the question. No one would have replied: "We worship images, idols." These words *idolator, idolatry,* are found neither in Homer, nor in Hesiod, nor in Herodotus, nor in a single author of the gentile religion. There has never been a single edict, a single law, ordering men to worship idols, to serve them as if they were gods, to regard them as gods.

When the Roman and Carthaginian commanders made a treaty, they called all their gods to witness. "It is in their presence," they said, "that we swear peace." Now the statues of all these gods, whose enumeration was very long, were not in the generals' tent. They regarded the gods as present at the actions of men, as witnesses, as judges. And surely it was not the image that constituted the divinity.

How, then, did they look upon the statues of their false divinities in the temples? With the same look—if we may express ourselves this way—as we regard the images of the objects of our veneration. Their error lay, not in worshiping a piece of wood or marble, but in worshiping a false divinity represented by the wood and marble. The difference between them and us is not that they had images and we don't: the difference is that their images represented the fantastic beings of a false religion, and that ours represent the real beings of a true religion. The Greeks had a statue of Hercules, and we have one of St. Christopher; they had Aesculapius and his goat, and we St. Roch with his dog; they had Jupiter armed with thunder, and we St. Anthony of Padua and St. James of Compostella.

When the consul Pliny addresses his prayers *to the immortal gods*, in the exordium of his *Panegyric to Trajan*, he does not address them to images. These images were not immortal.

Neither the most recent nor the most distant ages of paganism offer a single fact from which we could conclude that they worshiped an idol. Homer speaks only of gods who inhabit high Olympus. The *palladium*, although dropped from heaven, was merely a sacred pledge of the protection of Pallas; it was she who was venerated in the *palladium*.

The Romans and the Greeks knelt before statues, gave

them crowns, incense, flowers, paraded them in triumph in public places. But we too have sanctified these practices, and we are not idolators.

In times of drought, the women carried the statues of the gods after they had fasted. They marched barefoot, hair disheveled, and it rained buckets forthwith, as Petronius says, *et statim urceatim pluebat.* Haven't we consecrated this practice, illegal among the gentiles, and certainly legal with us? In how many villages don't we march barefoot, carrying corpses, to obtain the blessing of Heaven through their intercession? If a Turk, a learned Chinese, were to witness these ceremonies, he could at first sight accuse us of putting our confidence in the images we thus promenade in procession; but a word would be enough to set him straight.

People are astonished at the enormous number of declamations constantly made against the idolatry of the Romans and the Greeks; and then they are even more astonished to discover that they weren't idolators at all.

True, some temples were more privileged than others. The great Diana of Ephesus had a higher reputation than a village Diana. More miracles were performed in Aesculapius' temple at Epidaurus than in any other of his temples. The statue of Olympian Jupiter attracted more offerings than that of Paphlagonian Jupiter. But, since here we must always set the customs of a true religion against those of a false religion, haven't we had, for centuries, more devotion at certain altars than at others? Don't we carry more offerings to Notre Dame de Lorette than to Notre Dame des Neiges? We'll see if people will seize this pretext to accuse us of idolatry.

People imagined only a single Diana, a single Apollo, a single Aesculapius, and not as many Apollos, Dianas, and Aesculapiuses as they had temples and statues. Hence it is proved, as firmly as a point of history can ever be, that the ancients didn't believe that a statue was a divinity; the cult couldn't be attributed to this statue or this idol; consequently the ancients weren't idolators.

A coarse and superstitious populace which doesn't think, which knows neither how to doubt, nor to deny, nor to believe, which runs to the temples because it is idle and because in a temple the small man is equal to the great, which carries its customary offering, which talks continually of miracles without examining one of them, and which is hardly better than the sacrifices it brought; this populace, I say, might well be struck with religious awe at the sight of the great Diana or thundering Jupiter, and worship the statue itself without knowing it. That has sometimes happened to our rude peasants in our temples; they were consequently taught that it is the blessed, the immortals admitted into heaven, whose intercession they should ask, and not the images of wood and stone, and that they must only worship God alone.

The Greeks and Romans augmented the number of their gods by apotheoses. The Greeks deified conquerors, like Bacchus, Hercules, Perseus. Rome raised altars to its emperors. Our apotheoses are of a different breed; we have saints in place of their demigods, their secondary gods; but we pay attention neither to rank nor conquests. We have raised temples to men who were simply virtuous, who would for the most part be unknown on earth if they had not been placed in heaven. The apotheoses of the ancients were made out of flattery, ours out of respect for virtue. But these ancient apotheoses are yet another convincing proof that the Greeks and Romans were not, properly speaking, idolators. It is clear that they no more acknowledged a divine virtue in the statue of Augustus and Claudius than in their medals.

Nothing in Cicero's philosophical works permits even the slightest suspicion that the statues might be mistaken for gods and confounded with the gods themselves. His interlocutors violently attacked the established religion; but none of them thought of accusing the Romans of taking marble and brass for divinities. Lucretius, who reproaches the superstitious with everything, does not reproach anyone with this foolishness. Hence, once again, this opinion did not exist, people had no idea of it; there were no idolators.

Horace has a statue of Priapus speak; he has it say: "Once I was the trunk of a fig tree; a carpenter, not knowing whether to make a god or a bench of me, finally decided to make me into a god, etc." What can we conclude from this joke? Priapus was one of those little subordinate divinities handed over to scoffers; and that very joke is the strongest proof that the image of Priapus, which was set up in the vegetable garden to frighten away the birds, was not deeply revered.

Adopting the commentators' manner, Dacier observed that Baruch had predicted this little adventure when he said: "They will only be what the workmen want them to be"; but he might have observed too that one can say as much of all statues.

From a block of marble one might make a wash basin as well as an image of Alexander or Jupiter, or something else still more respectable. The material from which are formed the cherubim of the holy of holies could have served the lowest functions equally well. Is a throne, an altar, the less revered because the workman could have made it into a kitchen table?

Thus, instead of concluding that the Romans worshiped the statue of Priapus, and that Baruch had predicted it, Dacier should have concluded that the Romans made fun of it. Consult all the authors who mention the statues of their gods, you won't find a single one who speaks of idolatry: they expressly say the opposite. One reads in Martial:

Qui fingit sacros auro vel marmore vultus,
Non facit ille deos; . . .

[*He who in gold or marble sacred images*
Makes, does not make gods; . . .
Epigrams, VIII, xxiv, 5-6]

In Ovid:

Colitur pro Jove forma Jovis.

[*Jupiter is worshiped in Jupiter's shape.*
Epistulae ex Ponto, II, viii, 62]

In Statius:

Nulla autem effigies, nulli commissa metallo
Forma Dei; mentes habitare et pectora gaudet.

[*God's shape is not held by statues or metal;*
He is pleased to dwell in our hearts and minds.
Thebaid, XII, 503-504]

In Lucan:

Estne Dei sedes, nisi terra et pontus et aer?

[*Where is God's home but on earth and sea and air?*
Pharsalia, IX, 578]

One could make a volume of all the passages which testify that images were nothing but images.

The only instance which could make us believe that statues had something divine about them is that of statues giving out oracles. But surely the prevailing view was that the gods had chosen certain altars, certain images, in order to dwell there for a time, to give audience to men there, to answer them. In Homer and in the choruses of the Greek tragedies all we see is prayers offered to Apollo, who renders his oracles on mountains, in this temple, in that town; through all of antiquity there isn't the slightest trace of a prayer addressed to a statue.

Those who professed magic, who thought it a science, or who pretended to think so, claimed to have the secret of making the gods descend into statues; not the great gods, but the secondary ones, the genii. This is what Hermes Trismegistus called *making gods;* and this is what St. Augustine refutes in his *City of God.* But this, too, clearly demonstrates that the images had nothing divine about them, since it was necessary for a magician to animate them. And it seems to me it happened very rarely that a magician was clever enough to give a soul to a statue and to make it speak.

In a word, the images of the gods were not gods. Jupiter, and not his image, launched the thunder; it was not the statue of Neptune that raised the seas, nor that of Apollo that gave light. The Greeks and Romans were gentiles, polytheists, but not idolators.

Whether the Persians, the Sabaeans, the Egyptians, the Tartars, the Turks, Were Idolators, and of What Antiquity Is the Origin of the Images Called Idols.

HISTORY OF THEIR CULT

It is a great mistake to call nations who worshiped the sun and the stars idolators. For a long time these nations had neither images nor temples. If they were mistaken, it was in rendering unto the stars what they owed the creator of the stars. Moreover, the dogma of Zoroaster, or Zerdust, collected in the Sadder, teaches a supreme, rewarding, and avenging Being; and that is pretty far from idolatry. The state of China has never had an idol; it has always preserved the simple worship of the master of heaven, King-tien. Among the Tartars, Genghis Khan was not an idolator, and had no image. The Muslims, who crowded into Greece, Asia Minor,

Syria, Persia, India, and Africa, called the Christians *idolators, giaours*, because they believed that the Christians worshiped images. They smashed several statues they found at Constantinople in Santa Sophia and in the church of the Holy Apostles, and in other churches, which they converted into mosques. Appearances deceived them, as it always deceives men, and led them to believe that the temples dedicated to saints who had been men, the images of these saints which are revered on one's knee, and the miracles worked in these temples were insurmountable proof of the most complete idolatry. Still, nothing of the kind! In fact, the Christians worship only a single God, and revere in the blessed nothing but the power of God itself working in his saints. The iconoclasts and the Protestants have leveled the same reproach of idolatry against the Church, and they have received the same reply.

Since men very rarely have precise ideas, and still more rarely express their ideas in precise and unequivocal words, we give the name *idolators* to the gentiles, and above all to the polytheists. Enormous volumes have been written, a variety of views has been retailed, on the origin of this worship of God or of several gods in visible shape: this multitude of books and opinions proves nothing but ignorance.

We don't know who invented clothes and shoes, and we should like to know who first invented idols! How much do we care about a passage from Sanchuniathon, who lived before the Trojan war? What does he teach us when he says that chaos, spirit—that is, *breath*—in love with its own principles, derived mud from them, that it rendered the air luminous, that the wind Colp and his wife Bau begot Eon, that Eon begot Genos, that Chronos, their descendant, had two eyes in back as in front, that he became a god, and that he gave Egypt to his son Thout? Here is one of the most respectable documents of antiquity.

Orpheus, earlier than Sanchuniathon, teaches us no more in his *Theogony*, which Damascius has preserved for us. He represents the principle of the world in the shape of a dragon with two heads—one of a bull, the other of a lion—a face in the middle which he calls the-face-of-god, and gilded wings at the shoulders.

But you can derive two great truths from these bizarre notions: one, that visible images and hieroglyphs date from the most remote antiquity; the other, that all the ancient philosophers recognized a first principle.

As for polytheism, common sense will tell you that as long as there have been men—that is, weak animals, capable of reason and madness, subject to all accidents, to sickness and death—these men have felt their weakness and their dependence; they have readily recognized that there is something more powerful than they; they have felt a power in the earth which furnishes their nourishment, one in the air which often destroys them, one in the fire which consumes, and in the water which drowns. What more natural, for ignorant men, than to imagine beings who presided over these elements? What more natural than to revere the invisible force that made the sun and the stars glitter in our eyes? And again, since they wanted to form an idea of these powers that were superior to men, what more natural than to imagine them in a palpable manner? Was it even possible to do anything else? The Jewish religion, which preceded ours, and which was given by God himself, was filled with these images representing God. He deigns to speak human language out of a bush; he appears on a mountain; the celestial spirits whom he sends all come in human shape; finally, the sanctuary is filled with cherubim, who possess the bodies of men, with wings and animal heads. This led Plutarch, Tacitus, Appian, and so many others into the mistake of reproaching the Jews with worshiping a donkey's head. Despite his prohibition against painting and sculpting any likeness, God thus deigned to adapt himself to human weakness, which demanded images that spoke to the senses.

Isaiah, in chapter 6, sees the Lord seated on a throne, the train of his robe filling the temple. The Lord extends his hand and touches Jeremiah's mouth, in the first chapter of this prophet. Ezekiel sees a throne of sapphire in chapter 3, and God appears to him like a man seated on that throne. These images did not affect the purity of the Jewish religion, which never used pictures, statues, or idols to represent God to the eyes of the people.

The Chinese men of letters, the Parsees, the ancient Egyptians, had no idols; but soon Isis and Osiris were represented; soon Bel, at Babylon, became a huge colossus; Brahma was a bizarre monster in the Indian peninsula. The Greeks above all multiplied the names of the gods, statues, and temples, but they always attributed the supreme power to their Zeus, whom the Latins called Jupiter, master of gods and men. The Romans imitated the Greeks. These nations always placed all the gods in heaven, without knowing what they meant by heaven, and by their Olympus: it is not likely that these superior beings lived in the clouds, which are nothing but water. At first, they put seven of them into the seven planets, among which they counted the sun; but later the gods were made to dwell in the whole of heaven.

The Romans had their twelve great gods, six male and six female, whom they called *Dii majorum gentium*: Jupiter, Neptune, Apollo, Vulcan, Mars, Mercury, Juno, Vesta, Minerva, Ceres, Venus, Diana; Pluto was by then forgotten: Vesta took his place.

Later came the gods *minorum gentium:* the local deities, the heroes, like Bacchus, Hercules, Aesculapius; the infernal gods, Pluto, Proserpine; those of the sea, like Thetis, Amphitrite, the Nereids, Glaucus; then the Dryads, the Naiads; the gods of the gardens, those of the shepherds. There was one for every profession, for every act in life, for children, for nubile girls, for married women, for women in labor; they had the god Pet. Finally, they deified the emperors. To be sure, neither these emperors, nor the god Pet, nor the goddess Pertunda, nor Priapus, nor Rumina the goddess of breasts, nor Stercutius, the god of the toilet, were regarded as the masters of heaven and earth. The emperors sometimes had temples, the minor household gods did not; but all had their images, their idols.

There were little grotesque figures with which the populace decorated their rooms; they were the amusements of old women and of children, unauthorized by any public worship. The superstition of each individual was allowed to operate in its own way. These little idols are still found in the ruins of ancient towns.

While nobody knows when men began to make idols for themselves, we do know that they date from the remotest antiquity. Terah, Abraham's father, made them at Ur, in Chaldea. Rachel stole and carried off the idols of Laban, her father-in-law. We cannot go back farther than that.

But what precise notion did the ancient nations have of all these images? What virtue, what power, did they attribute to them? Did they believe that the gods descended from heaven to hide themselves in these statues, or that they communicated a portion of the divine spirit to them, or that they communicated nothing at all to them? A great deal has been written about this, too, to no purpose: it is clear that every man decided in this matter according to the degree of his reason, or his credulity, or his fanaticism. It is evident that the priests attached as much divinity to their statues as they could, to attract more offerings. We know that the philosophers disapproved of these superstitions, that the warriors laughed at them, that the magistrates tolerated them, and that the common people, always absurd, didn't know what it was doing. This, in a few words, is the history of all the nations to whom God has not made himself known.

We can draw the same conclusion about the worship all Egypt offered to an ox, and which several towns offered to a dog, a monkey, a cat, or to onions. It is very likely that these were emblems at first. Later, they worshiped a certain ox Apis, a certain dog named Anubis; they always ate beef and onions, but it is hard to know what the old women of Egypt thought of sacred onions and oxen.

Quite often the idols spoke. In Rome, on the feast day of Cybele, they commemorated the fine words the statue had pronounced when it was transferred from the palace of king Attalus:

Ipsa peti volui; ne sit mora, mitte volentem:
Dignus Roma locus quo deus omnis eat—

I wished to be taken away, come for me quickly; Rome deserves to have every god established there.

The statue of Fortuna spoke: to be sure, the Scipios, the Ciceros, the Caesars, believed none of this; but the old woman to whom Encolpius gave an écu to buy geese and gods might well have believed it.

The idols gave out oracles too, and the priests, hidden in the hollow interior of the statues, spoke in the name of the Divinity.

How is it possible that in the midst of so many gods and so many different theogonies and individual cults there was never a religious war among the nations that are called *idolatrous?* This peace was a good born of an evil, of error itself; for every nation, acknowledging several inferior gods, was pleased to have the neighbors have their own. If you except Cambyses, who is reproached with killing the ox Apis, we find not one conqueror in profane history who maltreated the gods of a vanquished nation. The gentiles didn't have an exclusive religion, and the priests thought of nothing but multiplying offerings and sacrifices.

The first offerings were fruit. Soon after that, they needed animals for the priests' table; they slaughtered them themselves; they became butchers, and cruel; finally they introduced the horrible practice of sacrificing human victims, and above all children and young girls. The Chinese, the Parsees, the Indians, were never guilty of such abominations; however, according to Porphyry, they immolated human beings at Hieropolis in Egypt.

In Tauris they sacrificed foreigners; happily, the priests of Tauris must have had few customers. The early Greeks, the Cypriots, the Phoenicians, the Tyrians, the Carthaginians all had this abominable superstition. The Romans themselves fell into this religious crime, and Plutarch reports that they immolated two Greeks and two Gauls to expiate the love affairs of three vestal virgins. Procopius, contemporary of Theodobert, king of the Franks, says that the Franks immolated human beings when they entered Italy with this prince. The Gauls, the Germans, generally practiced these terrible sacrifices. It is hard to read history without conceiving a horror of mankind.

True, among the Jews, Jephthah sacrificed his daughter, and Saul was ready to immolate his son; true, those who were pledged to the Lord under anathema could not be redeemed as one redeems animals, and had to perish. Samuel, a Jewish priest, used a sacred chopper to dismember king Agag, a prisoner of war whom Saul had forgiven, and Saul was condemned for observing the law of nations with this king. But God, master of men, can take away their life when he likes, how he likes, and because he likes, and it is not up to men to put themselves in the place of the Master of life and death and to usurp the rights of the supreme Being.

To console mankind for this dreadful spectacle, for these pious sacrileges, it is important to understand that in almost all the nations that are called *idolatrous* there was sacred theology and popular error, secret worship and public ceremonies, the religion of the sages and that of the multitude. A single God was taught only to those initiated in the mysteries; we need only cast a glance at the hymn attributed to ancient Orpheus, which was sung in the mysteries of Ceres Eleusinus, so famous in Europe and Asia: "Contemplate divine nature, illuminate your spirit, govern your heart, march in the path of justice; let the God of heaven and earth be always present before your eyes: he is unique, he exists by himself alone; all beings derive their existence from him; he sustains them all; he has never been seen by mortals, and he sees all things."

There are a thousand testimonies to the fact that the sages abhorred not only idolatry but even polytheism.

Epictetus, a model of resignation and patience, so great a man in so low a situation, never speaks of anything but a single God. Here is one of his maxims: "God has created me, God is within me; I bear him around everywhere. Should I soil him with obscene thoughts, unjust actions, sordid desires? My duty is to thank God for everything, to praise him for everything, and to cease blessing him only when I cease to live." All of Epictetus' ideas turn on this principle.

True, Marcus Aurelius, perhaps as great on the throne of the Roman empire as Epictetus was in slavery, often speaks of gods, whether to conform to accepted language, or to express the notion of intermediate beings between the supreme Being and men; but in how many places does he not show that he recognizes only one eternal, infinite God! "Our soul," he says, "is an emanation of the Divinity. My children, my body, my mind, come to me from God."

The Stoics, the Platonists, acknowledged a divine and universal nature; the Epicureans denied it. The pontiffs spoke of a single God only in the mysteries. Where then were the idolators?

However, it is one of the great errors in the *Dictionnaire de Moréri* to say that at the time of Theodosius the Younger idolators remained only in the remote lands of Asia and Africa. Even in the seventh century there were still many gentile people in Italy. Northern Germany from the Weser on was not Christian in the age of Charlemagne. Poland and all the north remained what is called *idolatrous* for a long time after him. Half of Africa, all the kingdoms beyond the Ganges, Japan, the populace of China, a hundred hordes of Tartars, have preserved their ancient worship. In Europe there remain only some Laplanders, Samoyedes, and Tartars who have persevered in the religion of their ancestors.

Let us conclude with the remark that in the period we label the Middle Ages, we called the country of the Mahometans *la Paganie;* we called a people which abhors images, *idolators, worshipers of images.* Let us concede once again that the Turks have a better excuse to think us idolators when they see our altars loaded with images and statues.

JEPHTÉ OU DES SACRIFICES DE SANG HUMAIN

JEPHTHAH OR HUMAN BLOOD SACRIFICES

It is obvious from the text of the Book of Judges that Jephthah promises to sacrifice the first person who comes out of his house to congratulate him on his victory over the Ammonites. His only daughter comes to meet him; he tears his clothes, and he immolates her after allowing her to go to the mountains to bewail the misfortune of her dying a virgin. Jewish girls celebrated this episode for a long time, weeping for Jephthah's daughter for four days.*

I'm not investigating in what age this story was written, whether it was imitated from the Greek tale of Agamemnon and Idomeneus, or whatever its model was; whether it came before or after similar Assyrian stories; I am keeping to the text: Jephthah consecrated his daughter as a burnt offering and carried out his vow.

The Jewish law expressly ordered the immolating of men consecrated to the Lord. "No one devoted, who is to be utterly destroyed from among men, shall be ransomed; he shall be put to death." The Vulgate translates: *Non redimetur, sed morte morietur.* (Leviticus, chapter 27, verse 29.)

It is by virtue of this law that Samuel cut king Agag, whom, as we have already said, Saul had forgiven, into pieces; indeed, Saul was condemned by the Lord and lost his kingdom for sparing Agag.

---

* See chapter 11 of Judges.

With this, human blood sacrifices are clearly inaugurated; no point of history is better verified. One can judge a nation only by its archives, and by what it reports about itself.

INONDATION · INUNDATION

Was there ever a time when the globe was completely inundated? That is physically impossible.

It could be that the sea has passed over every piece of ground, one after the other; but that could have happened only by a slow progression, during an enormous number of centuries. In five hundred years' time, the sea has withdrawn from Aigues-Mortes, Fréjus, and Ravenna, which were great ports, and left about five miles of dry ground. It is evident that, at this rate, the recession of the sea would require two million two hundred and fifty thousand years to travel round the globe. It is remarkable that this period should so closely approach the time needed by the earth's axis to straighten itself and coincide with the equator, a very likely movement which was first suspected about fifty years ago, and which could be completed in more than two million three hundred thousand years.

The beds, or layers, of shells which have been discovered several miles from the sea are incontrovertible evidence of the gradual deposit of these maritime products on terrain that was once the shore of the ocean; but that water should have covered the entire globe at one time is a chimera, scientifically absurd, demonstrated to be impossible by the laws of gravitation and of fluids, and by the insufficient quantity of water. We do not claim to be doing the slightest damage to the great truth of the universal deluge, reported in the Pentateuch: on the contrary, that is a miracle; hence we must believe it; it is a miracle, for it could not have been accomplished by the laws of physics.

In the history of the deluge everything is miraculous:

it is miraculous that forty days of rain should inundate the four quarters of the earth and that the water should rise fifteen cubits above all the highest mountains; miraculous that there should be cataracts, gates, openings in the heavens; miraculous that all the animals from every part of the world should betake themselves to the ark; miraculous that Noah should find enough to feed them for ten months; miraculous that the ark should be able to accommodate all the animals with their provisions; miraculous that most of them should not have died; miraculous that they should have found something to eat when they left the ark; miraculous still, but in a different way, that one Le Pelletier should have believed he could give a natural explanation of how all the animals fitted into Noah's ark and were fed.

Now since the history of the deluge is the most miraculous thing anyone has ever heard of, it would be insane to explain it: this is one of the mysteries we believe by faith; and faith consists in believing what reason cannot—which is still another miracle.

Hence the history of the universal deluge is like that of the tower of Babel, Balaam's ass, the fall of Jericho at the sounding of trumpets, water changed to blood, the passage through the Red Sea, and all the prodigies God deigned to perform on behalf of the elect of his people; these are depths the human understanding cannot sound.

INQUISITION

As you know, the Inquisition is an admirable and wholly Christian invention to make the pope and the monks more powerful and turn a whole kingdom into hypocrites.

St. Dominic is generally considered the first to whom we owe this sacred institution. In fact, we still have a patent granted by this great saint, which is in these very words: "I, brother Dominic, reconcile to the Church one Roger, bearer of these presents, on condition that he will let himself be whipped by a priest, on three consecutive Sundays, from the town gate to the church door, that he will abstain from meat all his life, that he will fast for three Lents a year, that he will never drink wine, that he will wear the *san-benito* with crosses, that he will recite the breviary every day, say ten Paters during the day and twenty at midnight, that he will henceforth keep chaste, and present himself to the parish curate every month, etc., all this on pain of being treated like a heretic, perjurer, and impenitent."

Although Dominic was the true founder of the Inquisition, Louis de Paramo, one of the most respectable writers and most brilliant luminaries of the Holy Office, nevertheless reports in the second chapter of his second book that God was the first founder of the Holy Office, and that he exercised the power of the preaching brethren against Adam. At first, Adam is summoned before the tribunal: *Adam, ubi es?* and in fact, he adds, the lack of a summons would have rendered God's proceeding void.

The clothing of skin God made for Adam and Eve was the model for the *san-benito* which the Holy Office makes the heretics wear. It is true that with this argument one can prove that God was the first tailor; but it is no less obvious that he was the first Inquisitor.

Adam was deprived of all the immovable property he possessed in the great terrestrial paradise: hence the confiscations of the properties of all those condemned by the Holy Office.

Louis de Paramo observes that the inhabitants of Sodom were burned as heretics, because sodomy is expressly a heresy. From this he moves on to the history of the Jews; there he finds the Holy Office everywhere.

Jesus Christ is the first Inquisitor of the new law; the popes were Inquisitors by divine right; and finally they communicated their power to St. Dominic.

Then he enumerates all those whom the Inquisition has put to death; he finds far more than a hundred thousand of them.

His book was printed in Madrid in 1598 and had the approval of the scholars, the praises of the bishops, and the permission of the king. Today we can't imagine such horrors, at once so extravagant and so abominable; but then nothing seemed more natural and more edifying. All men resemble Louis de Paramo when they are fanatics.

This Paramo was a plain man, very exact in his dates, who omitted no interesting fact and scrupulously calculated the number of human victims immolated by the Holy Office throughout the world.

With the greatest naïveté he recounts the establishment of the Inquisition in Portugal, and he is perfectly in agreement with four other historians who all sound like him. This is their unanimous report:

Long before, at the beginning of the fifteenth century, pope Boniface IX had delegated the preaching brethren to go from town to town in Portugal, to burn heretics, Moslems, and Jews; but they were itinerants, and the kings themselves several times complained about the annoyance they caused. Pope Clement VII wished to give them a settled establishment in Portugal, as they had in Aragon and Castile. There were difficulties between the courts of Rome and Lisbon; tempers got strained; the Inquisition suffered from this and was not completely established.

In 1539 a papal legate appeared at Lisbon; he had

come, he said, to establish the Holy Inquisition on unshakable foundations. He brought king John III letters from pope Paul III. He had other letters from Rome for the principal officials of the court; his patent as legate was duly sealed and signed: he showed the most ample authority to create a Grand Inquisitor and all the judges of the Holy Office. He was an impostor named Saavedra, who could forge every kind of handwriting and fabricate and affix false seals and false stamps. He had learned this trade in Rome and perfected it in Seville, where he arrived with two other rascals. His train was magnificent; it was composed of more than a hundred and twenty domestics. To subsidize this enormous expenditure, he and his confidants borrowed immense sums at Seville in the name of the apostolic chamber of Rome; everything had been planned with the most dazzling artifice.

At first the king of Portugal was astonished at the pope's sending him a legate *a latere* without notifying him in advance. The legate replied proudly that in a matter of such urgency as the solid establishment of the Inquisition, His Holiness could brook no delays, and that the king should be honored that the first courier to bring him the news should be a legate of the Holy Father. The king dared not reply. Thereafter, the legate established a Grand Inquisitor, sent around everywhere to collect the tithe; and before the court could receive an answer from Rome, he had already had two hundred people burned and collected more than two hundred thousand écus.

However, at Seville, the legate had borrowed a very considerable sum on forged bills from the marquis of Villanova, a Spanish nobleman, who now thought it best to repay himself with his own hands instead of going to Lisbon to get involved with the impostor. Villanova marched with fifty armed men to the frontiers of Spain, near which the legate was at that time making his circuit, kidnapped him, and brought him to Madrid.

The imposture was soon discovered in Lisbon, and the council of Madrid condemned Saavedra to a flogging and ten years in the galleys; but what is remarkable is that afterward pope Paul IV confirmed everything the impostor had done; he rectified, with the plenitude of his divine power, all the little irregularities of procedure, and made sacred what had been purely human.

> Qu'importe de quel bras Dieu daigne se servir?
>
> [What does it matter what arm God deigns to employ?]

This is how the Inquisition established itself in Lisbon, and the whole kingdom marveled at Providence.

Still, all the procedures of this tribunal are familiar; it is well known how it opposes the false equity and blind reason of all the other tribunals of the universe. It imprisons people on the mere denunciation of the most sordid persons; a son can denounce his father, a wife her husband; one can never confront one's accusers; property is confiscated for the benefit of the judges: that at least is how the Inquisition has behaved up to our time: there is something divine in it, for it passes reason how men should have borne this yoke patiently. . . .

And now at last count Aranda has been blessed by all of Europe for paring the nails and filing the teeth of the monster; but it still breathes.

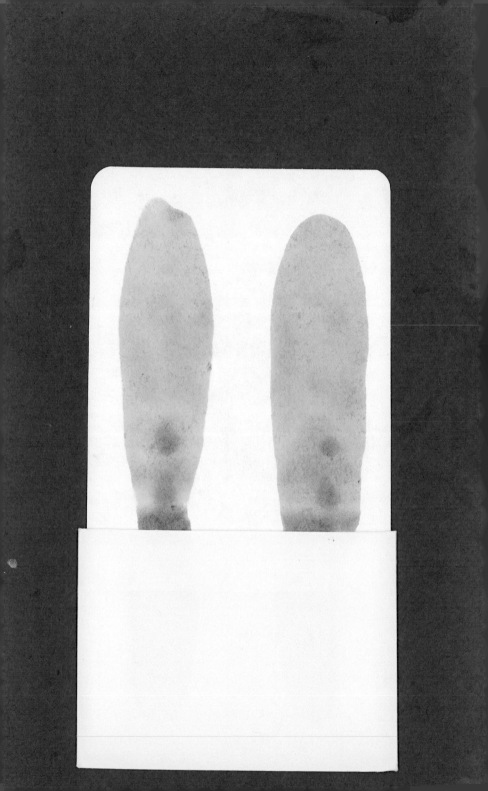